Murder in Tombstone

Murder in Tombstone

The Forgotten Trial of Wyatt Earp

Steven Lubet

Yale University Press

New Haven and London

Published with assistance from the Mary Cady Tew
Memorial Fund.

Set in Galliard type by Achorn Graphic Services.
Printed in the United States of America by R. R. Donnelley,
Harrisonburg, Virginia.

Library of Congress Cataloging-in-Publication Data

Lubet, Steven.
   Murder in tombstone : the forgotten trial of Wyatt Earp /
   Steven Lubet.
      p.   cm.
   Includes bibliographical references (p.) and index.
   ISBN 0-300-10426-X (cloth : alk. paper)
    1. Earp, Wyatt, 1848–1929. 2. Earp, Wyatt, 1848–1929—
Trials, litigation, etc. 3. Tombstone (Ariz.)—History—19th
century. 4. Peace officers—Arizona—Tombstone—Biography.
5. Outlaws—Arizona—Tombstone—History—19th century.
6. Trials (Murder)—Arizona—Tombstone. 7. Violence—
Arizona—Tombstone—History—19th century. 8. Frontier
and pioneer life—Arizona—Tombstone. 9. Tombstone
(Ariz.)—Biography. I. Title.

F819.T6L83 2004
978.02′092—DC22
[B]
                            2004045580

A catalogue record for this book is available from the British
Library.

The paper in this book meets the guidelines for permanence
and durability of the Committee on Production Guidelines
for Book Longevity of the Council on Library Resources.

10 9 8 7 6 5 4 3 2 1

To my father,
Fred Lubet ז״ל

Contents

Murder in Tombstone

1

Slap Leather

In American popular culture there may be no more enduring character than the western gunfighter. Popularized in dime novels, glamorized in Hollywood films, and serialized on television, his image is nearly synonymous with the frontier itself. Often a hero, sometimes a villain or outlaw (not at all the same thing), and lately an enigma or cynic, he is always quick on the draw—ready to stand his ground and shoot it out.

The gun duel has its own legendary structure. Armed men face each other on a dusty street, weapons holstered but trigger fingers taut. They stand ready, hands poised, each waiting for the other to make the first move. One of the combatants, usually a bad guy, reaches for his gun, sometimes shouting a taunt or challenge: "Slap leather." Then the firing begins, ending only when someone lies bleeding on the ground. The winner, either hero or antihero, walks slowly and quietly away. His work is done.

There is seldom, if ever, an aftermath to a fictional gunfight. No posse, no arrest, certainly neither a trial nor imprisonment. If the sheriff so much as arrives on the scene, the bystanders quickly assure him that it was a "fair fight" or perhaps "self-defense," which is sufficient to conclude the investigation.

The myth of the gunfight depends wholly on its form. When armed men openly confront each other, it is their business and only their business. As long as there is no sneaky ambush or ganging up, the larger community will remain more or less uninvolved. There will be no postmortem talk of prosecution, of police brutality, or even of protecting innocent bystanders from stray bullets. The bad guys smirk at the law's impotence, while lawmen (and their vigilante counterparts) revel in the cheers of the crowd.

The reality was sharply different. There were many murders and shootouts in the days of the Wild West, from the end of the Civil War until about 1890, but they were far from "the quick-draw duels in the street that form the climax of so many movies."[1] In fact, most shootings were committed in the course of robberies or during drunken brawls, with no hint of mannered choreography.

Lawmen in particular were unlikely to keep their guns holstered when facing armed criminals. It made far more sense—for both law enforcement and self-preservation—to approach the bad guys from behind or, failing that, with a maximum show of force. It could be nearly suicidal to wait for an adversary to draw first—far better either to knock him to the ground or intimidate him into surrendering.

And even standing face to face, it was virtually impossible to "slap leather." The quick-draw holster, invented in Hollywood as a movie prop, would have been worse than useless in real life because there could be no good way to keep a gun from falling out while walking or riding. In fact, men carried their pistols in their waistbands or their pockets, only occasionally wearing gunbelts (which were often equipped with straps to keep the weapons firmly in place). When it came to gunfights, displaying your weapon was the first move, not the last, of anyone who was seriously interested in surviving.

Also contrary to cinematic imagery, the Old West was not devoid of law and order. Along with settlement came social institutions such as churches, schools, and businesses, all of which required law enforcement. Most towns were run by business elites, who quickly enacted gun-control ordinances and established local police forces, some of which—as in Dodge City, Kansas—became well-known for their efficiency and professionalism. Consequently, shootings did not go unnoticed, and real-life murderers did not flaunt notches on their guns. Outlaws were apprehended, arrests were made, trials were held. Even famous figures such as Wild Bill Hickok and Wyatt Earp were charged with crimes following shoot-outs, though the courts in both cases proved keenly sympathetic to claims of self-defense.

Frontier policing was a distinct art, largely perfected in the Kansas cowtowns where rowdy Texas trailhands tended to get drunk and sometimes violent after weeks spent herding cattle north to railheads. The Texans weren't outlaws but they were armed and dangerous, and their carousing often involved serious damage to life and property. Town marshals faced a dilemma in places like Dodge City, Abilene, and Wichita. Texas drovers were the primary source of crime, but they were also the main source of income for the local saloons, gambling parlors, and dance halls. As Allen Barra points out, local business interests expected the constabulary to keep the Texans under control, but could not afford to see them driven away. Too much violence in law enforcement, especially gunplay, was bad for commerce, but too little law enforcement might lead to vigilantism, which could pose an even greater threat to a town's economic lifeblood. The compromise solution was frequently for the law officer to use his pistol as a club, rather than a shooting iron, isolating the leader in any group of troublemakers and "buffaloing" him across the head before he could do any substantial damage. Drunken cowhands might shoot at the moon, street lamps, or each other, but they had relatively few armed confrontations with lawmen, and almost none that involved quick-draw artistry.

In the entire history of the Wild West, perhaps the most famous "slap leather" gun battle occurred when the Earp brothers—Virgil, Wyatt, and Morgan—along with Doc Holliday encountered the Clanton and McLaury brothers in Tombstone, Arizona, on October 26, 1881. The basic outline of the story is well known, although subsequent pulp fiction exaggerated the role of Wyatt Earp at the expense of his older brother Virgil, who was actually in charge that day.

The trouble began in the late evening of October 25, when Ike Clanton and Tom McLaury rode into Tombstone with a wagonload of beef. Shortly after midnight, Ike got into a shouting match with Doc Holliday at the Alhambra Saloon (the reason for their quarrel would play an important part in the gunfight the next day). As the two men exchanged increasingly violent insults, Doc taunted Ike to make good: "You son-of-a-bitch, go arm yourself." Ike returned the threats in kind until Virgil Earp, Tombstone's town marshal, intervened and separated the two men.

Ike Clanton, drunk and bad-tempered, spent much of that night and the next morning wandering the streets and cursing the Earps and Holliday. At one point he confronted Wyatt with the warning that they would soon have to go "man for man." Wyatt was dismissive, replying, "Go home, Ike, you talk too much for a fighting man."

Ike continued to make his way from saloon to saloon, threatening the Earps in front of anyone who would listen. By noon, he was standing in front of Hafford's Saloon waving a rifle and continuing to spout off. In the meantime, Virgil and Wyatt, who had gone home to sleep, were alerted to Ike's tirade and the alarming fact that he was now brandishing firearms. Virgil tracked Ike down and tried to pound some sense into him, or more likely knock the fight out of him, clubbing Ike to the ground with the barrel of his gun.

It didn't work. Ike continued his threats, at one point warning Morgan Earp that, given the opportunity, he "would have furnished a coroner's inquest for the town." Not long afterward, Frank McLaury and Billy Clanton rode into town for what was probably a prearranged rendezvous with Ike and Tom. The four men headed to Spangenberg's gun shop, where they were observed ominously loading bullets into their cartridge belts. Sensing trouble, Virgil wasted no time walking to the nearby Wells Fargo office to borrow a short-barreled shotgun.

The Clantons and McLaurys next proceeded to the O.K. Corral, where they were overheard threatening to shoot the Earps on sight. For unknown but suspicious reasons, the four men, carrying six-guns and rifles, then moved to the other side of the block, stationing themselves in a vacant lot adjacent to Camillus Fly's photography studio and boardinghouse.

As long as the four men remained at the O.K. Corral, Virgil was willing to let them vent their anger—perhaps they were preparing to leave town. But when they moved toward the city street, he decided that matters had gone far enough. They were openly carrying arms in a public place, in violation of the law. Calling on Morgan, Wyatt, and Doc Holliday for assistance, Virgil determined to disarm the Clantons and McLaurys, by force if necessary.

Thus began the famous march toward destiny. Virgil, Wyatt, Morgan, and Doc walked slowly down Fremont Street toward the confrontation that would become known as the gunfight at the O.K. Corral. Virgil carried a walking stick in his right hand and a six-gun in his waistband. Wyatt and Morgan were carrying pistols, and Doc was concealing the Wells Fargo shotgun under his overcoat.

As they came within ten feet of the Clantons and McLaurys, Virgil called out, "Boys, throw up your hands, I want your guns." Then something went terribly wrong. Someone fired a shot, and as Ike Clanton put it, "the ball opened." Within thirty seconds six men had been shot. Billy Clanton and both McLaury brothers were dead or dying; Virgil and Morgan Earp were seriously wounded, and Doc Holliday was slightly hurt. Wyatt was unscathed. So was Ike, the instigator of it all, who had run away when the shooting began.

Who fired the first shot, and why? And could the tragedy have been avoided, even as the Earps faced down the Clantons and McLaurys in those last critical moments? Some witnesses lauded the Earps for confronting dangerous outlaws, while others accused them of assassinating innocent ranchers who were desperately trying to surrender. Were the Earps courageous lawmen or cold-blooded killers? It would take a trial to answer that question, and the controversial verdict has been debated for the past 120 years.

To the prosecutors, the Earps and Holliday were murderers—law officers out of control who abused their badges out of malice and revenge. For the defense, the Earps were steadfast heroes—willing to risk their lives on the mean, dusty streets of Tombstone for the sake of order and stability. The case against the Earps, with its dueling narratives of brutality and justification, played out themes of intrigue, betrayal, duplicity, revenge, and even adultery. As the witnesses contradicted and denounced each other, the lawyers used all of their considerable talents to shape the testimony and sway the court.

We tell ourselves that trials are about truth, but they are also very much about clarity. The most convincing case wins, not necessarily the truer one. As we will see, the prosecutors in Tombstone seemed at times to have a nearly airtight case, but their efforts were hampered by indecision, dissension, false starts, and conflicts of interest. At key moments, the prosecutors repeatedly overplayed their hand, allowing passion rather than judgment to determine their strategy. In fact, the prosecutors probably had a winning case, but it was not the one they ended up presenting.

In contrast, the defense team, led by the exceptionally capable Thomas Fitch, took advantage of every miscue and error by the prosecutors. He deftly employed loopholes in the territorial statutes, allowing Wyatt to testify without fear of cross examination. Most importantly, Fitch constructed a coherent, unified theory of defense that successfully exploited every flaw in the prosecution's case.

The hearing in the Tombstone court was not simply an epilogue to the gunfight, as most historians have tended to treat it. It was an independent event, in which tactics and maneuvers determined the outcome. After more than a century of argument, no one can say definitively whether Wyatt Earp was innocent or guilty of any crime, but we will be able to see exactly how his attorney out-lawyered the opposition.

One more thing is certain. Wyatt's own description of the events provided a reference point for the legend of the frontier gunfight that has lasted to this day. Testifying before Judge Wells Spicer in a Tombstone courtroom, Wyatt explained: "I did not intend to fight unless it became necessary in self-defense and in the performance of official duty. When Billy Clanton and Frank McLaury drew their pistols, I knew it was a fight for life, and I drew in defense of my own life and the lives of my brothers and Doc Holliday."

Everyone can imagine the scene. The stalwart frontier marshal, though facing death at the hands of outlaws, refuses to pull his weapon first. Then a bad guy makes a false move. Slap leather. The shooting begins.

2

From Dodge City to Tombstone

Wyatt Berry Stapp Earp headed west for the Arizona Territory in late 1879, with no reason to expect that his exploits in Tombstone would eventually establish him as one of the most famous frontier marshals in American history. For most of the previous four years he had worked as a deputy marshal or policeman in several Kansas towns, but his career as a lawman had an on-and-off quality. He was terminated amid controversy from his first full-time job in Wichita, and he served three different terms in Dodge City, interrupted by his efforts to find more lucrative opportunities in places such as Deadwood and Fort Worth. He tried his hand in a wood-hauling business and he also gambled and worked as an armed guard (or "shotgun messenger") for a stagecoach line, but he returned each time to Dodge City where he was always welcomed back to the force at a monthly salary of about seventy-five dollars.

Wyatt obviously had a natural affinity for law enforcement, which called upon his inner reserves of determination and self-control. The *Dodge City Times* observed, "He had a quiet way of taking the most desperate characters into custody which invariably gave the impression that the city was able to enforce . . . and preserve her dignity." And the *Ford County Globe* commended him for doing his duty "in a very creditable manner—adding new laurels to his splendid record every day."[1] Later, when Wyatt was on trial for his life in Tombstone, the Dodge City fathers would rally to his support, attesting that he was "vigilant in the discharge of his duties, and while kind and courteous to all, he was brave, unflinching, and on all occasions proved himself the right man in the right place."

But however much he was respected in Kansas, it was evident by the summer of 1879 that Wyatt, at age thirty-one, had grown tired of the low pay and continual danger that attended his lawman's job. While Wyatt himself had never been seriously injured, his friend Ed Masterson (Bat Masterson's older brother), then the Dodge City marshal, was killed by a drunken cowhand outside the Lady Gay Dance Hall in early 1878. Other officers and citizens were killed or wounded by the frequent gunplay in Dodge City streets, and several incidents surely combined to persuade Wyatt that he was no longer the right man in the right place.

James "Spike" Kennedy, the son of Captain Mifflin Kennedy, a wealthy and powerful Texas cattle baron, was in the habit of causing trouble when he brought his herd into Dodge City. In July 1878 Wyatt arrested him for carrying a pistol inside the town limits, and a month later Marshal Charlie Bassett arrested him again for disorderly conduct. Unaccustomed to such insulting treatment, Kennedy complained to Dodge City Mayor James "Dog" Kelley, no doubt expecting that his father's prestige and influence would prompt the mayor to call off the law. Kelley, however, further offended the young Texan, informing him that the officers were doing their duty and that Kennedy could expect another arrest if he continued to disobey the law. Infuriated, Spike Kennedy muttered a threat and angrily rode out of town.

Kennedy returned several nights later to make good his threats, firing four shots through the bedroom window of Mayor Kelley's house. The mayor was not home, but one of Kennedy's bullets struck and killed a houseguest, the popular actress Dora Hand.

Suspecting Kennedy as the murderer, Ford County Sheriff Bat Masterson quickly enlisted Wyatt Earp, Bill Tilghman, and Charlie Bassett to give chase—"the most intrepid posse ever to pull a trigger," in the words of the *Dodge City Times*.[2] Tracking Kennedy for nearly seventy-five miles, the posse finally cornered him before he could flee the state. When Kennedy refused to surrender—accounts vary as to whether he reached for his gun or his quirt—the posse had no choice but to fire, Bat Masterson wounding him in the shoulder.

Back in Dodge City, the local press was outraged, calling Kennedy a "cold-blooded assassin" and "a fiend in human form."[3] Two weeks later, however, Judge R. G. Cook held a preliminary hearing behind closed doors, discharging Kennedy for lack of evidence. The speedy release of a murderer embittered Wyatt, who would later blame the miscarriage of justice on the influence of Captain Kennedy's money.[4] As his own fate unfolded in Tombstone, Wyatt would benefit greatly from the social class and economic biases of a judge, but it is not known whether he appreciated the irony.

The following spring, Wyatt was nearly killed trying to disarm a bunch of rowdy Missourians when one of the men pulled a concealed gun. Wyatt was saved from "lead poisoning," as the *Dodge City Times* put it, when Bat Masterson managed to "use the broad side of his revolver" to knock the man senseless. Angered by the resistance, Wyatt and Bat seem to have lost control of their tempers, beating the fellows so badly that "their own mothers would have had a hard time picking out their sons." Wyatt's methods had always been rough—he had no compunctions at all about head-banging for the sake of peace, a practice that led the *Ford County Globe* to commend his "finest work" and "neatest polishes"—but this sort of gratuitous violence seemed to mark a new level of frustration with the endless eruptions of drunken trailhands.[5]

It did not help matters that the Dodge City economy was in sharp decline. As the railroads expanded, towns like Dodge lost their near-monopolies on the cattle trade. By the summer of 1879, business had fallen off dramatically in the saloons and dance halls, and so had the work of the police force. In an 1896 newspaper interview, Wyatt explained, "In 1879 Dodge City was beginning to lose much of the snap which had given it a charm to men of restless blood, and I decided to move to Tombstone, which was just building up a reputation."[6] Some writers suggest that Wyatt had simply grown bored with Dodge City, noting, for example, that he made only twelve arrests in the space of year and that Dodge's complement of dance halls, saloons, and whores had fallen to an all-time low.[7] It is more likely, however, that "snap" referred to economic vitality rather than excitement.

Wyatt had regularly abandoned police work in favor of fortune seeking, though with such poor results that he always ended up returning to his badge. This time, perhaps, he thought it would be different. His brother Virgil, five years Wyatt's senior, had already settled in Prescott, Arizona, and sent word back to Kansas that there were vast opportunities in the rapidly expanding Southwest. Tombstone especially held great promise, following several impressive silver strikes. It is doubtful that restlessness alone would have tempted Wyatt to go west—he was an adventurer, not a wanderer—but money was always a great motivator for the Earp brothers. He accepted Virgil's invitation and resigned his position in Dodge City for the third and final time.

Wyatt departed Kansas in early September, accompanied by his second "wife" Celia Ann Blaylock, whom everyone called Mattie. Wyatt's earlier marriage to Urilla Sutherland had ended when his young wife died of fever after less than a year. There is no evidence that he ever formally married Mattie, but the two lived together as husband and wife until he left her (or, as many say, abandoned her) in Tombstone. Wyatt's oldest brother, James Cooksey Earp, then thirty-eight, also made the trip, along with his wife Bessie and her children from a previous marriage. Stopping briefly in Las Vegas, New Mexico, where they were joined by John Henry "Doc" Holliday and "Big Nose" Kate Elder, the party arrived in Prescott on November 1, 1879.

Virgil Edwin Earp was an experienced lawman—he had served on the police force of Abilene, Kansas, and he was the town constable in Prescott—but he had his eye on bigger things. Along with Wyatt and James, he hoped to get rich from the silver mines of Tombstone, either by staking claims or, more likely, by running the businesses that served the miners. His wife Alvira, known as Allie, may have been less enthusiastic about the impending move. She was never fond of Wyatt—eventually she would grow to hate him—and she found civilized Prescott, the territorial capital, more congenial than the prospect of a rough-and-tumble mining camp. But the Earp brothers were deeply committed to each other, often to the discomfort of their wives, and they began making plans to strike it rich.

As happy as Virgil was to see Wyatt and James, however, he was surely uneasy about Doc Holliday, who was already notorious as a trouble-maker. Although educated at a Philadelphia dental college, Doc was a gambler and a drunk, living on the margins of frontier society. He was also reputed to be a killer, although there was never any hard evidence that the rumor was true. Wyatt and Doc had met in Texas and become friends in Dodge City—it was said that Doc once saved Wyatt's life, though again the facts are obscure—and they continued their unlikely friendship in Arizona. Doc's penchant for violence and erratic behavior would play a crucial role in the Earps' Tombstone troubles, but for now Virgil probably welcomed him as a necessary concession to Wyatt.

Pausing only briefly in Prescott, Wyatt and James, along with their wives, reached Tombstone on about December 1, 1879. They were accompanied by Virgil, who had taken some time to sell his property and quit his job, and the reluctant Allie. Morgan, youngest of the brothers at age twenty-eight, did not arrive until July 1880, with Doc Holliday showing up in the fall. In a place like Tombstone—said at the time to be more distant from New York City, by rail or telegraph, than any other town in the United States—almost anything seemed possible. Men could change their lives or begin new ones. Some would succeed in the arduous and frequently dangerous search for a new silver stake, while many others would attempt more dependable professions. Tombstone was filled with merchants, laborers, gamblers, bankers, saloonkeepers, journalists, entrepreneurs, politicians, engineers, lawyers, speculators, and thugs—typically in combination and often indistinguishable from one another. On the multi-occupational frontier it was not remarkable to encounter a gambler-lawman, a banker-miner, a judge-prospector, or even a gunslinging dentist.

Tombstone was a classic boomtown that grew haphazardly, almost recklessly, as long as silver ore was plentiful and easy to extract. The discovery of silver in the area had come as a surprise in 1877 when an eccentric prospector named Ed Schieffelin headed off on his own into the San Pedro River valley at the foot of the Huachuca Mountains. Warned by a soldier that he would find nothing in the arid territory except his tombstone, Schieffelin defied the odds by locating a rich vein of silver. Filing his first claim in August 1877, Schieffelin remembered the sardonic warning and named the place "Tombstone."

Word of the strike spread rapidly, and the area quickly filled with prospectors and other fortune seekers. As new mines were discovered, a small settlement developed on a mesa called Goose Flats. Initially not much more than a few canvas tents, the town of Tombstone was eventually established on the site. By early 1879, the first steps were taken toward the organization of an official municipality, and on November 24 of that year, Tombstone elected its first mayor and city council.

Although wooden storefronts and adobe houses steadily replaced the tents and shacks, Tombstone remained at the very edge of civilization. Even in its palmiest days, residents continued to refer to the town as a mining camp, recognizing the impermanence inherent in its near total dependence on the silver rush. Clara Spalding Brown, the wife of a mining engineer and one of the keenest observers of Tombstone life, sent regular dispatches to her hometown newspaper, the *San Diego Daily Union*, "thinking that a few notes regarding Tombstone and the journey thereto, from a woman's point of view, may be entertaining to some of the ladies of San Diego." Her initial impression of Tombstone, written on July 7, 1880, was of "an embryo city of canvass, frame and adobe." Filled with bothersome flies and hundreds of seemingly idle itinerants, "the only attractive places visible [were] the liquor and gambling saloons, which are everywhere present."[8] Pretensions abounded, but desirable food and fresh vegetables were nearly impossible to find.

A steady influx of capital from the East brought the veneer of development—hotels, theaters, gambling houses, oyster bars, an opera house, and even an ice cream parlor and a "New York style cigar shop"[9]—but the hardships and uncertainties of the frontier always remained. Surrounded by rugged mountains and only thirty miles from the Mexican border, the community found itself plagued by rustlers and bandits. Shootings were common and robberies more so, much to the dismay of civic leaders who realized that stability and order were essential to sustained prosperity. Law enforcement, therefore, was always a crucial issue, made difficult by the overlapping jurisdictions of the federal marshal, county sheriff, and city police, not to mention the evident negligence or outright apathy of some of the peace officers.

George Parsons, whose detailed journal is one of the best surviving accounts of life in Tombstone, frequently despaired of the "hard crowd" that made life so difficult for law-abiding citizens. Driven to desperation by one particularly wanton murder, he could barely contain himself even when writing in his own diary: "I believe in killing such men as one would a wild animal. The law must be carried out by the citizens, or should be, when it fails in its performance as it has lately done." Clara Brown made a similar, though far more genteel, observation in the summer of 1880, perhaps showing less outrage because she was writing for publication rather than reflection: "The boasted quietude of the camp has been disturbed of late, and fears are entertained that the end is not yet. Two murders have been committed within the last ten days, both the result of drinking and gambling. When saloons are thronged all night with excited and armed men, bloodshed must needs ensue occasionally."[10]

Like almost everyone else in southeast Arizona, the Earp brothers were attracted to Tombstone by the flush economy and the relative absence of established authority. Nor were they particularly choosy about how they would make their fortunes. Wyatt's original plan was to operate a stagecoach line; he brought with him a string of horses and a buckboard wagon that he intended to use for that purpose. Upon learning, however, that Tombstone was already well-served by two established stage lines, he turned his efforts elsewhere, though never, it seems, in a single direction.

Among other enterprises, Wyatt obtained a quarter interest in a faro game at the Oriental Saloon in exchange for his services as an enforcer. The saloon owner, Lou Rickabaugh, had invested considerably in making his gambling parlor the fanciest in Tombstone, if not in all of Arizona. As the story goes, another gambling house operator became worried about the volume of business he was losing to Rickabaugh's posh establishment, so he hired a local tough named John Tyler to harass Rickabaugh's patrons in an effort to drive customers away from the Oriental. It was Wyatt's job to rid the Oriental of the troublesome Tyler, a task that he accomplished quickly and with a minimum of violence.

One afternoon, as Tyler made his glowering threats at Rickabaugh, and everyone else within earshot, Wyatt walked quietly up behind the ruffian and grabbed him firmly by the ear. Then, as Stuart Lake put it in his adulatory and highly embellished biography: "Using the ear as a lever, Wyatt propelled Tyler to the door. With a shove and a boot he sent the gunman sprawling into Allen Street." Howling in pain, Tyler exclaimed, "I didn't know you had an interest in this place." "I have," answered Wyatt, "and you can tell your friends it's the fighting interest."[11]

The account may be apocryphal—Lake is the only source, and he frequently exaggerated or invented facts—but it is not uncharacteristic of

Wyatt's methods or temperament. He did not hesitate to use force, but he preferred to use the minimum amount necessary to accomplish his objective. Whether or not he obtained it in return for evicting John Tyler, it is certain that Wyatt ran a faro bank at the Oriental, which at the time was considered an honorable profession even for a once and future lawman.

The Earps also began staking mining claims within weeks of their arrival in Tombstone, naming one "Earp" and another "Mattie Blaylock," after Wyatt's wife. More interested in speculation than physical labor, they sold at least one of the claims and leased several others rather than work the mines themselves. In the meantime, James found work as a bartender and faro dealer, while Virgil, Wyatt, and Morgan all took occasional employment guarding stagecoach shipments for Wells Fargo. These were important jobs. No railroad reached Tombstone at the time—the nearest connection was twenty miles away in Benson, with another even farther in Tucson—so stagecoaches were an essential lifeline for commerce and industry, carrying both payrolls and bullion in and out of town. Robberies were a constant threat, and it took a good deal of courage to "ride shotgun."

In Tombstone, as in Kansas, it seemed that the Earps were always drawn back to law enforcement, if not for its "snap," then as a source of guaranteed income. Before leaving Prescott, Virgil was appointed deputy U.S. marshal by the territorial marshal Crawley Dake. The job did not pay much, but it established Virgil as the only resident federal authority in southeastern Arizona—a position that would not endear him to everyone in Tombstone. By the following July, Wyatt was also wearing a badge, having been appointed a deputy by Pima County Sheriff Charles Shibell. Since Shibell was headquartered in Tucson, this made Wyatt, at least temporarily, one of the most important lawmen in and around Tombstone. Moreover, the position was potentially a lucrative one, involving tax collection as much as law enforcement, with the deputy entitled to a percentage of the take.

The *Tombstone Epitaph* applauded Shibell's choice: "The appointment of Wyatt Earp as Deputy Sheriff by Sheriff Shibell, is an eminently proper one, and we in common with the citizens generally congratulate the latter on his selection. Wyatt has filled various positions in which bravery and determination were requisites."[12] No one, of course, realized at the time just how much bravery and determination would be required in the coming months, as tension mounted through a series of incidents leading to the Earps' showdown with the Clantons and McLaurys.

The Cowboy Menace

As the population of Tombstone grew, from perhaps a few hundred in late 1877 to as many as six thousand by 1881, the town successfully attracted investment from Boston, Philadelphia, Chicago, New York, and San Francisco, rapidly becoming one of the most vibrant economic centers in the Southwest. Men like George Parsons, a native New Yorker and San Francisco banker, and Richard Gird, another New Yorker by way of California, arrived to work the silver mines. Gird succeeded fabulously, becoming one of the principal mine owners in the territory; Parsons failed at mining but left behind his detailed journal, which is essential to our understanding of life in Tombstone. Others set up a variety of businesses and professional offices, often working in a bit of prospecting on the side. Many of the era's most prominent figures passed through Tombstone at least briefly, including Joseph Goldwater, a founder of the merchant family that produced Senator Barry Goldwater; George Hearst, California mining magnate and father of the publisher William Randolph Hearst; and the Rev. Endicott Peabody, who would return to the East to found the Groton School and later served as a tutor to Franklin Delano Roosevelt.

An eastern-oriented business establishment attempted to dominate political and economic life. Tombstone's first three mayors were all easterners, as were the first three city marshals. As with businessmen everywhere, they placed great value on stability, fearful that lawlessness might disrupt their enterprises and that even rumors of violence could drive away future investment. It was never easy to impose law and order on the frontier, and it was especially difficult in a place like southeast Arizona, where sudden wealth and the proximity of the Mexican border combined to attract men who were casual, at best, in their respect for the law. The Earp brothers, as we will see, were unyielding when it came to law enforcement, a trait that would put them immediately at odds with a certain element in Tombstone and its environs.

The so-called Cowboys were a loose band of "rootless ex-cowhands and saddle tramps [who] gravitated toward the small towns of south-eastern Arizona, attracted to the climate and the relative lack of law enforcement on either side of the [Mexican] border."[13] Many of them came from Texas, resembling the trailhands that the Earps so often man-handled in Kansas. More than a few were either Confederate veterans or their kin, harboring an abiding resentment of the law in general and fed-eral authority in particular. At the time, the term "cowboy" did not describe the men who drove cattle for a living—they were generally called stockmen or drovers—but rather was a derisive term that was syn-onymous with rustler, or worse.*

At their most benign, the Cowboys combined small-scale ranching with occasional cattle theft, primarily accomplished by raiding herds in Mexico and bringing the stolen cattle back across the border. Rustling Mexican cattle was barely considered a crime in Arizona, especially since the region's growing demand for beef could not easily be met otherwise. Local butchers were not particular about the origin of their stock, and many citizens, including some prominent politicians, were friendly to-ward the Cowboys, regarding them more as freebooting entrepreneurs than out-and-out thieves.

The Mexican authorities, of course, felt otherwise, especially when sev-eral of the Cowboy raids proved deadly. In July 1881, a band of Cow-boys, sometimes estimated to have been as many as fifty in number, attacked a group of Mexican traders who were doing business in Arizona, robbing them and leaving four dead. The wanton killings—known as the Skeleton Canyon massacre—created an international incident, prompt-ing Governor Luis Torres of Sonora to complain that his citizens had been murdered by "Texan Cowboys." The Mexican consul in Prescott protested vigorously to Arizona's acting Governor John Gosper, de-manding that he "use all the means at your command in order to effect the extermination of those who lay waste whole districts of my country, murder my countrymen and rob them when they come to contribute to

---

*Adopting Allen Barra's approach, I will capitalize Cowboy when referring to the rough and lawless crowd on the Arizona frontier to distinguish them from the hard-working ranch hands whom we all rightfully admire.

the commerce of this territory." Mexican General Adolfo Dominguez even traveled to Tombstone seeking U.S. assistance, saying, "We think that the American officials and a great majority of the citizens deprecate these acts of lawlessness, and believing this we have courage to hope that by united effort the outlaws may be suppressed."[14]

The Mexicans did not wait for U.S. authorities to solve the problem, however. On August 13, 1881, Mexican soldiers killed five suspected rustlers in the Guadalupe Canyon massacre, leading Clara Brown to fear that Cowboy retribution could result in a border war: "It is likely to lead to very serious trouble, and a war with Mexico would be a calamity greatly to be deplored, in more ways than one. While no one upholds the recent massacre, those who think dispassionately about the matter realize that the Mexicans were not the first to inaugurate the present unhappy state of affairs along the border. They have suffered greatly from the depredations of those outlaws who, under the guise of 'cowboys,' infest this country and pursue the evil tenor of their ways with no attempt at interference on the part of those whose duty it is to suppress crime."[15]

The prospect of hostilities with Mexico set off alarm bells in the Tombstone business community. Nothing could be worse for commerce and investment than open warfare. Fortunately, the Mexican government succeeded in calming the situation, at least temporarily, by sending additional troops and establishing forts in Sonora until rustling raids became more risky than rewarding. This, however, had the predictable effect of shifting Cowboy activity to the Arizona side of the border. The rustlers began stealing American cattle from the region's larger ranching operations, as well as robbing stagecoaches and citizens in outlying areas.

Contemporary writers have debated the actual extent of the "Cowboy problem," but it is evident that many residents were seriously alarmed at the time. George Parsons, for example, railed against the Cowboys in his journal, writing, "Be it understood in this journal, cowboy is a rustler at times, and rustler is a synonym for desperado—bandit, outlaw and horse thief." He recounted an incident when a friend of his was accosted at gunpoint: "Nick who shares a cabin with me had quite an adventure today with a cowboy on the Charleston road three or four miles out. The fellow rode up to Nick, who was on his good horse, and leveling a six-shooter at him, ordered him to dismount and hand over his horse. Nick dismounted, and while in the act of handing over the bridle reins, seized the fellow's revolver, and in the struggle, it was discharged causing the horses to jump apart, when Nick ran to his horse, jumped on him and was off like a flash while the cowboy fired two shots after him."[16]

Newspapers from Tucson to San Francisco reported on the Cowboys' depredations. A letter in the *Arizona Weekly Star* complained of "a visit from the 'cowboys,' as they are called [who] were guilty of grave outrages" including robbery and shootings. "The terror these men have caused the traveling public . . . is having a serious influence," the writer continued, "and this scab on the body politic needs a fearless operation to remove it." The *San Francisco Examiner* warned that "cowboys [are] the most reckless class of outlaws in that wild country . . . infinitely worse than the ordinary robber," and the *San Francisco Exchange* allowed that "two or three prompt executions and the cowboy will become as meek as the product of the animal from which he takes his name."[17]

There were persistent rumors of impending Cowboy invasions, sometimes said to involve scores of desperadoes. Acting Governor Gosper, following a visit to Tombstone, expressed his fear that "the cowboys will come to control and 'run' that part of our Territory with terror and destruction."[18] And while Tombstone itself never suffered an outright attack or takeover, the number of robberies and other crimes—especially in the surrounding countryside—created a constant level of anxiety and disquiet.

The two most notorious Cowboys were John Ringo and William "Curly Bill" Brocius, both of whom became adversaries of the Earp brothers. Ringo traveled from Missouri to California as a child, but as a teenager he moved to Texas, where he began developing a reputation as an outlaw and a killer. Charged with at least one murder (though never convicted), he spent time in several Texas jails before fleeing to Arizona, where he became known as a leader among the Cowboy rustlers. Ringo has sometimes been described as an educated man given to reading, perhaps even with a year or so of college, but this is probably a legend that developed in order to make him a more interesting foil for Doc Holliday.

No one has ever accused Curly Bill Brocius of having an education, but he certainly made his presence known across southeast Arizona. In one incident he and a companion terrorized the outlying town of Charleston on a Saturday night, at one point forcing the patrons of a saloon to remove their clothes at gunpoint and dance for the Cowboys' amusement. The next day he rode into neighboring Contention, where he disrupted a religious service, firing shots inside the church and perhaps at the minister. As Parsons put it, they "played the devil generally—breaking up a religious meeting by chasing the minister out of the house—putting out lights with pistol balls."[19]

Ringo and Curly Bill were professional criminals who made their livings at rustling and robbery. When Cowboys were excoriated in the press and condemned by upstanding citizens, it was usually with men like them in mind. They were prime suspects in the murderous attack at Skeleton Canyon, and they were known to have committed many other crimes. Curly Bill was the admitted killer of Tombstone Marshal Fred White, although he claimed it was an accident and charges against him were dismissed.

In addition to the full-time Cowboys, others combined legitimate ranching with trading in stolen cattle. Rustlers obviously had to dispose of their stock, and the easiest way was through middlemen—local ranchers who would combine the stolen cattle with their own herds. Some may have done this reluctantly, worried that their own cattle might be stolen next if they declined to cooperate, while others were more than eager to work closely with the rustlers.

Historian Paula Mitchell Marks places Tom and Frank McLaury in the latter category. They definitely held stolen stock, sometimes acting as virtual bankers for the rustlers, but they were "no desperados." Since it was common, almost unavoidable, for small ranchers to welcome cow thieves, Marks believes that it is unfair to call the McLaury brothers Cowboys, despite their frequent hospitality and financial association with rustlers. Other writers are not so generous, accepting the characterization of the McLaurys as dangerous Cowboys—"fences of the frontier" who assumed only the "veneer of respectability" in order to rebrand and sell stolen livestock.[20]

There is not much dispute about the Clantons. Newman Haynes "Old Man" Clanton established his family—including his sons Ike, Billy, and Phin—in the San Pedro River valley, not far from Charleston, which was one of the satellite mining towns that surrounded Tombstone. Even the most sympathetic sources agree that the Clantons went well beyond receiving stolen livestock; they were active rustlers who raided back and forth across the Mexican border. Old Man Clanton is sometimes referred to as a leader of the Cowboys, but this is at best an exaggeration. The Cowboys, in truth, were essentially leaderless—a recognizable group but far from an organized gang. Many of them, having fled Texas to avoid authority, were far too independent to acknowledge anyone as a boss. The best explanation was probably given by hotel keeper Tom Thornton, who told the *San Francisco Examiner* that the Cowboys could not possibly recognize a chief, "No sir, the 'cowboys' don't herd together in droves, but come and go about their own personal business wherever they desire to go."[21] On the other hand, Old Man Clanton may have appeared to be a ringleader, if only by virtue of his age and the number of his sons as well as the fact that other Cowboys tended to do business at the Clanton ranch.

A considerable myth has developed around the Cowboys, sometimes describing them as Robin Hood figures who stood up for local independence against the encroachment of federal authority and large-scale ranchers like John Slaughter. Social historian Richard Maxwell Brown goes so far as to characterize them as "social bandits" and "resistance gunfighters" who defended the "rural, pastoral, Southern cowboy" culture against the incorporating forces of "urban, industrial, Northern, capitalistic Tombstone."[22] It is unlikely, however, that the Cowboys would have seen themselves in those terms; certainly there is no record that they stole from the rich and gave to the poor. In fact, their preference was to steal from Mexicans and sell to the richest buyers possible, which made them quite obviously dependent on urban, industrial, capitalistic Tombstone. When it was no longer feasible to raid Mexico, many Cowboys were ready and willing to rob and occasionally even murder Americans, both urban and pastoral.

If anything, the Cowboys' relationship to Tombstone was symbiotic, not flatly antagonistic, at least when it came to rustled cattle. Their more serious crimes, especially stagecoach robbery, drew a much more severe response from the business and professional establishment, especially when it appeared—rightly or wrongly—that certain law officers were either unable or unwilling to track down the offenders.

Nevertheless, the Cowboys had many friends and supporters both in and around Tombstone. Butchers and other local merchants, who did not need to raise outside capital, depended on Cowboys for cheap provisions, and saloonkeepers enjoyed their freewheeling spending habits. Regional loyalties also played a part. The past might be reinvented in Tombstone, but it could not be completely forgotten. The Civil War was still a fresh wound in the early 1880s, especially for the many Confederate veterans who came to Arizona in order to rebuild their lives or to skirt federal authority. As Texans and southerners, the Cowboys were natural allies of the local Democrats, who formed a political counterweight to Tombstone's Republican business establishment.

Tombstone Politics

When the Goose Flats settlement began to change from a ragged collection of tents to a real town, the only source of local government was Pima County, which covered the vast reaches of southern Arizona— larger in area than many eastern states—and was seated in distant Tucson. It quickly became obvious that more immediate administration would be necessary to provide the services that the expanding population and dynamic economy required. Among the most pressing problems were public safety and the security of land titles—issues that often overlapped, as when speculators and squatters nearly took up arms against each other in what came to be known as the "town site" controversy.

The first steps toward establishing a recognized town were taken in March 1879 when five land dealers organized the Tombstone Town Site Company, which, under federal law, would eventually give way to a municipal government. The purpose of the company was to obtain title to the territorial land that would later be deeded over to residents and future purchasers. Of course, the potential for profiteering, not to mention outright corruption, was enormous, as the value of Tombstone property grew with every new load of silver ore from the mines.

William Harwood was elected Tombstone's first mayor on November 24, 1879; but he served for only a few months and was replaced the following January by Alder Randall, who soon became involved in a serious scandal. By law, the mayor held the town patent, issued by the U.S. Department of the Interior, which gave him the power to distribute land titles within the town site. Randall, however, was accused of conspiring to deliver property rights to speculators James Clark and Michael Gray, rather than to the citizens who already occupied the lots.

The ensuing controversy threatened to break into open violence, as Clark and Gray tried to collect "rent" from (and failing that, to evict) citizens who believed they held title to their own homes. The land dealers' resort to strong-arm tactics (sometimes assisted by Cowboys Ike Clanton and Curly Bill Brocius) was met with determined resistance, resulting in an uneasy standoff. George Parsons observed that ten men "had shotguns loaded" and "some rope to stretch" Clark and Gray's necks, if that proved necessary for the people to "assert their rights."[23]

A court in Tucson eventually issued an injunction against Mayor Randall, preventing him from granting additional deeds, and he was later prosecuted, though unsuccessfully, for malfeasance in office.

With so much money to be made by exploiting both the mines and the miners, political life in Tombstone was a "a maelstrom of opportunity and excitement."[24] Elections were frequently held and hotly contested, and they were often subject to charges of irregularity or fraud. Although factions tended to shift somewhat, the political parties were well developed and highly active. The Republican forces were concentrated in the town of Tombstone, primarily representing eastern-oriented business interests. The surrounding areas were dominated by Democrats, a fact that became particularly important when Cochise County was organized—it was split off from the immense Pima County in February 1881—with its seat in Tombstone. The Arizona Territory itself was controlled by the Republican administration in Washington, which appointed both the governor and the U.S. marshal. The result was a complex set of overlapping jurisdictions—federal, county, and municipal—each with its own law-enforcement authorities and political allegiances.

Perhaps the most important Republican in Tombstone was the publisher-politician John Clum. Born in New York's Hudson River valley, Clum attended a year of divinity school at Rutgers before heading west in 1871 as a member of the U.S. Signal Service. He served for two years at a weather station in New Mexico and then obtained an appointment from the Grant administration as the Indian Agent on the San Carlos Apache Reservation, although he was only twenty-two years old.

Clum's tenure with the Office of Indian Affairs was exceptionally progressive and humane. He established an Apache police force and appointed Apache judges to hear criminal cases on the reservation. At a time when many Indian agents were either corrupt or indifferent, Clum stood out for his honesty, dedication, and energy.

In 1877, Clum resigned from his position with the government and moved to Tucson, where he purchased the *Arizona Weekly Citizen,* which he managed to turn into the territory's first successful daily newspaper. By late 1879, however, Clum observed that "business in Tucson began to drag," and he made plans to move to Tombstone where, as he noted in his autobiography, "the future seemed alluring."[25] He sold the *Citizen* and ordered a small hand press for delivery in Tombstone. With the financial backing of Richard Gird, the region's most prominent mine operator, Clum published the first issue of the *Tombstone Epitaph* on May 1, 1880.

A devoted Republican—he was married to a niece of William Dennison, who served in Lincoln's cabinet as postmaster general—Clum used the pages of the *Epitaph* to encourage industry and investment, to promote law and order, and to condemn the cattle thieves and road agents, whom he called "the murdering cowboys." Reporting on an attack on a Mexican trading party, the *Epitaph* warned that the "cowboys" had "grown bold with the deeds of crime they have committed [and had] no fears of the civil authorities." Therefore, the story continued, "the people are justified in taking the law into their own hands and ridding themselves of the dangerous characters who make murder and robbery their business."[26]

An editorial published in April 1881 summarized Clum's, and probably the Republican business community's, view of life and commerce on the frontier: "There are many things and causes which militate seriously against the internal improvement of our territory, even in the face of the potent fact that we possess in a large measure everything calculated to attract attention and win capital. The cause to which we especially allude is the fact that our people as a class have not that reverence for the law necessary to induce men of money to cast their lot with us in an earnest endeavor to develop our wonderful mining and stock raising resources. [U]ntil we come to a just comprehension of the fact that civilized communities cannot exist without law and executed law at that, we cannot reasonably expect an influx of capital, which is always wary and circumspect."[27]

On January 4, 1881, John Clum was elected Tombstone's third mayor. In his dual positions as mayor and editorialist, he would be the Earps' most important supporter in Tombstone. After their gunfight with the Clantons and McLaurys, he would become their strongest and most vociferous defender.

The political opposition to the Republican establishment was led by John Behan and his backers. In a territory filled with newcomers, Behan was practically a native. Born in Missouri in 1845, he moved with his parents to Arizona at the age of eighteen. His family was prominent in commercial life in and around Prescott, but Johnny turned to Democratic Party politics at a young age. In 1864, when he was only nineteen years old, Behan was appointed clerk of the territorial legislature (where Democrats were the majority party). Later, he was elected to the legislature as a Democrat from Yavapai County, where at times he also served as sheriff and clerk of the district court.

In the summer of 1880, Behan was drawn to Tombstone, where he hoped to continue his political career while reaping financial gain. He invested in several local businesses while he surveyed the electoral landscape. Virtually every account of Behan describes him as a man with consummate interpersonal skills—smooth, friendly, outgoing, well-spoken, and popular—which he did not hesitate to use in as many ways as possible. When Cochise County was organized in February 1881, Behan managed to obtain the lucrative sheriff's position, even though the appointment was made by Republican Governor John Fremont. County sheriff was the plum political job in territorial Arizona because it involved tax collection as much as law enforcement and the sheriff's compensation included a percentage of the revenues. Estimates of the potential proceeds for Cochise County ran as high as thirty thousand dollars annually, a very impressive sum in those days.

Behan's primary ally in Tombstone was Harry Woods, his undersheriff (second-in-command) and the editor of the *Tombstone Nugget,* a newspaper that was as stoutly Democratic as the *Epitaph* was Republican. In fact, the two newspapers conducted a spirited rivalry, frequently trading accusations of bias and inaccuracy. Clum derisively referred to the *Nugget* as "the cowboy organ," and Woods responded by accusing the *Epitaph* of affinity with "stranglers" or vigilantes. There was truth to both charges. John Clum was indeed active in the Citizens Safety Committee, and the *Epitaph* regularly cautioned Sheriff Behan that his inability to deal with crime might cause the people themselves "to rid the county of these outlaws."

Behan's (and Woods's) association with the Cowboys was more controversial. There is no doubt that most of the Cowboys considered themselves Democrats, as did nearly all of the ranchers in rural Cochise County, and that Behan depended on them for electoral support. In 1880 John Ringo, Curly Bill Brocius, and Ike Clanton all worked for the Democrats in a crucial election for Pima County sheriff that was later overturned because of vote fraud. The real question is whether Behan rewarded his allies by turning a blind eye to their crimes. It was forgivable, under local morality at the time, to indulge the theft of Mexican cattle. But there was also much suspicion that Behan was at best uninterested in tracking down stagecoach robbers if they happened to be Cowboys and Democrats.

It was always clear which side the Earps would take when they arrived in Tombstone. They were staunch Republicans. Virgil and James were veterans of the Union Army; James took a musket ball in the shoulder that troubled him for the rest of his life and may have caused his preference for bartending over police work. Wyatt also tried to enlist but was too young. Coming from Kansas, the Earps were considered easterners by Arizona standards (then as now), and they had little patience for cattle thieves and outlaws, especially if they seemed to be Texans. Although they were far from "violent point men for the incorporating social and economic values" of industrial capitalism,[28] the Earps took an approach toward law enforcement that was indeed tough and inflexible, no matter who was involved. Virgil once arrested Mayor Clum for "fast riding" on the Tombstone streets, and Wyatt managed to do him one better—threatening to arrest a judge in his own courtroom.

It was probably inevitable that the Earps would find themselves at odds with Johnny Behan—not so much because of their party affiliations, but because he was a political opportunist while they were professional lawmen. As we will see, there were other, deeply personal reasons for the rivalry as well. As much as John Clum was the Earps' supporter, Johnny Behan would become their competitor, their antagonist, and ultimately their accuser.

3

Prelude to a Gunfight

The first confrontation between the Earps and the Cowboys came in the summer of 1880 when six mules were stolen from Camp Rucker, a U.S. Army outpost not far from Tombstone. Lacking authority to search private property, Lieutenant J. H. Hurst sought assistance from Virgil, the deputy federal marshal for the region, who enlisted Wyatt and Morgan to help track down the thieves. Acting on a tip, the posse rode to the McLaury ranch on the Babacomari River, where they found the mules, as well as a branding iron that was used to change "US" to "D8" on the mules' hides. Wary of resistance by the rustlers, Lieutenant Hurst apparently made a deal with a Cowboy named Frank Patterson, who agreed to return the mules the next day if the Earps left without making any arrests. Wyatt would later claim that he advised Hurst against the compromise, offering to fight for the government property if necessary, but the lieutenant insisted on heading back to Tombstone.

Predictably, the mules were never delivered as promised. Furious at having been first robbed and then deceived, Lieutenant Hurst posted notices in Tombstone offering a reward for the "arrest, trial and conviction" of the thieves. "It is known that the stolen animals were secreted at or in the vicinity of the McLaury Brothers ranch," the notice read, "and it is also believed they were there branded on the left shoulder over the Government brand." Hurst specifically charged that Frank McLaury assisted in hiding the mules.[1]

Frank McLaury reacted angrily, publishing a rejoinder in the pro-Cowboy *Nugget* in which he called the army officer "a coward, a vagabond, a rascal, and a malicious liar," suggesting that Hurst had stolen the mules himself. Frank audaciously derided Hurst as "unmanly," saying that he was incapable of hunting the mules himself and instead relied on "several citizens" for assistance.[2] Perhaps unwittingly, Frank also offended the Earps, who were acting not as "citizens" but under the authority of Virgil's federal badge. According to Virgil, Frank McLaury followed his published notice with a direct threat, accosting Virgil and warning him, "If you ever again follow us as close as you did, then you will have to fight anyway."

There is no corroboration for Virgil's account, but Frank McLaury's willingness to confront Lieutenant Hurst (and implicitly the Earps) reveals him as a hothead who would stand his ground against authority, even when he was in the wrong. That trait might come in handy when rustling livestock, but it would get him killed the following year. For the time being, however, Frank poured out insults at Lieutenant Hurst, confident of the antigovernment sentiment in the area. "I am willing to let the people of Arizona decide who is right," he said.[3]

In the midst of this quarrel between Hurst and McLaury, Charlie Shibell appointed Wyatt a deputy Pima County sheriff, ushering in a period of collaborative law enforcement in Tombstone. Wyatt and Virgil were on good terms with Fred White, the elected town marshal, meaning that the federal, county, and city officers were all able to work closely together. It would not last long. A killing, an election, and a double cross—all with Cowboy involvement—would combine to bring the brief season of cooperation to an end. Throughout the summer and into the fall, however, the three fighting Earps (Virgil, Wyatt, and Morgan—James was supportive but avoided gunplay) and Fred White did their jobs with courage and integrity.

Sometime around September, Doc Holliday and Big Nose Kate arrived in town from Prescott. Holliday would prove to be the wild card in the Tombstone deck. A native Georgian and the son of a Confederate officer, a gambler and shootist with little respect for the law, he might have been a natural ally of the Cowboys and their political associates but for his profound friendship with Wyatt Earp. Many years later, after Holliday had passed away, Wyatt would recall him as a philosopher and a wag, a "mad, merry scamp with a heart of gold." Such are the wishful reconstructions of memory and affection. In his lifetime, it is doubtful that anyone would have called Doc Holliday a scamp, at least not to his face. Nearly everyone but Wyatt regarded Doc as a reckless and quarrelsome troublemaker, known for a quick temper "which was bad when sober and worse when drunk."[4] Gaunt and mysterious in demeanor, Holliday brought with him to Tombstone a reputation as a gunslinger and killer. But even though the rumors about Doc were surely exaggerated, if not entirely invented, his notoriety reflected poorly on the Earps. Their connection to Holliday would be relentlessly exploited by their detractors.

Doc Holliday was diagnosed with tuberculosis at the age of twenty-one, which many believe prompted him to head west. He may have hoped that the climate would restore his health. Or, as the legend has it, he may have intended to "meet Death head on." In either case, his aggressive and volatile temperament has often been attributed to the fatalism of a man who expected to die young. Remarking on Doc's arrival in Tombstone, writer and publisher Bob Boze Bell observed, "Never have a municipality and a man been better suited to each other."[5]

Indeed, Holliday was barely in town for a month before he was involved in a gunfight, on October 10, 1880. While gambling at the Oriental Saloon, Doc got into a heated argument with another "local sport," as the *Epitaph* put it. The other man backed down, most likely intimidated by Doc's reputation for erratic violence. Next, however, Doc got into an even nastier quarrel with Milt Joyce, one of the saloon owners, who berated Holliday for causing trouble and ruining business. When Holliday argued back, Joyce ordered him out of the establishment, refusing to return Doc's pistol, which had been deposited with the bartender. Not one to suffer slights in silence, Doc returned after only a few minutes, having armed himself with a self-cocking, double-action revolver. Standing no more than ten feet from Joyce, Doc fired the first of several shots, at which point the saloon owner "jumped for his assailant and struck him over the head with a six-shooter, felling him to the floor and lighting on top of him."[6] More shots were fired, both by Holliday and bartender Gus Williams, until Fred White succeeded in separating the combatants. When the smoke cleared, Joyce had suffered a serious shot through the hand, and William Parker, another partner in the Oriental, had been shot in the left foot.

Holliday was initially charged with assault with a deadly weapon, but he was allowed to plead guilty to assault and battery and was fined twenty dollars. More significant than the sentence was the fact that Milt Joyce was a prominent Tombstone Democrat, whose anger toward Holliday would give him and his colleagues one more reason to resent the Earps.

Later that month there was another, far more serious shooting in Tombstone. Just after midnight on October 28, a bunch of "Texas cowboys," as the *Epitaph* reported, "began firing on the moon and stars on Allen Street."[7] As it happened, Marshal Fred White was nearby and hastened to put an end to the disturbance. Wyatt and Morgan Earp also heard the shots and ran to the scene, Wyatt stopping momentarily to borrow a pistol from Fred Dodge, the local Wells Fargo agent.

As most of the carousing Cowboys fled, White approached Curly Bill Brocius, who seemed to be one of the bunch. "I am an officer, give me your gun," White demanded, and then more forcefully, "Now, you Goddamned Son of a bitch, give me that pistol." Brocius seemed to comply, handing his weapon to the marshal when it suddenly discharged—either by accident or design—with the bullet striking White in the groin. Wyatt quickly ran up behind Brocius (by some accounts he was already holding the Cowboy when the gun went off) and knocked him to the ground with the barrel of his gun. Brocius protested his innocence, claiming for the first of many times that the pistol had misfired: "What have I done? I have not done anything to be arrested for."[8]

Fearing that Brocius might be lynched for shooting the popular town marshal, Wyatt took him to the local jail, where the three Earp brothers stood watch throughout the night. The next morning, before it was known whether White would live or die, Brocius was charged with assault to murder. As reports spread of a possible lynching, it was decided to transfer the prisoner to Tucson. Wyatt drove Brocius out of town, guarded for the first few miles by Morgan and Virgil.

Fred White died the following Saturday. On his deathbed, however, he made a statement that seemed to exonerate Brocius of murder, if not necessarily assault or manslaughter, explaining that the Cowboy's gun seemed to have fired accidentally when he grabbed it by the barrel. Presented with this evidence at a preliminary hearing, the court in Tucson dismissed the charges against Brocius, which by then had been increased to murder. True to his nature, Curly Bill did not react to his release with humility or contrition. Having essentially dodged a bullet, he

responded by firing dozens more, setting off on a shooting spree that terrorized citizens in Charleston and Contention, though he wisely avoided
Tombstone and the Earps. It may have been the killing of Fred White,
as much as anything else, that began to alter public opinion of the
Cowboys, changing their image, at least among the Tombstone elite,
from tolerated cattle thieves to violent and dangerous criminals.

The shooting of Fred White, and Brocius's subsequent release, had
other important implications in Tombstone, both recognized and un-
recognized at the time. Almost immediately after White's death, the
Tombstone town council appointed Virgil Earp acting marshal, briefly
consolidating all three levels of law enforcement in the Earps' hands. The
tragedy also prompted the council to enact a new ordinance, prohibiting
private citizens from carrying firearms within the city limits (previously,
only concealed weapons were illegal). Almost precisely a year later, it was
Virgil Earp's insistence on enforcing the gun law that led to the fatal
shoot-out with the Clantons and McLaurys.

The incident also provides several significant insights into Wyatt Earp's
character. First, it is interesting to note that he was unarmed on the night
of the killing, having to borrow a pistol from Wells Fargo agent Fred
Dodge, although he was a deputy county sheriff at the time. And even
though he was provoked by the shooting of his friend Marshal White,
Wyatt used his gun as a club to subdue Brocius, loath even in those circumstances to shoot an unarmed man. Finally, all three Earp brothers
obviously considered it their duty to protect Brocius from harm, bringing him to trial rather than exposing him to rough justice. Later, when
the Earps were themselves charged with murdering three men in cold
blood, their reputations for integrity, earned in the Brocius episode and
others, would stand them in good stead.

Elections

Political turmoil came to a head in Tombstone with the election
for Pima County sheriff, held on November 2, 1880. The incumbent,
Democrat Charles Shibell, faced a stiff challenge from Republican Bob
Paul. Wyatt Earp was in a difficult position. As Shibell's deputy he normally
would have been expected to support his boss, even if he was put off by

Shibell's Cowboy supporters. But as a Republican, Wyatt would have been well-disposed toward Bob Paul, not only out of political attachment, but also because the big man had earned an outstanding reputation as sheriff of Calaveras County, California. In the end, it seems that Wyatt determined to stay neutral and did not campaign for either candidate. But he was not able to maintain his neutrality once the results were announced.

When the ballots were first counted, it appeared that Shibell had eked out a narrow victory by only a handful of votes. Almost immediately, rumors began to spread of vote fraud, especially in the San Simeon valley, where election officials included Ike Clanton and John Ringo. Curly Bill Brocius, released on bond and still awaiting trial for the murder of Fred White, served as a sort of precinct captain, escorting people to the polls whether or not they were qualified voters, and apparently with the admonition that they "vote early and often."

The next morning, Brocius himself brought the ballots into Tombstone, where they reported a suspicious tally of 103 votes for Charlie Shibell (and an identical total for virtually every other Democratic candidate) and only one for Bob Paul. According to the *Epitaph,* "the odd vote is said to have been cast by a Texas cowboy who when questioned as to why he was voting the Republican ticket, said: 'Well, I want to show those fellows that there wasn't any intimidation at this precinct.'"[9] San Simeon produced more than enough votes to swing the election, although the ballots outnumbered qualified voters by a ratio greater than two to one.

Paul sought a recount and took the case to court. On November 9, less than a week after the disputed election, Wyatt Earp resigned as Shibell's deputy, some say in disgust, in order to support Bob Paul's bid. According to Stuart Lake, Wyatt played a crucial role in the election dispute, traveling to San Simeon in order to gather evidence of vote fraud. Perhaps that actually happened—it would be consistent with Wyatt's abrupt resignation—but there is no record of it, and no Earp-produced evidence was ever offered in court. With or without Wyatt's input, the result of the election was overturned on January 29, 1881, when a district court judge in Tucson ordered Shibell's entire San Simeon vote disqualified (there was Republican vote fraud as well, but not enough to affect the outcome). Shibell appealed that ruling, but it was affirmed by the territorial supreme court in April, and Bob Paul was finally sworn in as Pima County sheriff.

In the meantime, however, three events altered the balance of law-enforcement power in Tombstone, setting the stage for much of the violence that would follow. When Wyatt resigned as deputy county sheriff, Charlie Shibell appointed fellow Democrat Johnny Behan as his replacement. Then, on November 12, 1880, a special election was held for town marshal, the job that Virgil had filled on a temporary basis since Fred White's death.

Virgil threw his hat in the ring, quite reasonably expecting the support of the Tombstone establishment. He had already been appointed to the position and he was, after all, the most experienced lawman in town. Surprisingly, however, John Clum backed a different candidate—Ben Sippy, a part-time policeman with unimpressive credentials. The reason for Clum's endorsement has never been explained. He may have seen qualities in Sippy that have eluded historians, or he may just have made a poor choice. In any event, Sippy won the election and served until the following June,[10] when he disappeared from town, leaving behind no explanation, or even a letter of resignation, but numerous rumors about bad debts and missing funds.

With Ben Sippy's election, the Earps' official involvement in law enforcement was limited to Virgil's commission as deputy U.S. marshal, a position with narrow jurisdiction and slim remuneration. Nonetheless, they stood ready to help the local authorities when needed. For example, Virgil and Wyatt both assisted Sheriff Behan and Marshal Sippy in protecting the life of a tinhorn gambler known as Johnny-Behind-the-Deuce (named after his favorite play at the faro table), who was threatened by a lynch mob after he murdered a popular mining engineer.

The Earps were dedicated to law and order, both in and out of office, but they did not risk their lives out of sheer altruism. Wyatt had his eye on an important prize, and it made good sense for him to remain visible in law-enforcement matters. The territorial assembly had voted to subdivide Pima County, carving out Cochise County (originally spelled Cachise) with its seat in Tombstone, effective February 1, 1881. The sheriff of the new county would be the most important lawman in the area, not to mention the most highly compensated, and Wyatt Earp had good reason to think that he was the right man for the job. Upon the official organization of Cochise County, Governor John Fremont was to make initial appointments to all public offices, with elections to be held in November 1882. Since Fremont was a Republican—in 1856 he was the party's first-ever candidate for president—it stood to reason that he would select a fellow Republican, such as Wyatt Earp.

The other leading applicant for the position was Johnny Behan, who, though a Democrat, was far more politically astute than any of the Earps. It is easy to imagine the adroit Behan pleading his case to Fremont, pointing out that the designated sheriff would have to be confirmed by the Territorial Legislative Council, which was controlled by Democrats. Also, the new county would be heavily Democratic and there would be little point in naming a sheriff who would only be beaten in the next election. Virgil Earp had proved himself a poor candidate even within Republican Tombstone, so how good could Wyatt's chances be county-wide? Fremont was never especially popular in Arizona, so it might have seemed that he could enhance his standing by naming the well-liked Johnny Behan to the sheriff's job, rather than the dour Wyatt Earp.

Of course, this is speculation. There is no record of when or how the applicants approached the governor. But somewhere along the line it must have become obvious that Fremont was leaning toward Behan, because Wyatt and Johnny struck a deal that would not have made sense otherwise. As Wyatt would later explain it, he agreed to abandon his candidacy in exchange for Behan's promise to appoint him undersheriff, which would allow the two men to divide the proceeds of the office. Behan's version of the deal differed in the details, if not the general outline. He claimed that he was "satisfied that I would get the appointment" but still offered the undersheriff's position to Wyatt without requiring him to withdraw. Should Wyatt succeed in getting the job, however, Behan said there was no need to return the favor, recognizing that Wyatt would have to name one of his brothers second-in-command.

Neither story rings completely true, especially Behan's claim that he was already assured of receiving the position when he opened negotiations with Wyatt Earp. On the other hand, Wyatt was hardly the type to give up easily if he thought he had a good chance of prevailing. The best interpretation is probably that Behan was the clear front-runner but that both men were still in contention. In that case, each would have had an incentive to deal with the other, which is evidently what happened.

Johnny Behan was confirmed as the first sheriff of Cochise County on February 10, 1881. Rather than fulfill his bargain with Wyatt Earp, however, he quickly appointed Harry Woods as his undersheriff. An Alabama native and a stalwart of the Democratic Party, Woods had been active in lobbying the legislature to create Cochise County, and he was also the editor of the influential *Tombstone Nugget*. He was no lawman, but he brought political savvy and important connections to the office. Since Behan was far more interested in collecting taxes than in arresting rustlers, his promise to Wyatt Earp would just have to be ignored.

Ignored, perhaps, but not forgotten. The broken deal was also the beginning of the breakdown in relations between Behan and the Earps, who had little respect for the new sheriff as a lawman. They soon grew scornful of Behan's lax attitude toward law enforcement, and they became increasingly suspicious of his evident sympathy for Cowboys and rustlers. There was also a much more personal rivalry between Wyatt Earp and Johnny Behan, which may have played a more important role in the eventual confrontation than anyone was willing to acknowledge, at least in public, until decades later.

In the autumn of 1880, Behan began living with a beautiful young woman named Josephine Sarah Marcus. The daughter of middle-class German-Jewish immigrants, Josephine was born in New York City but moved to San Francisco with her family in the late 1860s, where her father worked as a baker. According to Josephine's memoirs, which were not published in her lifetime, she ran away from home in 1879 to join a troupe of actors that was about to bring a production of *HMS Pinafore* to Arizona. There she met Johnny Behan when, amid rumors of an impending Apache raid, he briefly escorted the troupe's coach. "He was a romantic, dashing cavalier," she said, "markedly handsome, with dark, flashing eyes and a ready smile."[11] The two became enamored of each other and began a courtship that would have far-reaching consequences.

Recent scholarship casts doubt on most of the details of this story, which appears to have been heavily romanticized. In any event, Josephine soon returned to San Francisco, where, again according to her memoir, she was pursued by the love-struck Behan, who traveled all the way from

Arizona to propose marriage. Josephine at first refused and Johnny left empty-handed, but he soon wrote to her from Tombstone, promising financial success and a good life. Josephine relented and again left her family for Arizona, intending to become the bride of Johnny Behan.

The two lived together as husband and wife, but Johnny did not make good on his promise of marriage. Details are sparse, but at some point Josephine's affections strayed in the direction of Wyatt Earp. In one version of events, she walked out on Johnny after catching him in bed with another woman; in another, Wyatt succeeded in "stealing" Sheriff Behan's woman. In either case, it seems clear that by the late summer of 1881, Wyatt and Josephine were romantically linked, and Wyatt had ended his uneasy "marriage" to Mattie Blaylock.

The more intriguing possibility is that Wyatt and Josephine became involved as early as the spring of 1881, provoking Behan or at least wounding his pride. There is evidence that he continued to carry a torch for Josephine even longer, as he turned up in San Francisco in March 1882, at a time when Josephine was known to be living there with her parents. What reason would the sheriff of Cochise County, Arizona, have for traveling all the way to San Francisco if not to pursue the woman Bat Masterson once called "the belle of the honky-tonks" and the "prettiest dame" in Tombstone?[12]

Whatever the specifics, the Johnny-Josie-Wyatt triangle must surely have caused tension between the two men—either because of Johnny's jealousy or because Wyatt shared Josephine's resentment at Behan's poor treatment of her. The commitment between Wyatt and Josephine would only grow stronger. They remained together for nearly fifty years, marrying in 1888 after the death of Mattie Blaylock.

The Benson Stage Robbery

On March 15, 1881, a band of outlaws attacked the Tombstone-Benson stagecoach, opening the final chain of events that would lead to the gunfight at the O.K. Corral. The stage was being driven by Eli "Bud" Philpot, with Bob Paul—still waiting for the outcome of his challenge to the Pima County sheriff's election—riding shotgun. As the stage ascended a small incline, a masked bandit stepped into the coach's path, demanding that the driver stop the horses. Paul raised his shotgun to resist, but the would-be robbers fired, killing Philpot and a passenger. The horses bolted and the bandits fled, leaving behind a Wells Fargo box containing twenty-six thousand dollars in silver.

Paul gained control of the frightened team and brought the stage safely into Benson. He sent a telegram to Tombstone, informing the authorities of the murders, and a posse was quickly assembled. As George Parsons described it in his journal: "Men and horses were flying about in different directions, and I soon ascertained the cause. A large posse started in pursuit—$26,000 in specie reported on stage. Bob Paul went as shot gun messenger and emptied both barrels of his gun at the robbers, probably wounding one. 'I hold for no one,' he said and let drive. Some 20 shots fired—close call for Paul."[13]

Once on the trail, the posse divided into two bands. One group, under the leadership of Virgil Earp, included Wyatt and Morgan, Bat Masterson, Doc Holliday, and a Wells Fargo agent named Marshall Williams. The other was headed by Sheriff Behan, accompanied by Harry Woods and several other men.

After three days, the Earp posse managed to track down a man named Luther King, who confessed his complicity in the holdup. Claiming that he had only held the horses, King named William Leonard, Harry Head, and James Crane, all of whom had Cowboy associations, as the men who had done the shooting. The Earps turned King over to the Behan posse for delivery back to Tombstone and set off on the trail of Leonard, Head, and Crane. After six days of hard riding, they admitted defeat and headed back to town, only to be stunned by developments in Tombstone.

The first bad news was that Luther King had managed to "escape," although that may be the wrong term given the shady circumstances in which he regained his freedom. The official story was that King had slipped out of the jailhouse while the deputy was distracted, but the details are telling. There had been many rumors of a Cowboy plan to rescue their confederate. Nonetheless, Harry Woods admittedly left King unattended—and the door to the jailhouse unlocked—while an attorney was drawing up a contract for the sale of King's horse to John Dunbar, who happened to be a business partner of Behan's as well as the Democratic treasurer of Cochise County. By "coincidence," there also happened to be a fresh horse waiting behind the jail, which King used to make good his departure.

King's escape caused an uproar. At a minimum, it was inexcusable for the sheriff's office to be so casual about the custody of a man being held in connection with a murder. Suspicions of complicity were unavoidable. Parsons probably summed up the views of many outraged citizens when he wrote, "Some of our officials should be hanged. They're a bad lot."[14]

Harry Woods's *Nugget* was predictably forgiving of the lapse, calling it a "well-planned job by outsiders to get [King] away."[15] The *Nugget's* story ignored an obvious question: How was it that King's confederate knew that Behan's undersheriff and partner would take their eyes off the prisoner on that day at that time? There might have been an innocent explanation, but one would have to pardon the Earps if they indulged their own suspicions about Behan's loosely guarded jail.

To make matters worse, Sheriff Behan refused to pay the Earps for their posse work. Although the county supervisors appropriated about eight hundred dollars to cover the expense, Behan did not share any of it with the Earps, claiming that they had never been officially deputized. Legally, he was on shaky ground. The territorial statutes took a rather loose approach to deputization, requiring no formalities and allowing peace officers simply to enlist "other persons who, by their command, act in their aid." In commonsense terms, Behan's case was even weaker. By tracking down and arresting Luther King, the Earps produced the posse's only positive accomplishment, which Behan's deputy proceeded to bungle, or perhaps sabotage, through inattention (the Earps also stayed on the trail six days longer than anyone else). Nonetheless, the county supervisors supported Behan, which incensed Virgil: "Everybody but myself and my brothers were paid, and we did not get a cent until Wells-Fargo found it out and paid us for our time."[16]

Most ominously, Tombstone was awash in rumors that Doc Holliday had participated in the Benson stage holdup. There is usually some basis for gossip, but in this case it was negligible—Doc had been seen riding into Tombstone on the night of the robbery, his horse "fagged out" with exhaustion. It was enough, however, to keep the stories alive, especially given Doc's unsavory reputation.

Johnny Behan was happy enough to pursue the rumors, either because he believed them (which was not very likely, given that even Luther King said nothing to implicate Holliday) or because he saw an opportunity to undermine the Earps. Karen Holliday Tanner, Doc's biographer (and distant niece), believes that Behan was also "influenced by his close friend Milt Joyce," Doc Holliday's nemesis and a Democratic Cochise County supervisor. Pro-Earp writers have suggested that Behan was hopeful of distracting attention from his own inability to arrest, or hold, the stage robbers, or even to "camouflage [his] own association" with the outlaws.[17]

Whatever his motive, Behan seized an opportunity that July when Kate Elder, evidently after one of her periodic fights with Holliday, became drunk and vindictive. Behan persuaded her to sign an affidavit charging Doc with taking part in the holdup, and Doc was promptly arrested and charged with murder.

The case came before Justice of the Peace Wells Spicer for a preliminary hearing, but the evidence against Holliday virtually dissolved. The now-sober Kate recanted her accusation, and Wyatt helped Doc produce several witnesses who supported his alibi that he had been gambling in Charleston on the evening of the robbery (hence his return to Tombstone on a lathered horse). District Attorney Lyttleton Price, a Republican appointed by Governor Fremont, announced that the evidence appeared to be insufficient and requested dismissal of all charges. As the *Nugget* sarcastically reported, "The court thereupon dismissed the case and discharged the defendant, and thus ended—what at the time was supposed to be—an important trial."[18] To the Earps' satisfaction, Behan could only have been embarrassed by the outcome. Judge Spicer and District Attorney Price, of course, had merely done their jobs. They were not lenient toward Holliday. The absence of evidence would have permitted no other result. But Price and Spicer would soon play crucial roles in the prosecution of the Earps, when they would both, to varying degrees, be charged with favoring the defense.

Another Bargain

Perhaps spurred by Johnny Behan's ineptitude and unreliability, Virgil and Wyatt were determined to get their badges back. Virgil's opportunity came quickly enough. In early June, the feckless Ben Sippy obtained a two-week leave of absence from Tombstone to attend to some financial matters. When he failed to return or send word, Virgil Earp was again appointed town marshal (although the town council had recently changed the title to the more urban-sounding chief of police).

For his part, Wyatt decided to renew his effort to obtain the Cochise County sheriff's job, setting his sights on the next election. Realizing that it would be an uphill battle to unseat the genial and well-liked Johnny Behan—in a Democratic county, to boot—Wyatt embarked on an ill-conceived scheme to increase his own popularity and visibility, with disastrous consequences.

Believing that Ike Clanton had information about Leonard, Head, and Crane—the robbers of the Benson stage—Wyatt approached the rustler with an offer. Wyatt proposed to give Ike the hefty reward offered by Wells Fargo for the three Cowboys if Ike would agree to lure his sometime-pals into an ambush. Wyatt could then bask in the glory of capturing the outlaws and probably exonerate Doc Holliday once and for all. Giving the reward money to Ike Clanton seemed like a small price to pay in exchange for bolstering Wyatt's chances in the election. As he would later explain in court, "I had an ambition to be sheriff of this county in the next election, and I thought it would be a great help to me with the people and businessmen if I could capture the man who killed Philpot."

Ike seemed to have no compunction about betraying his friends. He insisted on keeping the deal a secret, of course, since his life would be worthless if word got out that he had conspired to inform on fellow Cowboys. Equally important, Ike was certain that Leonard, Head, and Crane would not give up without a fight—so he needed to know whether the reward was offered "Dead or Alive." Wyatt agreed to send a telegram to the Wells Fargo headquarters in San Francisco seeking confirmation that the Cowboys did not need to be captured alive. He received an affirmative reply on June 7, 1881, and showed it to Ike to seal the deal.

As it turned out, Ike Clanton had no opportunity to keep the bargain or reap the reward. Leonard, Head, and Crane all died that summer before Clanton could spring the trap. Leonard and Head were killed in early June in a gunfight with Ike and Bill Haslett in New Mexico. According to an anonymous letter in the *Epitaph,* the Cowboys intended to drive the Hasletts off their ranch, but the brothers got wind of the plot and managed to shoot first. Within weeks, both Hasletts were also dead, murdered in revenge by Jim Crane and as many as half a dozen friends.

The killing of the Hasletts was terrifying. It was one thing for someone to be shot in a drunken brawl, or even a holdup, but a reprisal killing was far worse, raising the risk of violence to an entirely new level. It also meant that the Cowboys took vengeance seriously, making it impossible for the Earps to ignore Ike Clanton's tirade later that year when he stormed from one end of Tombstone to the other threatening their lives. As the Haslett brothers learned, when Cowboys threatened someone, they meant it.

There was one more incident that deepened the antagonism between the Earps and the Cowboys, and it implicated Johnny Behan as well. Late at night on September 8, the stagecoach from Tombstone to Bisbee was robbed by two masked men. After they seized a mail sack and the Wells Fargo box, one of the bandits made a fatal slip, going through a passenger's pockets to see whether he had "some sugar." As a slang term for money, it seems that "sugar" was a favorite saying of Frank Stilwell, one of Johnny Behan's deputy sheriffs, which immediately made him a prime suspect.

The robbery was reported the next morning, and a posse set out from Tombstone that included Wyatt and Morgan Earp. Picking up the outlaws' trail, Wyatt found a boot heel that matched the tracks at the scene of the robbery. In Bisbee, Wyatt located a shoemaker who was able to identify Stilwell as the owner of the suspect boot. Wyatt arrested Stilwell, as well as his accomplice Pete Spence (sometimes also called Spencer), and brought them to Tombstone charged with robbery.

The arrest of Behan's deputy was potentially explosive, even more damaging than the earlier escape of Luther King. Clum's *Epitaph,* which had once warned, "There is altogether too much good feeling between the Sheriff's office and the outlaws infesting this county," chose this time to make its point through acid understatement: "The evidence against Deputy Sheriff Stilwell is circumstantial, and rests principally upon the tracks made by his boot heels in the mud, which corresponded with those he had removed by a shoemaker upon his return to Bisbee. The *Epitaph* has no desire to prejudge the case, but if it turns out as now anticipated, that the officers of the law are implicated in this nefarious business, it would seem to be in order for Sheriff Behan to appoint another Deputy."[19]

Brought before Judge Spicer for a preliminary hearing, Stilwell and Spence produced several witnesses to support their alibis. Demonstrating that he was an equal opportunity skeptic when it came to circumstantial evidence, Spicer dismissed the charges against the defendants, just as he had discharged Doc Holliday earlier in the year. Virgil Earp, however, promptly rearrested the pair on a federal charge of robbing the mail and took them to Tucson for arraignment.[20] Pro-Earp writers generally assume that Stilwell was guilty, although the known evidence against him was pretty thin. Judge Spicer's ruling was impeccable; a trademark phrase and a new boot heel leave plenty of room for reasonable doubt.

If Stilwell had indeed robbed the stage, then the Earps obviously had one more reason to mistrust Sheriff Behan. If he had not—something that we will never know—then Virgil's rearrest would have looked much like a vendetta, both to Behan and to the other Cowboys. Nothing that we know about Virgil Earp suggests that he would intentionally have pursued an innocent man, but everyone makes mistakes and Virgil's judgment might easily have been influenced by his resentment of Behan and his suspicion of anyone who seemed to have Cowboy connections. In either case, the repeated prosecution of Stilwell surely increased the level of tension in Tombstone.

Wyatt would later testify that Frank McLaury reacted angrily to the arrest of Stilwell and Spence, offering the incident as proof that the McLaurys were in league with outlaws: "The McLaurys and Clantons have always been friends of Stilwell and Spencer, and they laid the whole blame for their arrest on us. . . . Frank McLaury took Morgan Earp into the street in front of the Alhambra [and] commenced to abuse Morgan Earp for going after Spencer and Stilwell. . . . He said to Morgan: 'If you ever come after me, you will never take me.'" We do not have Frank's version of the incident, but even Wyatt's account is ambiguous. McLaury could have been just as indignant about a vindictive arrest as a legitimate one.

Whatever the truth about Stilwell, the rift between the Earps and Behan continued to widen. As summer turned to fall, the law enforcement situation in Tombstone had deteriorated so badly that acting Governor John Gosper came to town to conduct a personal investigation.

Discouraged by almost everything he found, yet unwilling to take sides, Gosper reported the following to Secretary of State James Blaine:

> [T]he officers of the law are at times either unable or unwilling to control this class of out-laws, sometimes being governed by *fear*, at other times by a hope of *reward*. At Tombstone . . . I conferred with the Sheriff . . . upon the subject of breaking up these bands of out-laws, and I am sorry to say he gave me but little hope of being able in his department to cope with the power of the cowboys. He represented to me that the Deputy U.S. Marshal, resident of Tombstone, and the city marshal for the same . . . seemed unwilling to heartily co-operate with him (the Sheriff) in capturing and bringing to justice these out-laws.
>
> In conversation with Deputy U.S. Marshal, Mr. Earp, I found precisely the same spirit of complaint existing against Mr. Behan (the Sheriff) and his deputies.
>
> And back of this unfortunate fact—rivalry between the civil authorities, or an unwillingness to work together in full accord in keeping the peace—I found the two daily newspapers published in the city taking sides with the Deputy Marshal and Sheriff respectively; each paper backing its civil clique and condemning the other.[21]

Presciently, Gosper concluded that "*Something must be done,* and that right early, or very grave results will follow." It would only be a few weeks before he was proved correct.

4

Thirty Shots in Thirty Seconds

By the fall of 1881, all three of the Benson stage robbers were dead. Bill Leonard and Harry Head were dispatched by the equally ill-fated Haslett brothers, and Jim Crane was later killed by Mexican troops in the Guadalupe Canyon massacre, along with Old Man Clanton and several other rustlers. Wyatt Earp's deal with Ike Clanton never amounted to anything. It probably would have been forgotten without further incident if Ike had been able to keep his mouth shut. Instead, it became the catalyst for a gunfight.

At age thirty-three, Joseph Isaac "Ike" Clanton was the oldest son in a notorious family. Wyatt Earp would later maintain that Ike was a "sort of chief among the cowboys," but there is no evidence for this claim apart from Wyatt's assertion. Still, the Clanton family played a central role in cross-border cattle theft, with their ranch on the San Pedro River providing something of a headquarters for rustling activity, so Wyatt obviously had good reason to believe that Ike had significant contacts among the Cowboys. Whatever his position in the outlaws' vague hierarchy, most researchers agree that Ike was given to fits of temper and erratic behavior, especially when drinking.

Late on the evening of October 25, 1881, Ike Clanton and Tom McLaury rode into Tombstone with a wagonload of beef, which they left at the West End Corral. Shortly after midnight, Ike headed to the Alhambra Saloon for lunch (meaning a light meal), where he ran into Doc Holliday. The meeting was not entirely a coincidence.

Some time earlier—the date is uncertain—Ike apparently had an unsettling encounter with Wells Fargo agent Marshall Williams, who seems to have guessed that Clanton had some sort of deal working with Wyatt Earp. In fact, it is not impossible that Wyatt would have shared his plan with Williams, who was responsible for Wells Fargo's business in Tombstone. Or Williams might have figured it out for himself, having seen the "Dead or Alive" telegram that Wyatt requested from San Francisco. Either way, Ike was gravely alarmed at the possibility of being revealed as a snitch, and he accused Wyatt of spilling the beans to Doc Holliday. Why Ike would impute Williams's knowledge to Holliday is unclear; perhaps he was simply jumping to a frightened conclusion. Wyatt assured Ike that the deal was still a secret and summoned Holliday (who was gambling in Tucson) back to Tombstone in order to calm the worried Cowboy.

But if Wyatt showed poor judgment when he made his bargain with Ike, he showed ruinous judgment when he thought that Doc Holliday would do anything other than make the situation worse. In fact, the whole idea seems questionable. Why would Wyatt Earp care a whit about Ike Clanton's accusations, much less make any substantial effort to assuage his fears? Leonard, Head, and Crane were already dead, so Wyatt certainly did not need any more cooperation from the Cowboy. And it was Ike who had to worry about exposure, so he obviously had no leverage over Wyatt. Moreover, even if Holliday insisted that "Wyatt never told me about your deal," he would simultaneously be acknowledging that he knew there was a "deal" to deny. And that would only confirm Clanton's deepest fear. To Ike, especially if he was already drunk, Holliday's protestations would have to seem more like provocation than reassurance.

The source for this vignette is Stuart Lake, who interviewed Wyatt several times in the 1920s before publishing *Wyatt Earp, Frontier Marshal.* Lake frequently improved his story, and Wyatt, of course, would have been inclined to polish his own image forty years after the fact. So even if the basic outline of events is accurate, there is at least one alternative scenario. Perhaps Doc Holliday was called to Tombstone in order to intimidate Ike Clanton rather than to mollify him. Although the Benson stage robbers were dead, Wyatt might have wanted to maintain Ike as an informant. Lacking the inducement of reward money, a tough warning from Doc Holliday—whose reputation for violence was much fiercer than Wyatt's—would help keep the Cowboy in line. This is only a hypothesis, but it does provide a better explanation for Ike's furiously hostile reaction.

Not surprisingly, the meeting was far from conciliatory. Ike was facing the prospect of exposure (or maybe extortion), while still grieving his father's death in the Guadalupe Canyon massacre, so his unsteady nerves were no doubt frayed when he encountered Holliday at the Alhambra. The parlay soon dissolved into insults, as Ike refused to believe Doc's protestations of ignorance, and Holliday called Ike a "damned liar" and cursed him as a "son of a bitch of a cowboy." According to Ike, Holliday kept his hand "in his bosom," presumably holding a gun, while continuing his taunts: "You son-of-a-bitch, if you ain't heeled [armed], go heel yourself."

Morgan Earp, working as a "special deputy" in the Alhambra, managed to get both Ike and Doc to leave the saloon. Not long after, Ike confronted Wyatt on the street, still seething about his exchange with Holliday. Wyatt described Ike as angry and combative: "He said that in the morning he would have a 'man for man.'" Wyatt responded calmly, "I told him I would fight no one if I could get away from it, because there was no money in it."

Then, in what can only be described as a continuation of the feud by other means, many of the principals repaired to the Occidental Saloon for an all-night game of poker. Ike Clanton, Johnny Behan, Virgil Earp, Tom McLaury, and perhaps Wyatt, Morgan, and Doc, all sat around the same table for nearly five hours with no resort to violence (although Ike later complained that Virgil kept his pistol on display). History does not record the name of the big winner, but it is unlikely to have been Ike, whose foul humor remained. Following Virgil after the game ended, Ike continued his threats, this time against Doc Holliday. "That damned son of a bitch has got to fight," he said. Virgil cautioned Ike not to make a disturbance but only received another threat in reply, "You may have to fight before you know it."

Virgil and Wyatt each went home to sleep for a few hours, but Ike Clanton was in no mood to rest. Instead, he roamed the streets of

Tombstone, openly carrying a gun and continuing to curse the Earps and Holliday. Numerous witnesses heard Clanton's threats, some taking him seriously and some shrugging him off. Ike did succeed in alarming bartender Ned Boyle, telling him that "as soon as the Earps and Doc Holliday showed themselves on the street, the ball would open" and they would "have to fight." The colorful metaphor may have convinced Boyle that Ike meant business, so he hastened to Wyatt's house to warn him. At about the same time, deputy marshal A. G. Bronk was at Virgil's house delivering the same message. Eventually, at least half a dozen people would report Ike's threats to the Earps, including attorney Harry Jones, who told Wyatt, "Ike Clanton is hunting you boys with a Winchester rifle and six-shooter."

It may not have been the Earps whom Ike was hunting. He was soon seen standing outside Camillus Fly's rooming house, where Doc Holliday was living with Kate Elder. Doc was asleep, but Kate and Mary Fly saw Ike waving his Winchester. Kate ran upstairs and woke Doc, telling him, "Ike Clanton was here looking for you, and he had a rifle with him." With characteristic fatalism, Doc replied, "If God will let me live long enough, he will see me."

As noon approached, Ike Clanton was at the corner of Fourth and Fremont Streets holding his rifle and carrying a pistol in his waistband. Unaware of Ike's morning fulminations, John Clum greeted him rather cheerfully. "Hello, Ike," he said, "any new war?"[1] The publisher of the *Epitaph* continued walking, not realizing that the biggest story of his career was about to unfold.

By now, Wyatt and Virgil were out of bed and, along with Morgan, were on Ike's trail. Virgil and Morgan caught up with him first, near Allen Street. Virgil took the initiative, quickly grabbing Ike's rifle and just as quickly using his own revolver to club Clanton to the ground. Virgil would later claim that Ike was trying to draw his revolver, though Ike insisted that he was buffaloed from behind without warning.

Virgil and Morgan dragged the bleeding Cowboy to the courtroom of Judge Albert Wallace, charging him with carrying firearms within city limits. The charge was legitimate enough, but Tombstone's weapons ordinance was seldom rigorously enforced. Only moments earlier, for example, Mayor Clum had considered it unimportant when he observed Clanton fully armed.

Finding the courtroom empty, Virgil left to look for the judge while Wyatt and Morgan guarded Ike. The war of words continued, with Wyatt's temper boiling. "You damned dirty cow-thief," he said, "if you are anxious to make a fight, I will go anywhere on earth to make a fight with you." Clanton was equally belligerent, showing either courage or foolhardiness under the circumstances. "Fight is my racket," he replied, "and all I want is four feet of ground." Then, turning to Morgan, he continued, "If you fellows had been a second later, I would have furnished a coroner's inquest for the town." Deputy Marshal Dave Campbell managed to separate the men just as the judge arrived in the courtroom. Clanton was fined twenty-five dollars on the spot, which he paid immediately. Ike was free to go, minus his firearms, which Virgil deposited with the desk clerk at the Grand Hotel.

Leaving the courthouse, Wyatt nearly ran into Tom McLaury, who may have been looking for Ike either to help or to restrain him. Accounts differ as to whether the two men exchanged harsh words, with Wyatt reporting threats that bystanders denied hearing. According to witnesses, Tom was not visibly armed. But Wyatt, still fuming over Ike's outbursts, was taking no chances. Slapping McLaury with one hand, Wyatt pulled his revolver and used it to knock the Cowboy off his feet.

Nearly everyone in Tombstone knew that trouble was brewing. Stories flew around town of Ike's gun-waving histrionics and the Earps' brutal ripostes—not only against the disreputable Ike Clanton, but also against the seemingly innocent Tom McLaury. Even then, everything might have blown over if Billy Clanton and Frank McLaury, both heavily armed, had not chosen that moment to ride into Johnny Behan's Dexter Corral.

As we have already seen, Frank McLaury was not inclined to back down from a fight, whether he was right or wrong. Billy Clanton, at age nineteen, was already an experienced rustler. Only a year earlier, Wyatt caught him trying to remove a stolen racehorse from a corral. Billy did not resist returning the horse, but his cocky response—"Do you have any more horses to lose?"—showed him to be as brash as he was young. Most researchers agree that Billy and Frank were simply riding into town in order to meet up with their brothers, but their arrival must have seemed suspicious to the Earps. Both men had Winchester rifles in saddle scabbards, and both had six-guns on their hips, which they continued to carry in at least temporary violation of the Tombstone ordinance.

Billy and Frank soon learned of their brothers' rough treatment by the Earps. They may have told two friends, Billy Allen and Billy Claiborne, that they intended to get out of town, but instead they headed for Spangenberg's gun shop, where they were seen, along with Ike, loading ammunition into their gunbelts. As it turned out, the proprietor refused to sell a gun to Ike Clanton, whose weapons were still at the Grand Hotel, but that would not have been obvious to the many people watching from the street.

Citizens continued to warn the Earps about the Clantons and McLaurys. A miner told Virgil that the armed Cowboys "mean trouble," urging the marshal to disarm them. More ominously, a newcomer in town, completely unaware of the bad blood, informed Virgil that he had overheard four or five men saying "they would kill the whole party of Earps." Members of the Citizens Safety Commission offered their assistance, but Virgil declined the vigilantes' help, still assuming that he could bring the situation under control. As a precaution, however, he walked over to the Wells Fargo office, where he borrowed a short-barreled shotgun. By this time, the Clanton and McLaury brothers had gathered at the O.K. Corral. They had two horses with them, so they may have been thinking about leaving town. At least it seemed that way to Virgil Earp, who decided to leave the men alone as long as they remained in the corral and stayed out of the street.

For most of the day, Johnny Behan was nowhere to be seen. Having played poker all night, he slept late, as did Virgil and Wyatt, and evidently no one thought to wake him when the trouble began. Finally, in mid-afternoon, he heard the news while taking a shave at Barron's barbershop. Another customer said "there was liable to be trouble between Clanton and the Earp boys," so Behan told the barber to finish his shave in a hurry because he intended to "disarm the parties."

Leaving the barbershop, Behan encountered Virgil Earp near the corner of Fourth and Allen Streets, outside Hafford's Saloon and about a block from the O.K. Corral. Virgil and Johnny later told conflicting stories about their meeting, each claiming that the other was reluctant to assist in attempting to disarm the Cowboys. The upshot, however, was that Behan agreed to approach the Cowboys alone, and he set off to talk with them.

Although Virgil did not yet realize it, the Clantons and McLaurys had moved from the O.K. Corral, through an alley, into a vacant lot adjacent to Fly's rooming house on Fremont Street, bringing two horses with them. There has never been a good explanation for their move. Some writers have suggested that they intended to stake out Doc Holliday, although he was by that time long gone (in fact, he had already joined Virgil in front of Hafford's). Others believe that they were preparing to leave Tombstone, since they did have Frank and Billy's horses. But Ike and Tom's wagon was still at the West End Corral, across town in a different direction, and Ike's guns were still on deposit at the Grand Hotel, making the vacant lot an unlikely staging ground for departure. A third possibility is that they just wanted to get out of eyeshot of the Earps. The O.K. Corral was directly down Allen Street from Hafford's, where Virgil and company had gathered. Backing through the alley would give the Cowboys an opportunity to get out of sight while considering their options—whether to fight or flee.

Johnny Behan found the McLaury brothers standing outside a butcher shop that bordered the alleyway as it intersected Fremont Street. The Clanton brothers were slightly farther down the street, in the fifteen-foot-wide lot, where they had been joined by Billy Claiborne, another Cowboy. Behan asked Frank to surrender his arms, but Frank refused. Walking McLaury toward the vacant lot next to Fly's, the Cochise County sheriff again requested his gun. True to his character, Frank stubbornly insisted on keeping his weapons "without those other people [the Earps and Holliday] being disarmed" as well. Joining the other Cowboys outside Fly's, Behan patted down Ike Clanton for weapons but found nothing. Tom McLaury opened his coat to show that he was unarmed, but Behan did not search him. There was no need to search Billy Clanton, whose gun was in plain view but who claimed that he was headed out of town. Behan ignored Claiborne, who said he was not involved in the quarrel. Then, for some reason, he told the McLaurys and Clantons that he was going to "disarm the other party," and he left to find the Earps. Behan would later testify that he "considered the Clanton party under arrest, but I doubt whether they considered themselves under arrest or not, after I turned to meet the other party."

Behan's fruitless negotiations with Frank McLaury took about twenty minutes while Virgil Earp waited outside Hafford's, having been joined by his brothers and Doc Holliday. During this time, he was informed that the Cowboys had in fact left the corral and were standing on Fremont Street. That was a provocation Virgil decided he would not ignore, and he signaled the others that it was time to go to work. Ironically, the Cowboys had no reason to know that leaving the corral violated Virgil's unspoken ultimatum. They might even have thought that their retreat down the alley could avoid a confrontation, but instead it triggered everything that followed.

The Gunfight at the O.K. Corral

Wyatt and Morgan Earp were clearly Virgil's authorized deputies, but Doc Holliday was a different story. He had his own score to settle with Ike Clanton, having been threatened the previous evening and apparently stalked earlier that day. He showed up unbidden at Hafford's, mysteriously carrying a walking stick, and volunteered his help. Wyatt at first declined the offer, saying "This is our fight." But Doc persisted. "That's a hell of a thing for you to say to me," he replied. Virgil was apparently convinced that Holliday's assistance would be useful, handing him the shotgun to conceal under his long coat and taking the walking stick in exchange. Virgil would later be castigated for enlisting Holliday, but his choices were somewhat limited at the time, especially if he wanted to make an intimidating show of force. Some writers have questioned whether Holliday was ever actually deputized, but the territorial statutes required no specific formalities in cases where the public peace was threatened. In fact, Doc was a legitimate, if ill-chosen, member of Virgil's posse.

The Earps and Holliday began their march down Fourth Street to Fremont, where they turned left toward the alleyway. Dozens of people lined the street, with more watching from their windows, as the tension built. Virgil carried Doc's walking stick and kept his pistol in his waistband, while Wyatt and Morgan held their six-shooters in their hands. Doc tried to keep the shotgun out of sight—Virgil was worried that it would cause too much excitement if carried in plain view—but a stiff wind kept blowing his coat open, making concealment impossible. As they approached the vacant lot, a frantic Johnny Behan came rushing toward them.

"I am the sheriff of this county," he said, "and I am not going to allow any trouble if I can help it." As the Earps brushed past him, he called out a warning: "For God's sake, don't go down there or you will get murdered." Following after them, Behan then apparently contradicted himself, shouting, "I have disarmed them all." At least that is what Wyatt and Virgil believed they heard. Behan's version would be different, claiming that he said, "I was there for the purpose of arresting and disarming them." The discrepancy was crucial. Thinking that Behan had taken the Cowboys' guns, Wyatt and Virgil both relaxed their guard, only to be rudely surprised when Billy and Frank came into sight.

The Earps and Holliday stopped when they got to within about ten feet of the Cowboys. Billy Claiborne hurried out of the way, but the Clantons and McLaurys stood their ground. Billy and Frank still had their six-guns in open view and Tom McLaury was standing next to a horse with a rifle hanging from its saddle.

The Earps relied on years of experience as they faced the Clantons and McLaurys, surely expecting that the four men could be bullied into submission. Similar tactics had worked with countless Texans in Kansas, and they had worked equally well during the Earps' two years in Tombstone. Other men were not inclined to gamble with their lives, so they would usually back down at Virgil's command rather than test his intentions.

The Cowboys appeared edgy and frightened—a natural response, given the Earps' well-deserved reputation for rough justice. Ike and Tom, recalling their pistol whippings earlier in the day, did not want to be beaten again. The four men were cornered, but there was no way to tell how they would react. Would they surrender their weapons, trusting the Earps not to handle them too badly? Or would they make a fight of it? Either way, they had to act quickly in the face of Virgil's approach. But a sharp movement can easily be misunderstood in a tense situation, and the Earps were not inclined that day to give anyone the benefit of the doubt.

Virgil raised the walking stick in his right hand, calling out, "Boys, throw up your hands, I want your guns." Then, realizing what was about to happen, he shouted desperately, "Hold! I don't want that." It was too late. Two shots went off almost simultaneously, and, in Ike Clanton's phrase, "the ball opened." There would soon be great controversy over who started the gunfight, and in what circumstances, but there is no dispute that after a short pause the firing "became general."

Frank McLaury was the first man shot, taking a bullet in his right side and then staggering into the street. Morgan Earp was hit in the shoulder, by either Frank McLaury or Billy Clanton. As he fell to the ground, Morgan fired another round at Frank. Standing by one of the horses, Tom McLaury may have been trying to remove a rifle from its scabbard. If so, he did not act quickly enough, as Doc Holliday wheeled around and caught him under the right arm with a load of buckshot.

Ike ran toward Wyatt, whose own pistol was raised, grabbing him by the right arm in a gesture of either fear or courage. Seeing that Clanton was unarmed, Wyatt shoved him roughly to the side. "The fight has commenced," warned Wyatt. "Go to fighting or get away." Ike's fear triumphed, and he ran headlong into Camillus Fly's nearby house as Wyatt returned to the gun battle. The younger Clanton did not run. Although shot in the chest and again in the right wrist, Billy switched hands and continued firing as he slumped against a wall, shooting Virgil in the leg and inflicting a serious flesh wound.

In the meantime, Frank McLaury tried to shield himself behind a horse that he led across Fremont Street. Though severely wounded, he was not through fighting. Seeing Doc Holliday in his path, he lifted his gun and shouted, "I've got you now." Doc had thrown down his empty shotgun and drawn a pistol. "Blaze away," he replied, "you're a daisy if you have." Frank's unsteady shot grazed Doc's hip, just as both Holliday and Morgan Earp took more careful aim at the stumbling Cowboy, fatally striking him in the head and chest.

In less than half a minute, the most famous gunfight in American history was over. At least thirty shots had been fired, including two blasts from Doc Holliday's shotgun. Frank McLaury was killed on the spot; Tom McLaury and Billy Clanton were mortally wounded, to die within the hour. Virgil Earp's leg wound was painful, but not life threatening, while Morgan's wound was more serious, passing laterally from one shoulder to the other and chipping a vertebra. Wyatt Earp, the only participant who was not hit, silently surveyed the carnage. Ike Clanton, the man who started it all, was probably still running.

The dying Billy and Tom were taken into Camillus Fly's house. Dr. William Millar examined Billy, but finding his condition hopeless he treated him only with an injection of morphine. According to the *Nugget,* the younger Clanton was "game to the last," bravely saying, "Goodbye boys, go away and let me die."[2] Beyond even palliative care, Tom McLaury died without saying a word.

Before the bodies were moved, Coroner Henry Matthews arrived for a medical examination. Frank had two mortal pistol wounds, one in "the cranium beneath the right ear; another penetrating the abdomen one inch to the left of the navel," the latter most likely having caused his death. Billy Clanton also had two serious wounds—one in the abdomen and another "two inches to the left of the left nipple—as well as a bullet through his right wrist." Tom McLaury had a dozen buckshot wounds on the right side, covering an area as large as the coroner's hand. Matthews also searched the three bodies, finding six-shooters on Frank and Billy, but neither a weapon nor a cartridge belt on Tom—a fact that would be given much attention in the proceedings to come. Loosening Tom's shirt and belt, the coroner did find nearly three thousand dollars in cash, checks, and certificates of deposit in the Pima County Bank.

Too weak to stand, Virgil and Morgan were taken home by wagon. Wyatt and Doc stayed on the street, soon to be accosted by a trembling Johnny Behan. "Wyatt, I am arresting you for murder," he said, showing considerably more decisiveness than he had when negotiating with Frank McLaury. Wyatt was stunned, and then outraged. "I won't be arrested," he said. "You deceived me Johnny, you told me they were not armed. I won't be arrested, but I am here to answer what [*sic*] I have done. I am not going to leave town."

As Behan hesitated, realizing he was no match for Wyatt, the first of many citizens spoke up in the Earps' behalf. Sylvester Comstock, a saloonkeeper and hotel owner, pushed to the front of the crowd. "There is no hurry in arresting this man," he told the sheriff. "He done just right in killing them, and the people will uphold them." Wyatt seized the opportunity to back down the wavering Behan. "You bet we did right," he added. "We had to do it. And you threw us, Johnny. You told us they were disarmed." Whether he was persuaded, intimidated, or merely prudent, Johnny Behan made no arrest that day.

Sylvester Comstock was not the only Tombstone resident who supported the local police. Immediately after the gunfight, local sentiment was strongly in favor of Virgil and his brothers. Even as the smoke cleared, a signal from the Vizina mine whistle called dozens of armed vigilantes to the streets, ready to help protect "life and property" from a feared Cowboy "raid," as George Parsons put it.[3] So great was the sentiment for law and order that Ike Clanton—later joined by his brother Phin—was taken into protective custody to prevent a rumored lynching.

Predictably, John Clum's *Epitaph* led the chorus of justification. Its three-part headline the next morning ended with a telling phrase— "Yesterday's Tragedy; Three Men Hurled Into Eternity in the Duration of a Moment; The Causes That Led to the Sad Affair." In other words, the "tragedy" could only be understood in relation to its "causes," which the *Epitaph* quickly identified as the arrival in town of the "fractious and much dreaded cowboys." The *Epitaph* then recounted the killing of Marshal White, the robbery of the Bisbee stage, and the murder of Bud Philpot before even addressing the fatal gunfight.

The *Epitaph*'s report was based largely on an interview with R. F. Coleman, a miner who witnessed most of the fight. According to the published account, Virgil called upon the Cowboys "to throw up their hands, that he had come to disarm them. Instantaneously Bill Clanton and one of the McLaurys fired, and then it became general."[4] There was a thin line between opinion and news reporting in the 1880s, and the *Epitaph* frequently blurred it completely. Its report on the gunfight ended with a stern editorial:

> The feeling among the best class of our citizens is that The Marshal was entirely justified in his efforts to disarm these men, and that being fired upon they had to defend themselves, which they did most bravely.
>
> If the present lesson is not sufficient to teach the cowboy element that they cannot come into the streets of Tombstone, in broad daylight, armed with six-shooters and Henry rifles to hunt down their victims, then the citizens will most assuredly take

such steps to preserve the peace as will be forever a bar to further raids.[5]

Surprisingly, the *Nugget*'s story of the same day was also favorable to the Earps, a turn of events that is sometimes attributed to the fact that undersheriff-cum-editor Harry Woods was fortuitously absent from town. Instead, the article was written by the exceptionally professional Richard Rule, an objective reporter who apparently obtained his most crucial information from Johnny Behan. After reporting the sheriff's conversations with both the Cowboys and the Earps—for which the only possible source was Behan himself—Rule described the beginning of the gunfight, from the point where Virgil and his deputies proceeded down Fremont Street:

> [Behan] stepped out and said: "Hold up boys, don't go down there or there will be trouble: I have been down there to disarm them." But they passed on, and when within a few feet of them the Marshal said to the Clantons and McLaurys: "Throw up your hands boys, I intend to disarm you."
>
> As he spoke, Frank McLaury made a motion to draw his revolver, when Wyatt Earp pulled his and shot him, the ball striking on the right side of his abdomen. About the same time Doc Holliday shot Tom McLaury in the right side using a short shotgun, such as is carried by Wells-Fargo & Co. messengers.[6]

On the morning of October 27, the Earps probably thought that their only problem would be to recover from their wounds. Even the *Nugget*—known for its anti-Earp, pro-Cowboy sentiment—seemed to agree that the killings were prompted by Frank McLaury's move for his gun. Given the newspaper's strong connection to Behan, it must have seemed that the sheriff had reconsidered his plans to arrest them for murder.

On the next day, however, everything changed for the worse—including Johnny Behan's story.

5

—

Invitation to an Inquest

If the day's newspapers brought the Earps a sense of relief, they would quickly realize that their difficulties were far from over. Tombstone was a rugged place, so hardened to occasional shootings that the *Epitaph* ran a regular feature called "Death's Doings." But the town had never before experienced anything like a pitched battle in the street—in broad daylight and in front of scores of bystanders. The florid first sentence of the *Nugget*'s story underscored the impact of the gunfight on the community's sensibilities: "The 26th of October, 1881, will always be marked as one of the crimson days in the annals of Tombstone, a day when blood flowed as water, and human life was held as a shuttlecock, a day always to be remembered as witnessing the bloodiest and deadliest street fight that has ever occurred in this place, or probably in the Territory."[1]

Even people well-disposed toward the Earps could not avoid doubts as they reflected on the accounts of the witnesses, whether reported in the *Nugget* and *Epitaph* or passed from friend to friend in the saloons and shops. So what if Frank McLaury made a false move in the half-moment before the firing began? How could the Earps have been so sure that he was reaching for his gun? And even if Frank was foolishly starting to draw, couldn't the posse have backed him down without killing nearly everyone in sight? Then there was the problem of Doc Holliday. Virgil Earp may have had the authority to deputize him, but it was obviously a terrible misjudgment. The sight of Holliday was sure to provoke the

Clantons and McLaurys since he was known as a gunslinger rather than a lawman. Why did the Earps bring him along if their intentions were peaceable? Frank and Billy might not have resisted Marshal Virgil Earp, but they were sure to react angrily to the presence of Holliday. Even worse, there were already rumors that Doc fired the first shot. Known for his erratic behavior, Holliday might well have touched off the fight by pulling his gun while the Cowboys were still sizing up the situation. Whether or not that possibility—perhaps it was even a likelihood— weighed heavily on Virgil's conscience, it certainly roused suspicions among the citizens of Tombstone.

The corpses of Frank, Tom, and Billy were taken to an undertaker's parlor where they were "handsomely laid out" in formal clothing and displayed in open coffins under a bold sign that read "MURDERED IN THE STREETS OF TOMBSTONE." The authors of the sign are unknown, but it clearly conveyed a sentiment that would only grow in the course of the next days and weeks, much to the Earps' dismay.

The funeral for the McLaurys and Billy Clanton, held the following day, brought forth an astonishing show of sympathy for the slain men. Although the *Epitaph* had reviled them as "fractious and much dreaded cowboys," it turned out that they had many friends and sympathizers who grieved their violent deaths. More than three hundred people joined the procession on its way to Boot Hill, with as many as two thousand more said to have watched along sidewalks that "were densely packed for three or four blocks." Tombstone's brass band led the cortege, which the *Nugget* called "the largest ever witnessed in Tombstone." Even the *Epitaph* added a tolerant word, allowing that it was a most "saddening sight and such a one as it is to be hoped may never occur again in this community."[2]

Clara Brown was both impressed and disheartened by the spectacle. Although she observed that a "stranger . . . would have thought that some person esteemed by the entire camp was being conveyed to his final resting place," she was ultimately appalled: "No one could witness this sight without realizing the solemnity of the occasion and desiring proper regard to be observed for the dead, but such a public manifestation of sympathy from so large a portion of the residents of the camp seemed reprehensible when it is remembered that the deceased were nothing more or less than thieves."[3]

She may have thought it reprehensible to mourn the Cowboys, but Brown still allowed herself to attend the parade. As Casey Tefertiller has pointed out, "death often became a show in late nineteenth-century America."[4] Like Clara Brown, many of the onlookers must have come for diversion or entertainment, curious to see the well-dressed corpses in their "handsome caskets with heavy silver trimmings." Still, it could hardly have escaped notice that the Cowboys' burial drew a larger crowd than did Marshal White's funeral the previous year. People cared about the shootings and were not willing to let them pass quietly. The McLaury brothers were interred in a single grave, while Billy Clanton was buried separately. Then public attention turned to the law.

On October 28, 1881, only two days after the shootings, Coroner Henry Matthews convened a formal inquest. Born in Virginia, Matthews originally came west as an army surgeon in 1873. After a brief period in private practice in Tucson, he opened his Tombstone office in 1879, quickly becoming recognized as the dean of local physicians. He was appointed coroner by Governor Fremont upon the organization of Cochise County.

Historians have generally assumed that the inquest was held as a matter of course, but it was not quite that simple. While it may have been inevitable that there would be an inquiry into the unprecedented gun battle, the relevant Arizona statute provided for an inquest only when a person had been killed under "such circumstances as afford a reasonable ground to suspect that his death has been occasioned by the act of another by criminal means."[5] It is not known whether Coroner Matthews was reluctant or eager to hold the inquest, or whether either side pressured him. The determination to go forward, however, was a bad sign for the Earps. Notwithstanding the initial favorable reports in the *Nugget* and *Epitaph*, there would be no quick vindication.

Matthews's first statutory duty was to select a coroner's jury of nine to fifteen men. An active Republican—at one point he was chairman of the local party organization—he took some evident care to assemble ten jurors who represented a cross section of the business community. In addition to Charles Reppy, John Clum's business partner at the *Epitaph*, the jury also included saloonkeeper R. F. Hafford, who would later testify for the prosecution.[6]

An inquest is not a trial, or even an adversary proceeding. The coroner, rather than a judge, presides over the hearing. No lawyer presents a case or delivers an argument. Instead, the coroner has primary responsibility for interrogating witnesses, though the jurors may ask questions as well. Under Arizona law, the coroner was required to "summon and examine as witnesses every person who, in his opinion, or that of any of the jury, has any knowledge of the facts."[7] Matthews, however, engaged in substantial winnowing, calling only nine witnesses over two days, in contrast to the thirty who would eventually testify in the criminal case. His list showed a decided anti-Earp bias, including two witnesses—Ike Clanton and Billy Claiborne—whose veracity was open to question.

The first witness was Sheriff Behan, whose version of events had apparently changed markedly in less than forty-eight hours. Behan testified that Virgil Earp had been spoiling for a fight all afternoon. When they first met near Hafford's Saloon, for example, Virgil disclaimed any intention of disarming the "sons-of-bitches," saying that if the Cowboys "wanted to fight he would give them a chance." After trying to calm down the marshal, Behan left to disarm the Clantons and McLaurys. Before he could finish the job (Frank McLaury "rather demurred"), he saw the Earp party coming down the street, threatening trouble.

So far, Behan's testimony was fairly consistent with the newspaper accounts, though with a decidedly anti-Virgil spin. Within minutes, however, he would introduce an entirely new twist:

> When they got to the party of cowboys, they drew their guns and said, "You sons of bitches, you have been looking for a fight and you can have it!" Someone of the party, I think Marshal Earp, said "Throw up your hands! We are going to disarm you!"
>
> I heard Billy Clanton say, "Don't shoot me! I don't want to fight," or something to that effect.
>
> Tom McLaury said, "I have got nothing," and threw his coat back to show that he was not armed. This was instantly with the shooting, almost at the same time. The order to throw up their hands and this remark and the shooting were almost simultaneous.

Richard Rule, the *Nugget* reporter, must have been shocked to hear the sheriff testify so sharply at odds with the published account. Behan was saying that the Earps shot down men who were trying their best to surrender, with no mention of Frank McLaury's move for his gun.

Enhancing his own authority, Behan also testified that he considered the Clanton party under arrest when he searched Ike and requested the weapons of the others, although he had to admit that he doubted "whether they considered themselves under arrest or not." Doing his best to characterize the entire shoot-out as a private feud between the Earps and the Cowboys, Behan even denied that Virgil, the town marshal, was "acting in an official capacity" at the time.

Before leaving the stand, Behan made another new, and extremely important, claim that would influence both the inquest and the criminal case that followed. Asked who started the firing, he said: "I can't say who fired the first shot. It appears to me that it was fired from a nickel-plated pistol. There was two shots very close together. I know that the nickel-plated pistol was on the side of the Earps. I won't say which one of the Earp crowd fired it."

The witness was being disingenuous. Everyone in Tombstone knew that Doc Holliday favored a short-barreled nickel-plated pistol (the better to conceal in his "bosom," as when he confronted Ike in the Alhambra Saloon). Behan was blaming Doc for starting the fight, not necessarily Virgil Earp. After all, "the order to throw up their hands . . . and the shooting were almost simultaneous." The clear implication was that Virgil called for the Cowboys to surrender, but Doc literally jumped the gun, beginning the fight even as the cornered men raised their hands. Virgil would be culpable, of course, for bringing Holliday along in the first place. But Johnny Behan stopped short of accusing the town marshal of cold-blooded murder.

Intentionally or otherwise, this version of the story served a strategic purpose, both at the inquest and in the later criminal prosecution. By making Doc the primary bad guy (or maybe the scapegoat), Behan could avoid making wild accusations against the otherwise upright Earps while still presenting an account in which Virgil and Wyatt were indirectly responsible for the killings. As we will see, Behan's claim about recognizing a nickel-plated pistol would become untenable, although he would stick with it to the bitter end. Doc was carrying a shotgun at the beginning of the fight, and it would have been virtually impossible for him to have started the firing with a previously concealed pistol. Nonetheless, the "Doc fired first" theory would continue to be pressed, seemingly to the advantage of the prosecution.

Two other witnesses—Ike Clanton and Billy Claiborne—repeated Behan's claim, though they both lacked the sheriff's authority and credibility.

Ike Clanton told his whole story, beginning with the late-night incident in the Alhambra Saloon when "Doc Holliday came in and commenced abusing me [with] his hand on his pistol," with the apparent approval of Virgil, Wyatt, and Morgan. Ike admitted that he "heeled" himself, "expecting to meet Doc Holliday on the street." Instead, Virgil buffaloed him from behind.

When it came to the gunfight, Ike's testimony echoed Behan's, down to the detail of the nickel-plated pistol (again declining to say who held it). The Earps shouted "you sons-of-bitches, you ought to make a fight," while Virgil gave the order to raise their hands. Then, according to Ike, "Billy Clanton, Frank McLaury and myself threw up our hands at the order from the Earp party, and Tom McLaury threw his coat open and said, 'I have got no arms.'" To no avail. "At the same instant, Doc Holliday and Morg Earp shot," as Ike made his grab at Wyatt's gun hand.

In his inquest testimony, Ike offered only the vaguest reason for his "abuse" by the Earps and Holliday, much less the shootings that followed. "I never had any previous trouble with the Earps," he said, yet for some unstated reason, "they don't like me." As to the deal to betray the Benson stage robbers, Ike was still apparently wary of exposure, saying, "We had one transaction—I mean, myself and Earps—but it had nothing to do with the killing of these three men." It would later occur to Ike that the "transaction" had everything to do with the killings, but not until he had an opportunity to organize his story with the assistance of counsel.

Billy Claiborne, another Cowboy, testified that he helped Ike obtain medical treatment for his head injury before accompanying the Clanton brothers first to the Dexter Corral ("Johnny Behan's stable," he called it) and then through to the O.K. Corral. He saw Behan talking to Frank McLaury but could not hear what was said, and the next thing he saw was the approach of the Earps and Doc Holliday.

Unlike the other witnesses Claiborne testified that it was Virgil who first shouted, "You sons-of-bitches, you have been looking for a fight and now you can get it," before ordering the men to "throw up your hands!" After that implausible sequence, Claiborne's testimony was completely in line with Behan's and Clanton's. Billy, Ike, and Frank all raised their hands, as Billy cried, "Don't shoot me, I don't want to fight." At the same time, "Tom McLaury took hold of the lapels of his coat and threw it open and said, 'I have not got anything.' " It was "at that instant the shooting commenced by Doc Holliday and Morgan Earp," with Doc using his "nickel-plated six-shooter." After the first few shots, Sheriff Behan pushed Claiborne into Fly's photo studio—out of the way of danger—and he did not observe the rest of the fight.

Johnny Behan's testimony was essential, of course, given that the county sheriff witnessed nearly the entire gunfight. Although his political rivalry with Wyatt Earp was well-known, that alone would not have cast much, if any, doubt on his testimony. His romantic rivalry with Wyatt was potentially more damaging, but we have no way of knowing whether that was an open secret at the time; certainly no one remarked on it.

Ike Clanton, on the other hand, had very obvious reasons to distort his testimony, both to implicate the Earps and to absolve himself of responsibility for his brother's death. Even the most credulous observer would have to doubt his story that the Earps and Holliday threatened him, buffaloed him, and then tracked him down—killing three men in the process—all for no apparent reason other than "they don't like me." No one could have listened to Ike's testimony without wondering what he was hiding.

Billy Claiborne was not implicated in the killings, though he had been in the company of the Clantons and McLaurys right up until that last moment. Sometimes called "Billy the Kid," Claiborne was a known Cowboy who, barely three weeks earlier, had shot and killed a man in a saloon brawl in Charleston.

Neutral Witnesses

In addition to Behan, Clanton, and Claiborne, the jury heard from five "neutral" witnesses who had no connection with any of the participants. Their testimony was generally unfavorable to the Earps, but none of them corroborated either the "Cowboy surrender" or the "Doc fired first" theories.

R. F. Coleman, the miner whose account was quoted in the *Epitaph*, was called to the stand immediately following Behan, probably on the assumption that he would provide exculpatory evidence. Coleman was one of many Tombstone residents who kept an eye on Ike Clanton throughout the day. He saw Virgil arrest and buffalo Ike in the morning, followed them to Judge Wallace's courtroom, and then heard Ike's renewed challenge to Wyatt—"all I want is four feet of ground"—out on the street. Coleman watched the Cowboys gather at the O.K. Corral and concluded that they "meant mischief," which he reported to both Marshal Earp and Sheriff Behan, asking both officers to "go and disarm those men."

Continuing to trace the Cowboys' steps, Coleman returned to the O.K. Corral, passed through the alleyway, and ended up near the vacant lot in time to see the Earps brush past Johnny Behan. He heard the posse's order "throw up your hands" or "give up your arms," although he incorrectly attributed the command to Wyatt. At that moment, however, Coleman turned away and therefore could not see whether the Cowboys raised their hands. He heard the first two shots fired, but he was not in a position to see who did the shooting. He was able to say only that Billy Clanton "had his hand on his pistol which was in the scabbard" just after the first two shots were fired.

Coleman was asked about the slight discrepancy between his testimony and the story attributed to him in the *Epitaph*, in which he seemed to say that the firing began in response to Virgil's command to "give up your arms or throw up your arms." The witness affirmed, however, that his account in the *Epitaph* was "pretty near correct as published," leaving the jurors to resolve any lingering inconsistencies on their own. It is interesting to note that Johnny Behan was not asked a similar question, perhaps because no one identified him as the unnamed source of the *Nugget*'s report.

Two of the neutral witnesses, William Cuddy and C. H. Light, had relatively little to add, neither implicating the Earps nor exonerating them. The remaining two, however, provided potentially damaging details.

Housewife Martha King was shopping for dinner in Bauer's butcher shop just as the Earps and Holliday marched past on Fremont Street. Standing near the door, she heard one of the Earps say, "Let them have it," to which Doc Holliday replied, "All right." Frightened, she ran to the back of the shop and did not see the shootings.

P. H. Fellehy, a laundryman, delivered the most devastating—and enigmatic—testimony of the entire hearing. Like so many others, Fellehy was aware of the trouble brewing between the Earps and the Cowboys, and he did his best to follow the action. Most importantly, he saw and heard the discussion between Virgil and Johnny Behan just before Behan repaired to the vacant lot in his futile effort to disarm Frank McLaury. According to Fellehy, "The Marshal, Virgil Earp, said, 'Those men have made their threats. I will not arrest them, but will kill them on sight.'"

One can only imagine the impact of this explosive and unexpected testimony on the jurors and spectators. Behan, Clanton, and Claiborne had basically accused the Earps of shooting too quickly as the Cowboys tried to surrender. That would amount to homicide—either manslaughter or, at worst, second-degree murder—but Fellehy added evidence of premeditation. If Virgil really intended to "kill them on sight," then the applicable crime would have to be first-degree murder, which carried mandatory capital punishment under Arizona law.[8] It was one thing to wonder whether the Earps acted recklessly or irresponsibly, but it was an entirely different matter to suggest that they were deliberate assassins.

Tellingly, Johnny Behan made no mention of such a statement in his inquest testimony, or at any time thereafter, even though it was allegedly made directly to him. Throughout the legal proceedings Behan would be among the Earps' leading antagonists, but he always stopped short of accusing them of premeditated murder. As an experienced politician, Johnny was adept at telling people what they wanted to hear, and he must have realized the difficulty, if not impossibility, inherent in characterizing the well-regarded Virgil Earp as a wanton murderer. Whether it was real or imagined, laundryman Fellehy's account—"I will kill them on sight"—was never repeated. Curiously, Fellehy was the only witness from the inquest who was not called to testify again in the criminal case. And Johnny Behan, for reasons he never explained, would neither deny nor confirm Fellehy's account.

The Coroner's Verdict

At the close of the evidence, Coroner Matthews delivered a spare and strangely incomplete verdict: "William Clanton, Frank and Thomas McLaury, came to their deaths in the town of Tombstone on October 26, 1881, from the effects of pistol and gunshot wounds inflicted by Virgil Earp, Morgan Earp, Wyatt Earp, and one—Holliday, commonly called 'Doc' Holliday."

The verdict satisfied no one because it left the most important question unanswered: Was the homicide criminal or justified? The *Nugget* was especially sarcastic in its criticism of Matthews and his jury: "The people of this community are deeply indebted to the twelve [in fact, ten] intelligent men who composed the coroners [*sic*] jury for the valuable information that the three persons who were killed last Wednesday were shot. Some thirty or forty shots were fired, and the whole affair was witnessed by probably a dozen people, and we have a faint recollection of hearing someone say the dead men were shot, but people are liable to be mistaken and the verdict reassures us. We might have thought they had been struck by lightning or stung to death by hornets, and we never could have told whether they were in the way of the lightning or the lightning was in their way."[9]

If anything, the *Nugget* actually understated the inadequacy of the verdict. It was the coroner's statutory obligation to decide not only the cause of death, but also whether the killings were occasioned "by criminal means," in which case the jury also had to determine "who is guilty thereof." The law allowed the jurors to find either that the deaths were "criminal" or that they were "excusable or justifiable by law,"[10] but it did not authorize them in effect to abstain.

There is no good explanation for the coroner's failure to make the necessary findings, one way or the other. Perhaps the jury was badly split and unable to reach a verdict, with Reppy and Hafford conceivably canceling each other's votes. Perhaps Republican Matthews was unwilling to issue a warrant for the Earps, notwithstanding the weight of the evidence. Or perhaps the inconsistencies between Behan's testimony and Fellehy's made everyone hesitant to proceed.

By leaving the most important issue unresolved, however, the verdict was at least in part an implicit rejection of Johnny Behan. The sheriff asserted that the Earp party began firing without provocation at men who were pleading for their lives. He was corroborated by two witnesses, however shady, and contradicted by no one. If Behan was truthful, there was no way to characterize the events as anything less than involuntary manslaughter, which Arizona law defined as the "killing of a human being without malice" in the course of "a lawful act without due caution or circumspection."[11] For whatever reason, the coroner's jury expressed its unwillingness to act on the basis of Behan's testimony. If nothing else, this must have made the politician-sheriff wary. Having failed to persuade the coroner's jury, what would happen in a real trial, where he would be subjected to cross examination and confronted by defense witnesses?

Historians have more or less ignored the non-verdict, treating the inquest as a good source of information but without legal significance. In fact, it was a pivotal event. A favorable verdict for the Earps, declaring the shooting justified or excusable, might have ended the matter then and there. On the other hand, a finding of "criminal means" would have resulted in the execution of a warrant, defining the crime and placing the case firmly in the hands of the district attorney. In the absence of a clear resolution, however, the legal situation remained unsettled, opening the door to prosecution by other means. It was not long before the vacuum was filled.

Premeditated Murder

Within a day of the coroner's inconclusive report, Ike Clanton filed first-degree murder charges against the Earps and Holliday, alleging that they killed William Clanton and the two McLaurys with malice aforethought. It was the maximum charge and a capital offense.

Historians have long puzzled over the fact that it was Ike, rather than Sheriff Behan, who initiated the complaint. As Casey Tefertiller put it, "Oddly, Behan did not make the charge himself, which would have carried far more weight than the claims of a cowboy troublemaker." Allen Barra also wondered why the credible sheriff demurred in favor of the loutish Ike.[12]

The answer may lie in the nature of the charge itself. Behan was clearly willing to testify against the Earps, and perhaps even to embellish his story in order to convict them, but there is no reason to think that he was ready to make a fool of himself. His political position in Tombstone was delicate, especially since the arrest of Deputy Stilwell, and he was subjected to frequent criticism for his friendliness toward the Cowboys. It would serve his purposes to discredit the Earps, thus eliminating them as competition, but he had to be careful not to end up looking like a Cowboy shill.

The coroner's jury had been skeptical enough about Behan's basic story, without adding the elusive element of premeditation. It was fairly easy for Behan to contend that the mercurial Doc Holliday triggered the gunfight, shooting precipitously or intentionally, but without Virgil Earp's connivance. That could still make Virgil criminally liable for the irresponsible act of arming Holliday and bringing him into the confrontation. But it would be far more difficult—and controversial—to maintain that the town marshal was a deliberate party to an outright execution. Nothing in Behan's story, taken at its worst, could make the more serious allegation stick, and he was evidently unwilling to stake his reputation on such an extreme claim.

Ike Clanton would have no similar qualms. The Earps were his blood enemies, the killers of his brother and friends, and he had no political career to worry about. Of course, the uneducated Ike had no way of understanding the details of criminal law, much less the degrees of homicide and their different burdens of proof. He would simply want the maximum amount of retribution—call it either revenge or justice, depending on whether his story was true—in any way it could be achieved.

By the end of the inquest, however, it seems likely that Ike was already in touch with a lawyer, probably Ben Goodrich, who may have helped negotiate his release from protective custody. Ike would later acknowledge that he engaged an attorney "to prosecute this case," which would presumably include drafting the complaint. Given that Goodrich counseled Ike in the subsequent proceeding (and continued to defend him afterward when he was charged with complicity in shooting Virgil Earp), it is a safe assumption that the Texas-born Democrat was influential in charging the Earps and Holliday with first-degree murder, rather than a lesser crime.

It is uncertain whether Johnny Behan acquiesced in this strategy or was preempted by it, but he does not seem to have been behind it. For example, notwithstanding Behan's careful efforts to focus the blame on Doc Holliday, it appears that Ike Clanton's complaint did not differentiate among the four defendants, charging them all as equally culpable.[13] From the very beginning, then, the prosecution of the Earps and Holliday was a divided venture. Johnny Behan represented what might be called the moderate wing, providing testimony consistent with a murder case against Holliday and lesser charges against the others. Ike Clanton and Ben Goodrich, however, pressed for capital punishment without discrimination, however sparse the proof of premeditation might be. In fact, as the case unfolded, the prosecution would become increasingly dominated by extremists who were determined to see the Earps hang.

Of course, none of this was known in late October 1881. Tombstone residents were influenced more by the damning testimony at the inquest than by the jury's dubious and much derided verdict. Eight witnesses had charged the Earps with homicide of some degree, and no one testified unequivocally in their defense. On the strength of that information alone, the city counsel suspended Virgil from his position as marshal (although he was injured too seriously to do the job in any event).

In less than a week, public support for the Earps had slipped badly. Despite her own condemnation of the Cowboys, Clara Brown observed that general opinion was "pretty fairly divided": "You may meet one man who will support the Earps, and declare that no other course was possible to save their own lives, and the next man is just as likely to assert that there was no occasion whatever for bloodshed, and that this will be 'a warm place' for the Earps hereafter." George Parsons was even more pessimistic. His journal entry for October 31 read: "Met Wyatt Earp in hotel who took me in to see Virgil this evening. He's getting along well. Morgan too. Looks bad for them all thus far."[14]

In the end, however, only one person's opinion would really matter. The case was scheduled for a preliminary hearing before the Honorable Wells W. Spicer, justice of the peace.

6

Judge Spicer's Court

The hearing before Judge Wells Spicer could well have been a quick and tidy matter, leading to a nearly foregone conclusion. The court's only job was to determine whether a "public offense [had] been committed" and if so, whether there was "sufficient cause to believe the defendant[s] guilty thereof." The legal standard—"sufficient cause"—was minimal, since the only purpose of the hearing was to decide whether the case warranted further proceedings. Even the Arizona statutes anticipated that the hearing would be relatively brief and completely straightforward, providing that "the examination must be completed at one session, unless the magistrate for good cause shown adjourn [*sic*] it."[1]

At first, it must have been hard to see how the defendants could avoid facing trial. The prosecutor did not have to present a complete case at the preliminary hearing, much less prove it beyond reasonable doubt. Technically, Johnny Behan's testimony alone could have provided "sufficient cause" to believe that the Earps had committed a crime. He was prepared to testify, after all, that the Earp party had fired at men who were raising their hands in an attempt to surrender—and other witnesses would paint an even grimmer picture. Confronted by a pointed and measured case, many defense lawyers would have all but conceded the preliminary hearing, perhaps cross examining the prosecution witnesses, but otherwise holding their fire for the real trial. When court opened, Judge Spicer had every reason to believe that he would hear from only a handful of prosecution witnesses, and few or even none from the defense.

On the first day of the proceeding, the *Epitaph* optimistically reported that the matter would "probably occupy the court for several days."[2]

It did not happen that way. Instead, the proceeding turned into the equivalent of a full-scale trial, with thirty witnesses testifying over nearly a month, making it the longest preliminary examination in Arizona history. The prosecution and defense both called their most important witnesses, keeping little if anything in reserve. Both sides evidently realized that the Spicer hearing could resolve the entire case, one way or the other. As befit a bunch of Arizona gamblers, everyone decided to go for broke. It is not hard to figure out why.

In Tombstone's brief existence, it was fairly common for criminal charges to be dismissed at preliminary hearings, so prosecutors had to be particularly worried about losing cases without ever being able to bring them to trial. When Johnny Behan arrested Doc Holliday for robbing the Benson stage, the charge was dismissed after a preliminary examination, and the same thing happened when Wyatt Earp arrested Frank Stilwell for robbing the Bisbee stage (although Virgil immediately rearrested Stilwell for a federal offense).

Another such incident involved two of Wyatt's friends from Dodge City, Bat Masterson and a gambler named Luke Short. In February 1881, Short was dealing faro in the Oriental Saloon when he got into a fight with a drunken gunman named Charlie Storms. Bat Masterson managed to separate the two men temporarily, but Storms would not back down. He waited outside the saloon, where he accosted Short by grabbing his arm and pulling him off the sidewalk. Both men reached for their guns, but Luke Short managed to draw first. As Bat Masterson put it, Charlie Storms was "too slow, although he succeeded in getting his pistol out. Luke stuck the muzzle of his own pistol against Storms' heart and pulled the trigger. The bullet tore the heart asunder, and as he was falling, Luke shot him again. Storms was dead when he hit the ground." George Parsons, who arrived on the scene almost immediately after the shooting, noted that Short was "very unconcerned," assuming it was a case of "kill or be killed."[3] Luke Short was right not to worry. Although he was arrested, he never had to face trial. His claim of self-defense was accepted by a magistrate, and he was discharged following a preliminary hearing.

A slightly older case, however, was probably the greatest influence on prosecution strategy. On the evening of June 22, 1880, Buckskin Frank Leslie, a frontiersman and bartender with a reputation as a ladies' man, was keeping company with a married woman named May Killeen. Mike Killeen, May's cuckolded husband, watched angrily from the shadows as the lovers embraced on the porch of the Cosmopolitan Hotel. George Perine, a friend of Leslie's, saw what was happening and started to warn him. He was too late. Armed with a six-shooter, Killeen confronted his rival, who had taken the precaution of keeping his own pistol at his feet (courting a married woman could be dangerous business on the frontier). Both men fired, and so did Perine. Only Killeen was seriously wounded, dying several days later.

Frank Leslie and George Perine were both charged with the murder of Mike Killeen. When the two men were brought before a magistrate for a preliminary hearing, Leslie testified that he fired the fatal shots—but only after Killeen attacked him first. The magistrate accepted Leslie's claim of self-defense, and promptly discharged both defendants. The release of Leslie was not controversial, but the prosecutor was immediately blamed for blowing the case against Perine. As the *Epitaph* reported, it was thought "that if the prosecution had brought out the evidence at hand [Perine's] commitment would certainly have followed."[4]

It certainly appeared that the prosecutor had bungled the case by holding back evidence. Killeen had made a deathbed statement that was never presented at the hearing. According to the victim, Leslie's only shot went wild, but Perine intervened without cause and fired the two fatal shots. Although the statement seemed to cinch the case against Perine, the prosecutor evidently decided to withhold it in an effort to obtain rulings against both defendants. The tactic backfired, however, and Leslie and Perine were both discharged.

Following a public outcry, Perine was rearrested (by Wyatt Earp) and charged again with Killeen's murder. This time Killeen's statement was introduced, but its impact was blunted when Leslie testified for the defense, accepting full responsibility for the shooting. Nonetheless, the magistrate ruled against the defendant, remanding him to jail (though for manslaughter, not murder). After George Perine had been incarcerated for several months, the grand jury refused to indict him, and he was freed once and for all. Buckskin Frank married the widowed May Killeen, making it a happy ending for everyone still alive—except the thwarted prosecutor, who had to contemplate the possibility that Frank Leslie might not have been so quick to protect his friend if Mike Killeen's statement had been introduced at the first hearing.

The prosecution gambled by withholding evidence in the Killeen case, and lost. Other prosecutors would naturally be wary of making the same mistake.

The defense had its own reasons for putting all of its cards on the table. Judge Spicer was a Republican and part of the Tombstone establishment, well-inclined toward business interests and law enforcement. The Earps could expect decent treatment, if not outright favoritism, in his courtroom. In contrast, a Cochise County jury, if the case got that far, might well be dominated by rural Democrats and Cowboy sympathizers (juries were chosen countywide). It was clearly in the Earps' interest to end the case as quickly as possible, rather than take their chances later in a much less favorable forum. True, that strategy had drawbacks. By presenting their entire case before Judge Spicer—including the testimony of both Wyatt and Virgil—the defendants gave the prosecution a free, and otherwise unnecessary, preview. The defendants evidently believed that the risk was worth taking. Perhaps they recalled Frank McLaury's confident retort when Lieutenant Hurst caught him stealing army mules: "I am willing to let the people of Arizona decide who is right."[5] The Cowboy had little doubt that his friends would back him up against the government. The Earps were unwilling to bet their lives that he was wrong.

Finally, both sides had to worry about the long-term availability of their witnesses. Unlike today, cases in the late nineteenth century did not drag out for years, or even months. But people tended to pick up and move on the frontier, either chasing good fortune or escaping ill fate. Virtually everyone in Tombstone was a migrant, and the population was constantly shifting. In an age of limited communication and poor transportation, it could be difficult to summon distant witnesses for trial, if their whereabouts were even known. Consequently, the Arizona statutes allowed preliminary hearing testimony, if appropriately transcribed and preserved, to be used as evidence at trial.[6] Calling a witness at the preliminary examination, therefore, was a sort of insurance policy, preserving the testimony in case of later unavailability or disappearance.

Between the two sides, the prosecution had fewer concerns about producing its most important witnesses. Johnny Behan and Ike Clanton had strong incentives to testify, and they would obviously make a point of remaining available whenever needed. The prosecution also intended to call several other Cowboy witnesses—including Billy Allen and Wes Fuller (who did not testify at the inquest)—who were itinerant by nature, making it desirable to preserve their testimony, although they were not absolutely essential to the case. On the defense side, of course, the defendants were at all times either in custody or released on bail, so there was no additional strategic value in getting their testimony on paper. But the defense also had a surprise witness, unknown to the prosecution, whose testimony could blow the case wide open. He was a transient in Tombstone, however, and there was no guarantee that he would be willing to remain in town for an extended period of time. Therefore, caution dictated that the defense had to call him to the stand before Judge Spicer. Once that decision was made—to reveal their most important witness—there was no reason for defense counsel to hold back on anything else.

The Unkilled of Mountain Meadows

Judge Wells W. Spicer has been unfairly maligned as a partisan "crony" of the Earps, possibly related to them by marriage.[7] While it is true that he was a Republican who "leaned toward . . . the law and order crowd,"[8] there is no meaningful evidence that he was biased in favor of the defense. In fact, Spicer was an exceptionally capable jurist who ran a scrupulously impartial proceeding. Like every judge—indeed, like every human being—Spicer's interpretation of facts was influenced by his past experiences, to which Earp researchers and historians have not given sufficient attention.

Born in New York, Wells Spicer grew up in Iowa, where he began a career in newspaper publishing. At the same time, he read law with a local practitioner and was admitted to the Iowa bar in 1853. He continued to practice both law and journalism for a number of years until the lure of prospecting drew him to the West. After a brief stay in Colorado, Spicer arrived in the Utah Territory in 1869, where, typical of men on the frontier, he pursued his multiple interests. He continued to work as a lawyer and journalist while trying—unsuccessfully—to strike it rich by mining.

Professional life was difficult for a gentile (non-Mormon) lawyer in territorial Utah, where law and politics were dominated by Brigham Young and the Mormon Church. For a time, Spicer wrote for the vigorously anti-Mormon *Salt Lake Tribune*, but he later switched to the Salt Lake *Daily Herald*, which was friendlier to the Latter-day Saints. Spicer was active in the local Liberal Party, which opposed Young's theocracy, but he was careful to avoid anti-Mormon stances and he eventually gained Young's favor.

By 1874, Spicer was on the brink of great success. His law practice was thriving, and he had carved out a niche as a man who could maintain profitable relations with both Mormons and gentiles. All of that changed when he undertook the defense of John D. Lee in the Mountain Meadows massacre case. Although it is little remembered today, the Mountain Meadows prosecution convulsed the entire country in 1874–76. According to historian Will Bagley, the case drew national attention "unequaled until the Lindbergh kidnapping case and exceeded only by the O. J. Simpson trial," and Wells Spicer was right in the middle of it.

Two aspects of the Lee case are essential to an understanding of Wells Spicer's legal experience, and both would be mirrored later in Tombstone. First, the entire defense was riven by conflicts of interest, as Lee was eventually betrayed by the people he trusted most. Perhaps even more significant, Lee was tried before a jury that was stacked against him, making a fair trial impossible.

The crime occurred in 1857 when a wagon train bound from Arkansas to California—called the Fancher party after its leader—was attacked by a party of Mormons disguised as Paiute Indians. More than one hundred men, women, and children were murdered, leaving no one alive older than the age of six. The genesis of the attack lay in the undeclared "Utah war" of the 1850s. Following a series of disputes, Brigham Young had succeeded in virtually expelling all federal officers from the areas under his control. It was rumored, not without reason, that Young intended to secede from the Union, declaring the independence of "Deseret." President Buchanan responded by sending a detachment of the Union Army to the territory with orders to restore federal authority. In turn, Young threatened to shut down the overland trails to California that passed through Utah.

The doomed Fancher party was caught in the crossfire while they were resting and reprovisioning at a location in southern Utah called Mountain Meadows. Today it is widely accepted that Young himself gave the command to wipe out the emigrants in a show of strength, though numerous other stories were circulated at the time. In one version, the Fancher party had caused their own destruction by poisoning wells and provoking the local Indians. In another version, a band of Mormons tried to rescue the wagon train, only to be overwhelmed by the Paiutes, who then forced the Mormons into complicity. National outrage followed, but it was difficult to separate fiction from reality, much less bring a successful prosecution, in the face of rigid obstruction by the Mormon hierarchy. Soon, the crisis over slavery, and then the Civil War, consumed the attention of the federal government, and the case was not effectively pursued for more than a decade.

With the end of the Civil War came restoration of federal authority in Utah, along with a renewed interest in prosecuting the murderers of the Fancher party. Nine Mormons—including several midlevel leaders—were indicted, but the church establishment succeeded in spiriting almost all of them out of the territory or otherwise protecting them from arrest. Only one man was actually brought to trial.

John D. Lee was the reputed leader of the massacre, alleged to have organized the attack on the Fancher party, and to have killed emigrants with his own hands. Lee was arrested in late 1874 and brought for trial to Beaver City, not far from the site of the massacre. It is not known how Lee made contact with Wells Spicer, but they met in Lee's cell in late November to begin an attorney-client relationship that would last through two trials until the defendant was executed. Some histories have downplayed Spicer's role in the case, but his biographer asserts that he was always senior counsel, following Lee's insistence that no other lawyers could "meddle in the case without the consent of Spicer."[9] Whether or not he was the lead attorney at every phase of the two trials, it is certain that Spicer stayed at Lee's side and counseled him until the very end.

There was enormous pressure on Lee to turn state's evidence by implicating Brigham Young and other Mormon elders. Spicer at first advised Lee to save his own life by taking the deal, but Lee remained loyal to the church. To ensure Lee's allegiance, the church assigned two prominent lawyers—George Bates and Jabez Sutherland—to the defense team. Although nominally representing Lee, their real job was to protect the interests of the Mormon Church by keeping "church leaders from becoming embroiled in the case."[10] The plan worked, at least for awhile. No Mormon witnesses were willing to testify against Lee, who reciprocated by maintaining his silence. The jury—composed of nine Mormons and three gentiles—failed to reach a verdict, dividing along religious lines. The interests of the church were safeguarded, but Lee was still in jeopardy. His resolute silence gained him nothing but a second trial.

In the second trial, as Spicer must have feared, Lee was betrayed. The Mormon hierarchy made a deal with the U.S. attorney's office. The prosecutor, whose political survival depended on a conviction, however obtained, "agreed to impanel a Mormon jury [and] exonerate Mormon authorities of complicity in the massacre. In exchange, [Brigham] Young would deliver witnesses and documents—and guarantee the conviction of John D. Lee."[11] Most important, the prosecutor also agreed to drop charges against the other indicted Mormon leaders.

Once the deal was sealed, Bates and Sutherland decamped for Salt Lake City, leaving Spicer to defend Lee (with the assistance of two other, lesser known attorneys). An all-Mormon jury was empaneled in September 1876, leading a former federal prosecutor named Robert Baskin to remark that Lee was doomed. Although positive of Lee's guilt, Baskin believed that even a murderer "was entitled to a trial by a jury which was not subject to any outside influence, and had not been packed for the purpose of securing his conviction."[12]

Although not a single faithful Mormon testified against Lee at the first trial, the second case was far different. All seven of the prosecution witnesses were Mormons, including some who had participated in the massacre themselves (something they denied on the witness stand). Many of the witnesses had received explicit instructions from Mormon leaders. Typical of them was Jacob Hamblin, who swore that he saw Lee slit the throat of a young girl, implying that he had raped her as well. On cross examination, Spicer asked the witness why he had kept quiet about the crime for nearly twenty years. "I kept it to myself until it was called for in the proper place," was the feeble reply.[13] It did not matter, of course.

No matter how much the witnesses contradicted each other, the signal from the church was unmistakable. John Lee could not be acquitted.

After the inevitable conviction, Lee was taken to Mountain Meadows to be executed. Seated on the edge of his own coffin, Lee was allowed to make a final speech. "I have been sacrificed in a cowardly, dastardly manner," he said. He was shot by a firing squad and buried at the site. Wells Spicer was present throughout the macabre ceremony.

For his efforts, Spicer was all but driven out of Utah. Gentiles reviled him because of his conduct in the first trial, while Mormons resented his constant efforts to persuade Lee to testify against Young and others. It was not long before he fled to Arizona.

John Lee was guilty, of course, but not as charged. While he was certainly a participant in the massacre, he was framed for a crime much larger than the one he actually committed. Then he was convicted by perjured testimony before a rigged jury. The Lee case made a lasting impression on Wells Spicer. He saw firsthand what could happen when lawyers abandoned their clients, and he must have come to appreciate the importance of a vigorous and loyal defense. Perhaps most significantly, he saw the brutal power that a prosecutor could wield, abetted by false testimony in front of a hand-picked jury. So unsettling was the experience that Spicer began referring to himself as the "unkilled of Mountain Meadows."

It is unsurprising, then, that as a judge in Tombstone Spicer would be wary of prosecution claims, skeptical of contrived and exaggerated testimony, and hesitant to turn defendants over to partisan jurors. This does not mean that he prejudged cases or that he was biased against prosecutors. But he was inclined to look long and hard at evidence, taking seriously his duty to protect the rights of defendants. It would take a measured and coherent case to persuade him to commit the Earps for trial before a Cochise County jury.

Enter Tom Fitch

If there was one lawyer in Arizona who knew how to try a case before Wells Spicer, it was Thomas Fitch, defense counsel for Virgil, Wyatt, and Morgan Earp. He was well-acquainted with Spicer's involvement in the Mountain Meadows trials, and he understood exactly how a judge's outlook on law and evidence could be influenced by his past experiences. Moreover, Fitch was a gifted advocate, sometimes called the "Silver Tongued Orator of the Pacific," at a time when declamation was considered the height of the lawyer's art.[14]

Fitch was a colorful and noteworthy character in his own right, one of the best-known legal and political figures on the frontier in the 1880s, although he is hardly remembered today. Born in New York City in 1838, Fitch left home as a teenager and spent his formative years in the Midwest, working at various jobs in Chicago, Milwaukee, and St. Louis. As a reporter for a Milwaukee newspaper, he attended the June 1860 Republican convention, becoming a staunch supporter of Abraham Lincoln. Later that summer, he moved to San Francisco, where he actively campaigned for Lincoln and was given some credit for the narrow Republican victory in the 1860 election.

Tom Fitch began his own political career in California, where he was elected to the state legislature in 1862 at the age of twenty-four. Eventually, he would hold public office in four jurisdictions—two states and two territories—earning a reputation as a carpetbagger. The charge of opportunism did not impede his success. By 1864 he was living in Nevada, where he served as a district attorney and was later elected to the U.S. Congress. It was also in Nevada that he edited a literary journal called *The Weekly Occidental,* which counted Mark Twain among its contributors. Fitch served only one term in Congress (1869–71), where he "spoke out against federal oppression of the Mormons in Utah, and [in favor of] a harsh Southern Reconstruction."[15] Defeated for reelection, he moved to Utah, where he served as counsel to Brigham Young and handled all of the civil and criminal litigation for the Church of Jesus Christ of Latter-day Saints. In 1872, when Utah petitioned for admission to the Union as the state of Deseret, Fitch was named "senator-elect." He traveled to Washington, D.C., where he lobbied for statehood without success. Although Fitch moved back to San Francisco in 1874, he maintained a lifelong interest in and sympathy for the Mormon Church.

By 1877, Fitch was living in Prescott, Arizona, where he continued to practice law and dabble in politics. When John Fremont arrived as the newly appointed governor, he and his family stayed in the Fitches' home until their own quarters were ready. The two men shared a long commitment to the Republican Party, and their wives—Jessie Benton Fremont and Anna Fitch—became close friends. Fitch's association with Fremont served him well, and he became one of the most successful attorneys in the territory. After a term in the territorial legislature (where he served alongside John Behan), Fitch moved to Tombstone to take advantage of the silver boom, quickly becoming prominent in the legal and business communities. He delivered the town's Fourth of July oration in 1881, an important honor in those days. Always a Republican, Tom Fitch was never in the pocket of the business establishment. He considered himself a populist and was proud of his opposition to railroad interests. He used his Independence Day speech, for example, to "let himself loose on corporations and monopolies."[16]

There is no doubt that Fitch closely followed the trials of John Lee in 1875–76. He believed that Brigham Young had no responsibility for the massacre but recognized that Lee "never could have been convicted if the consent of the Mormon [sic] had not been given."[17] Fitch's memoirs do not mention Wells Spicer, but it seems impossible that he would have been unaware of Spicer's crucial involvement in the Mountain Meadows case, which gave him a decided advantage in representing the Earps.

While he may not have shared Spicer's abhorrence at the execution of John Lee, Fitch surely understood that the experience of the Mountain Meadows trials would heavily influence Spicer's conduct as a judge. The two cases were far from identical, but there were themes common to both prosecutions that were deftly exploited by Fitch. In his later years, he wrote a series of "Recollections and Reflections" for the *San Francisco Call* in which he reminisced about his days as a frontier lawyer. Although he did not write about the Earp trial, many of his reflections centered on the idiosyncrasies of individual judges and the important use that counsel can make of that sort of knowledge. He quoted one respected judge as saying, "When my enemy swore one way and my friend another, I always believed my friend."[18] Fitch was clearly impressed by that wisdom, and his trial work showed a determined effort to characterize himself—and his clients—as friends of the court.

Because of a conflict of interest, Tom Fitch represented the three Earp brothers but not Doc Holliday, who was separately represented by

T. J. Drum. Little is known of Drum,[19] although he was sufficiently well-regarded to be appointed a U.S. commissioner. It is obvious from the record that the case was tried under Fitch's leadership, with little or no active input from co-counsel. As we will see, the defense team was unified in its approach, never wavering from its theory of the case. That was not a small accomplishment, and it must have taken considerable effort on the part of the attorneys and their clients. Not only was there an evident conflict between the Earps and Holliday, but there were also potential conflicts between the brothers themselves—a tactic that was good for Wyatt might not have helped Virgil or Morgan—that had to be resolved for a successful defense. The outcome of the trial was very much determined by defense counsel's ability to present a united front, while the prosecution case was a study in dissension.

Counsel for the Prosecution

Nominally, the chief prosecutor in Tombstone was Lyttleton Price, a Republican who was appointed to the job by Governor Fremont amid great controversy. When Cochise County was first organized, Fremont compromised with the Democratic majority in the legislative council by naming a number of Democrats—including Johnny Behan—to key positions. His nomination of Price, therefore, drew substantial opposition, and Democrats made repeated efforts to prevent him from taking office. Price himself complained bitterly that he was "maligned and insulted" by local Democrats in their efforts to capture every position for themselves.[20] The Cochise County board of supervisors, in fact, went so far as to name another local lawyer, John Miller, district attorney, and soon there were dueling prosecutors in Tombstone. The situation was not resolved until the autumn of 1881, with Price taking undisputed control of his office only weeks before the Spicer hearing.

Nonetheless, Price was hobbled in his work. His Republican ties made him suspect to Ike Clanton and his supporters—it had been Price, after all, who agreed to drop charges against Doc Holliday following the Benson stage robbery. At the same time, vigorous prosecution of the Earps could only alienate his political backers and friends. There is no reason to think that Price was anything other than diligent and responsible, but his situation was difficult—and it was soon made more difficult by the addition of co-counsel.

Obviously mistrustful of the Republican Price, friends of the deceased Cowboys raised a fund—said to have been as much as ten thousand dollars—to hire additional counsel for the prosecution. The most prominent lawyer to join the prosecution team was Ben Goodrich, who also served as Ike Clanton's personal attorney. He would continue to represent Ike long after the Spicer hearing, in his continuing efforts to revive charges against the Earps. The Texas-born Goodrich was a Confederate veteran and a lifelong opponent of federal authority. Nearly two decades later, Goodrich would successfully defend the so-called Wham Payroll Case, playing on "prejudice in the territory against prosecutions by the federal government" to obtain the acquittal of eight stockmen who were accused of robbing an army gold shipment.[21]

A politically active Democrat—Ben would later be elected to the territorial assembly, and his brother Briggs served as Arizona's attorney general—Goodrich could be depended on to counterbalance any reluctance on the part of Lyttleton Price. As an advocate for Ike Clanton, he would surely see the case exclusively from the perspective of the victims, uninfluenced by considerations of law enforcement or social stability. Nonetheless, Goodrich and Price might well have been able to cooperate in the conduct of the case. The men were well-known to each other and, of course, they would have to continue to practice in the same community once the Earp trial was over. Both had political careers to consider, and neither would want to be blamed for obstructionism or incompetence. Indeed, for the first few days of the hearing it did seem that Price and Goodrich had worked out a reasonable accommodation.

All of that was blown apart, however, when a new attorney arrived in town from Fort Worth, Texas. Will McLaury, brother of the slain Frank and Tom, joined the prosecution team on the third day of the hearing, altering the balance of power between Price and Goodrich and ensuring that the case would be presented in its most extreme form. McLaury's fervor would mean heightened danger for the Earps, but it would also provide Tom Fitch with just the opening he needed.

7

"I Don't Want to Fight"

The first legal issue to come before Judge Spicer was the question of bail for Wyatt and Doc. (Virgil and Morgan were still incapacitated from their wounds, so they were not expected to attend court and they were not required to post bond.) Spicer initially "denied bail as a matter of right," which was appropriate in a capital case. Relying on his statutory discretion, however, "upon a showing of facts by affidavits," the judge granted bail to the two defendants in the amount of ten thousand dollars each. At that point, the prosecution might have requested a further hearing under another statute that prohibited bail in capital cases "when the proof is evident or the presumption great."[1] But there is no record that Price and Goodrich tried to invoke that statute by presenting witnesses or offering counter-affidavits. In effect, the prosecution seems to have accepted the ruling, even though that could have been taken as an admission that their evidence—at least of first-degree murder—was insufficient to deny bail. There are many possible strategic explanations for such a decision. Perhaps it was a compromise between Price and Goodrich; perhaps it was an effort to ratchet down the level of confrontation; or perhaps the prosecutors were still unsure about how their case would play out—it could be risky to rely too heavily on the first-degree murder charge, given the earlier indecision of the coroner's jury. For whatever reason, the prosecution approach at this point could not be called aggressive, which would enrage Will McLaury when he learned about it upon his arrival.

In any event, Wyatt had no difficulty raising bail. He received generous contributions from many members of the local business and mining
community, as well as from Tom Fitch. Interestingly, Wyatt himself
posted seven thousand dollars of Doc Holliday's bond (and James Earp
added a bit more), suggesting that business leaders were not so enthusiastic about getting the unpopular Holliday out of jail. Wyatt's assistance
to Doc was no doubt motivated by friendship, but it might also have
been a gesture of solidarity, indicating that all four defendants would
stick together even if their legal interests were not identical.

With the question of bail resolved, the case was ready to proceed—
virtually a murder trial in all but name.

The testimony began on October 31, 1881, only five days after the
shootings. At the very outset of the hearing, Judge Spicer excluded the
public and the press from the courtroom. As the *Epitaph* reported: "The
investigation was conducted with closed doors. No one, except the officers
of the court, and the witness whose testimony was being taken up, were
allowed inside." Spicer has been criticized for trying "to keep the proceedings secret," which presumably indicated his wariness of public opinion. In
fact, an Arizona statute gave the defendants an absolute right to a closed
hearing, requiring a magistrate, "upon the request of the defendant, [to]
exclude from the examination every person except his clerk, the prosecutor, and his counsel, and the attorney-general, the defendant and his counsel and the officer having the defendant in custody."[2]

We cannot know precisely why the defense initially chose to exclude
the press. Casey Tefertiller suggests that they may have wanted to avoid
the need for a change of venue in the case of a full trial. That seems
doubtful, however, since the defendants should have preferred trial outside Cochise County, where Cowboy sympathy was at its highest and
security would be provided by Sheriff Johnny Behan. In nearby Pima
County, for example, they would have enjoyed the protection of Wyatt's
friend, Sheriff Bob Paul. It is more likely, therefore, that defense counsel
wanted to prevent the prosecution witnesses from coordinating their testimony. Tom Fitch was extremely suspicious of potential collusion, and
he would have done everything possible to prevent it. It would have
done little good to exclude witnesses from the courtroom if they could
read about the proceedings in the next day's *Nugget* and *Epitaph*. For all

his effort, though, the attempt at secrecy failed. The *Nugget* managed to obtain and publish a full account of the hearing's first day, and Fitch realized that the exclusion order was futile. He moved to rescind it after only a day, "as it appeared impossible to curtail the enterprise of the press."[3]

The Evidence Begins

The first witness was Coroner Matthews, who repeated his conclusions from the inquest. Describing the wounds on the bodies of Tom, Frank, and Billy, he testified to the obvious fact that the cause of the deaths was "gunshot or pistol wounds." The only significant detail in Matthews's testimony was his observation of twelve buckshot wounds on Tom's right side, meaning that he was killed by a shotgun rather than a revolver. There was no cross examination of Matthews, as all of his testimony was either beyond dispute or helpful to the defense.

Billy Allen took the stand the next morning, ready to begin the prosecution case in earnest. Unfortunately, the surviving records do not disclose which attorneys conducted which examinations, so we do not know whether Price or Goodrich (or, conceivably, one of several other lawyers who assisted the prosecution) was responsible for Allen's testimony. In any case, Allen was an excellent lead-off witness. The direct examination was restrained and concise, suggesting a compromise approach by the prosecutors. Allen supported Behan's testimony at the inquest without going over the top. If Judge Spicer was on the lookout for exaggeration or guile, he would not find it in Allen's direct.

Allen testified that he was acquainted with all of the participants in the fight. A friend of the McLaurys and Clantons, he greeted Frank and Billy when they arrived in Tombstone, joining them for a drink at the Alhambra Saloon. It was Billy Allen who informed Frank that "Tom McLaury had been hit on the head by Wyatt Earp." Frank's shocked reaction was to put down his drink and head out of the saloon, apparently looking for his brother. "I will get the boys out of town," were his last words to Allen.

Later, the witness saw the Clantons and McLaurys convene at the O.K. Corral and cross through the alley toward Fly's rooming house. He saw the Earp party begin their walk down Fremont Street, encountering Johnny Behan, who "did not use any very great exertions" to stop them.

Allen claimed to have seen most of the fight, which he described in what would become familiar detail:

> When the Earp party got down to the Clantons, the Earp party said "You sons-of-bitches, you have been looking for a fight!" The same instant, Virgil said, "Throw up your hands."
>
> Tom McLaury threw his coat open and said, "I ain't got no arms!" He caught hold of the lapels of his coat and threw it open. William Clanton said, "I do not want to fight!" and held his hands out in front of him.
>
> Just as William Clanton said, "I ain't got no arms," the firing commenced by the Earp party.

The direct examination was also notable for what the witness did not say. Allen was tentative about who fired the first shot. He thought it was Holliday, judging from the smoke, but he admitted that the Earp party's "backs were to me. I was behind them." He made no mention of a nickel-plated pistol, and he offered that the second shot was from a shotgun. Perhaps most significantly, Allen stated that he "did not notice what Frank McLaury did" just before the shooting started. This left open the possibility that Frank was trying to reach for his pistol (or appeared to be), although the witness did say that Frank had no gun in his hand as the shooting began. Allen also admitted that he ducked behind a building and did not see the entire fight. "If the McLaurys shot at all," he concluded, "it was after I got in behind the building" and could no longer see the action.

Allen said nothing about premeditation by the Earps, so his direct testimony could be used in support of charges ranging from manslaughter to first-degree murder, depending on the balance of the evidence. In fact, his testimony was not inconsistent with the defendants' innocence, given his inability to see Frank McLaury's hands at the most crucial moment of the encounter.

As with the direct, the various reports do not say which lawyer conducted the cross examination of Billy Allen. Most writers have avoided this question, referring collectively to the work of "Fitch and Drum" or obliquely to defense counsel. Internal references in other examinations, however, all indicate that Tom Fitch was lead counsel for the defendants (with a single possible exception, discussed later).[4] We also know that Fitch was a famous and flamboyant character, as well as an amateur actor and playwright, disinclined to share the stage with lesser lights. And unlike the prosecution, there was no open dissension in the defense ranks, so it is a fair conclusion that Tom Fitch cross examined most, if not all, of the prosecution witnesses, including Billy Allen.

Even before the cross examination began, Fitch made a small and easily overlooked maneuver that fit into his overall strategy. He objected twice during Allen's direct examination, both times to hearsay statements about Wyatt's rough treatment of Tom McLaury. At first glance, the objections seem almost pointless. There was no doubt that Wyatt had buffaloed Tom, and in fact, Allen later testified without objection that he informed Frank about the incident. Moreover, the incident itself was not particularly damaging to the defense. True, it showed Wyatt clubbing a (possibly) unarmed man, but it also explained why Frank might have been angry and fearful enough to reach for his gun when the Earps approached him. A very real possibility, therefore, is that Tom Fitch made his first two objections in order to sound out the judge, rather than to exclude the evidence itself. If so, the tactic worked. Spicer showed himself to be a strict interpreter of the rules of evidence, sustaining the seemingly innocuous objections. That sort of information was helpful to Tom Fitch, and he would make unorthodox use of it the very next morning.

But first, there was a cross examination to complete. After some preliminaries, Fitch was careful to establish Allen's precise vantage point as the fight developed. It turns out that Allen heard the Earps' conversation as they passed Bauer's butcher shop, the very location where Martha King claimed to hear Morgan Earp tell Doc Holliday to "let them have it." Allen, however, testified to no such statement, and Fitch wisely allowed the omission to speak for itself—following the cross examiner's maxim to avoid asking "one question too many."

Allen insisted that the first shot was from a pistol, with the smoke coming from Doc Holliday. Fitch got him to repeat his statement that the second shot was from a shotgun, this time emphasizing that the blast appeared to hit Tom McLaury, who "threw his hands up to his breast."

Although he did not see the shotgun, Allen suggested that it might have been in Morgan's hands, which of course undermined his credibility. There was no question that Doc Holliday held the shotgun.

Having elicited much helpful information with the witness's cooperation, Fitch finally went on the attack. Hadn't the witness used an alias while living in Colorado? Hadn't he been indicted for larceny while passing by the name of L. Brand? Didn't he escape from Colorado and flee to Tombstone? The witness refused to answer, and the court upheld his "legal right to decline to answer." But of course, the damage was done.

On redirect examination, the prosecutors revealed just how closely they were tied to the "Doc fired first" theory. Rather than emphasize Allen's candid admission of uncertainty, which would have given their case some flexibility, the prosecutors tried to get a six-shooter into Holliday's hand by any means possible. The only question on redirect was whether the witness saw Doc fire a pistol. Allen replied that he "heard a shot, saw smoke, but did not see the pistol," although he did see Doc Holliday raise his hand. The contradiction may not have been immediately evident, but it would come back to haunt the prosecution. It was not possible for Doc Holliday to fire the first shot with a pistol (nickel-plated or otherwise) *and* to kill Tom McLaury with a shotgun, virtually at the same time.

Another witness—R. F. Hafford, the saloonkeeper and inquest juror—testified that afternoon, but he did not add anything of great significance. The case was adjourned until the next morning.

Tom Fitch had another card to play when court convened for the third day of the trial. To almost everyone's consternation (then and since), the defense moved to severely restrict the scope of Judge Spicer's authority. According to the defense argument, "a Justice of the Peace sitting as an examining court was entirely without any judicial function; that he was merely a ministerial officer, and as such has no power to pass on the relevancy or materiality of any evidence offered. Or, in other words, he was only a clerk whose only duty was to write down such evidence as was offered, and when an objection or exception was taken, to note the same on the deposition."[5]

The motion was almost directly contrary to the applicable statute, which clearly required the examining magistrate to rule on the sufficiency of the evidence, not just to record it. More than that, it seemed odd for

Tom Fitch to try to place that sort of limit on Spicer, who was thought to be well-disposed toward the defense. By turning the judge into a glorified clerk, whose sole duty was to write down the evidence, Fitch almost seemed to be conceding the inevitability of a full trial. That is hardly likely, not only because of its devastating consequences for the defendants, but also because Fitch had just done such a masterful job with the first prosecution witness. Historian Gary Roberts, for example, has questioned Fitch's tactic, "in view of the ultimate outcome and oft-repeated charges [of pro-defense bias] against Spicer."[6]

There may have been a much more sophisticated motive for Fitch's motion. As we will see, the defense trial theory would ultimately be based on establishing a lengthy chronicle of threats against the Earps by the Clantons and McLaurys. That history could be used to justify and explain Virgil and Wyatt's harsh reaction to Ike Clanton (and their unwillingness to wait and see when Frank McLaury seemed to reach for his pistol), but it would first have to meet the test of legal relevance. Remote events, such as the theft of some government mules the previous year, might well be ruled inadmissible at a preliminary hearing. Judge Spicer had already revealed himself to be a stickler regarding evidence—recall the sustained objections during Allen's testimony—so Fitch needed to lay the groundwork for a broad theory of admissibility.

There was no chance, of course, that Judge Spicer would rule against his own authority to decide evidentiary questions. So Fitch's motion might be better understood as a pitch for latitude, suggesting to Spicer that the court was in such a sensitive position—the transcript of the preliminary examination, after all, might be used as evidence at trial—that he should err on the side of admissibility.

If that was Fitch's plan, it worked beautifully. As was inevitable under the statute, Judge Spicer ruled that he did have the power to exclude testimony, "but intimated that he would . . . exercise a great liberality in admitting testimony."[7] That was exactly what Tom Fitch wanted to hear.

Johnny Behan Takes the Stand

When Johnny Behan was called to the stand in the afternoon of the third day, it was clear that his testimony would be one of the major turning points in the case. As the county sheriff, his word carried great authority; as an affable and popular politician, he was likely to be very persuasive. If Behan could testify convincingly—and if he could withstand cross examination—it would be hard to see how Judge Spicer could avoid finding sufficient evidence to support at least some degree of homicide.

Testifying for the second time in less than a week, Behan again described how he had first learned about the situation while sitting in the barber's chair: "Someone in the shop said there was liable to be trouble between Clanton and the Earps; there was considerable said about it in the shop and I asked the barber to hurry up and get through, as I intended to go out and disarm and arrest the parties."

The sheriff was impressive as he described his efforts to disarm the Clantons and McLaurys, including his body search of Ike and his visual inspection of Tom. He told Frank McLaury at least four times to turn over his weapons, but McLaury refused, insisting that the Earps be disarmed as well. Behan continued his efforts to persuade Frank until he was interrupted by the approach of the Earps. Instructing the Cowboys to stay put, Behan told them that he would "disarm the other party." He walked up Fremont Street to stop the Earps, encountering them in front of Bauer's butcher shop. "I was down there for the purpose of arresting and disarming the Clantons and McLaury's," he told the Earps as he ordered them not to go any farther. "I'm the Sheriff of this county and am not going to allow any trouble if I can help it." The Earps brushed past him without heed, and Behan followed the party—"expostulating with them all the time"—as they approached the vacant lot.

When the Earps got to within a few feet of the Cowboys, Behan heard Wyatt say, "You sons of bitches you have been looking for a fight and now you can have it," just as Virgil called for the Cowboys to "throw up your hands." At that very moment, the nickel-plated pistol made its first appearance, aimed at Billy Clanton. Behan's "impression at the time was that Holliday had the nickel-plated pistol; I will not say for certain that Holliday had it."

Billy cried, "Don't shoot me, I don't want to fight," and Tom threw open his coat, shouting, "I am not armed." Behan couldn't see the position of Billy's hands because his attention was drawn to the nickel-plated pistol, which was the first to fire—followed instantly by another shot from the Earp party, and then six or eight more before the Cowboys returned fire.

Behan believed that the nickel-plated pistol was aimed at Billy Clanton, but the only men he saw fall were Frank McLaury and Morgan Earp. He testified that Ike Clanton "broke and ran," but he could not see where he was going. He had seen a shotgun in the hands of Doc Holliday, who was trying to conceal it as he walked down the street, but he did not see it used in the fight and did not know what became of it. Behan did not see Tom McLaury until after the fight was over.

The prosecutors had good reason to be pleased when Johnny Behan finished his direct examination. It gave them almost everything they might have hoped for. He was precise and unequivocal, making the case against the defendants without overstating it: the Cowboys raised their hands in surrender just as Virgil ordered, but Doc Holliday began firing and the fight "became general." Behan's testimony raised two possibilities, one bad for the Earps and the other worse. At a minimum, Johnny established Virgil's recklessness in bringing Holliday into the confrontation. There was also at least a suggestion that Virgil planned the whole thing, intending all along to goad the Cowboys into "making a fight." As with any witness, there were a few problems in Behan's testimony— he made a total of seven references to the "nickel-plated pistol," which must have seemed almost obsessive—but they probably appeared fairly inconsequential at the time.

Interestingly, Behan did not elaborate on the history of bad blood between the Earps and the Cowboys, which could have been used to prove motive. The Earps, predictably, would put a different spin on that history when they presented their case, but that was all the more reason for the prosecution to get the sheriff's side of it first. As it was, however, Behan did not develop the evidence of premeditation. That would have to come later—if at all. Now everyone's attention was turned to cross examination.

Tom Fitch had an easy time cross examining Billy Allen, but he was facing a more formidable adversary in Johnny Behan. He did not bother trying to secure the witness's cooperation but began instead with a little ridicule about Behan's lack of attention to his job. Every alert citizen in Tombstone realized that a fight was brewing between the Earps and the

Cowboys, yet the county sheriff had to hear about it from a bunch of hangers-on at the barber shop: "You being in town and assumedly mingling with the people, if those difficulties were a matter of common comment, how did it happen that a report of it did not reach you?" The prosecutors made an immediate objection, which the judge sustained. The defense would not get complete license from the court.

For all of that day and much of the next, Tom Fitch laced into Behan, using all of the means at his disposal. One line of attack went to the witness's bias against Wyatt. Wasn't it true that Wyatt and Johnny had both applied for appointment as sheriff, and hadn't Behan backed out on the deal? Behan's answer was equivocal. Yes, they had both been applicants at first, but Behan was assured that he would get the office. He offered Wyatt the job of undersheriff, but not as part of any deal. Then, the witness added cryptically, "Something afterward transpired that I did not take him into the office."

But Fitch would not let it go that easily. He had a trap to set. Wasn't Wyatt still Behan's chief rival for the sheriff's office? Glib politician that he was, Behan did not understand the dynamics of cross examination, in which a witness's sincerity is always on the line. His instinct was to put himself in the best light—almost like making a campaign promise for which he would never be called to account. So Johnny took the bait and denied the obvious, claiming that he did not regard Wyatt as an aspirant for the sheriff's job. It was the first small crack in his credibility, but it would not be the last.

Tom Fitch used the same technique to even better effect later in the examination. "Once or twice in your direct examination," he pointed out to the witness, "you spoke of cowboys. What is a cowboy?"

In fact, Behan had used the term only once, and quickly withdrew it. But he thought he saw where Fitch was going and figured he could deflect the question. "My idea of a cowboy is men who deal in cattle—stockmen," he said.

Again, the answer was too clever by half. Everyone in Tombstone knew that "cowboy" was used as a synonym for rustler (or worse). Judge Spicer certainly did not think of "cowboys" as simple ranch hands, and Tom Fitch would make sure of that understanding when he later presented his own witnesses. But he was not yet finished with Behan.

Well, then, Fitch continued, "Do you regard the Clantons and McLaurys as cowboys?"

The witness's dilemma was exquisite. If a "cowboy" was merely a stockman, then there was no way to deny the cowboy-ness of the Clantons and McLaurys. But if the Clantons and McLaurys were in fact "cowboys," then nothing would keep Judge Spicer—Republican, businessman, and *Epitaph* reader—from jumping to the painful conclusion. A timely objection was sustained by the court, saving Behan from the discomfort of choosing an answer. But that only underscored the significance of Behan's predicament. Having tried to outsmart the cross examiner (almost always a mistake), he ended up outwitting himself. It would have made much more sense to concede that a "cowboy" was a criminal, which would then have allowed him to deny that the term applied to the Clantons and McLaurys. Of course, it is hard to think ahead when you are under cross examination, and sometimes harder still for an especially well-prepared witness.

The cross examination also turned to the crucial question of the nickel-plated pistol, which Behan had taken such pains to describe during his direct examination. The first step was to show how much of Behan's credibility rested on that part of his testimony:

> (Q) I understand you to say you had your eye on a nickel-plated pistol. Did you see the nickel-plated pistol before you heard the expressions?
>
> (A) I saw the nickel-plated pistol at the same time the expressions were made.
>
> (Q) Did you see it in any interval before the expressions were made?
>
> (A) I saw it at the same time.
>
> (Q) Was it pointed the first time you saw it?
>
> (A) Yes, it was pointed at Billy Clanton.
>
> (Q) Was it the commencement of the expressions, "You sons-of-bitches," that diverted your attention from the Clanton crowd and concentrated it upon the Earp crowd?
>
> (A) My attention was on the Earp crowd.
>
> (Q) How long had your attention been especially on the Earp crowd?
>
> (A) From the time I turned to go with them.

The witness had been led to insist that he kept his eyes constantly on the Earps, watching them as the nickel-plated pistol fired the first shot. Then came the hammer:

> (Q) Did you see the shotgun in the hands of the Earp party, and if so, which one of them?
> (A) The last time I saw the shotgun, [it] was in the hands of Doc Holliday.
> (Q) Did you see the shotgun employed in that difficulty?
> (A) I did not.
> (Q) Holliday having a shotgun just preceding the difficulty, and on the way to the difficulty, and your attention being especially directed to the Earp party, how does it happen that you do not know what became of the shotgun?
> (A) I do not know—it might have been used and I not know of it.

Behan's answer was feeble. The coroner had already testified that Tom McLaury was killed with a shotgun, and no one except Doc Holliday was ever seen with a shotgun. Nonetheless, the sheriff insisted that he kept his eyes glued to the Earp party but somehow managed to miss seeing the heavy artillery, while at the same time managing to keep sight of the nickel-plated pistol. The inconsistency was obvious, and Behan's refusal to back down only made it worse.

> (Q) Do you still insist that the first shot was fired from the nickel-plated pistol?
> (A) Yes.

The witness was cornered again. For his testimony to make any sense, the court would have to believe that Holliday marched down Fremont Street carrying a shotgun; put it aside in order to pull out his nickel-plated pistol; fired the first shot, presumably at Billy Clanton; and then picked up the shotgun in order to kill Tom McLaury—all in the space of a few seconds.

Many writers and historians have tried to substantiate Behan's claim. Some have suggested that Doc's aversion to shotguns led him to rely first on his nickel-plated pistol (although even that does not explain why he would turn back to the shotgun later). Alford Turner, the respected researcher who first compiled the transcripts of the inquest and the Spicer hearing, posited, "It was no trick for the ambidextrous Holliday to whip up the shotgun as an attention getter with his left arm and immediately follow with a shot from his nickel-plated pistol held in his right hand." Paula Mitchell Marks also apparently believes that Doc began shooting with both hands, "first firing the nickel-plated pistol at Frank, then . . . swinging the shotgun up and hitting Tom with a load of buckshot." Allen Barra, however, rightly points out that the sequence is unbelievable: "Ambidextrous or no, this would seem beyond the powers of even the man Wyatt Earp called 'the fastest, deadliest man with a gun I have ever seen.' "[8] After all, a shotgun is a two-handed weapon. It might conceivably have been possible for Doc to hold the shotgun with one hand, but it would have been impossible to fire it that way. Even Wyatt Earp, bigger and stronger than the tubercular Doc Holliday, made sure to hold his shotgun with both hands when he faced down the mob threatening Johnny-Behind-the-Deuce.[9]

But even if the two-gun feat were physically imaginable—something that Johnny Behan never claimed—there would still be an unanswerable question. Why? What would possibly motivate Doc Holliday to switch weapons not once, but twice, while fighting for his life (and the Earps' lives as well)? And why abandon a shotgun—the most effective weapon there is in close quarters—for a handgun? And not just any handgun. Doc Holliday favored a snub-nosed, self-cocking pistol. A gun like that was great for concealing in his bosom during a card game but notoriously inaccurate at any distance greater than point-blank range.[10]

Judge Spicer may not have been a gunfighter, but he would have recognized an implausible story when he heard one. In his eagerness to blame Doc Holliday, Behan undermined his own credibility yet again. In case it was not absolutely clear, Tom Fitch pressed the point home.

> (Q) Is it not a fact that the first shot fired by Holliday was from a shotgun; that he then threw the shotgun down and drew the nickel-plated pistol from his person and then discharged the nickel-plated pistol?

Uncharacteristically, the politician-turned-sheriff had no answer.

From what we have seen so far, the cross examination of Johnny Behan would be impressive to any modern lawyer or courtroom observer. Tom Fitch relied heavily on the classic approach of luring the witness into a series

of increasingly implausible assertions. One aspect of his technique, however, would today seem oddly ineffective, as it appeared to ignore two
nearly inviolable commandments of cross examination: Never ask a question if you do not know the answer, and never ask a witness for an explanation. For modern lawyers, cross examination is an exercise in tight
control, intended to give the witness as little maneuvering room as possible. Tom Fitch, however, continually asked open-ended questions, inviting
the voluble Behan to deny, disagree, expand, and explain. A few examples:

(Q) If anything, how much have you contributed or have promised to contribute to the associated attorneys who are now prosecuting this case?
(A) I have not contributed a cent, nor have I promised to.

(Q) After you followed or accompanied the Earps from under
the awning of the butcher shop, and the fight commenced, did
you occupy one position until the shooting ceased?
(A) No sir, I did not stand still. I moved around pretty lively.

(Q) When you left the Clanton party, as you stated, and
ascended Fremont Street to meet the Earps, did you not say,
addressing Wyatt Earp and Morgan Earp: "I have got them disarmed." Or words to that effect?
(A) No sir.

(Q) Did not the Earp party, after some remark made by you to
them, put their pistols farther back in their pants and did not
Holliday pull his coat over his gun?
(A) No sir. Holliday pulled his coat over his gun before I spoke
to him.

(Q) Have you, since the difficulty, had any interview with
William Allen, to compare your recollections with him in regard
to the difficulty?
(A) I had no interview with Allen about the matter; have met
him and talked about it on the street.

(Q) During the progress of the fight, did you see Ike Clanton take hold of Wyatt Earps [*sic*] left arm and hear Wyatt Earp say to him, "This fight has commenced, either fight or get away!"?
(A) No sir.

In each of these instances, and many others, it looks at first as though Behan thwarted Fitch's efforts by refusing to provide the expected answer. Yet Fitch continued in the same vein. Was he unreasonably optimistic, hoping that Behan would somehow experience a change of heart and start cooperating? Or was he desperate, trying anything that might possibly blunt the impact of Behan's forceful direct examination? In fact, Fitch was operating under the constraints of his day and age, using an extremely sophisticated, and potentially very powerful, approach to cross examination that modern lawyers may not immediately recognize.

Working without extensive pretrial preparation or discovery of the opposing party's files, nineteenth-century trial lawyers relied on a technique that might best be called "propositional" cross examination. Adverse witnesses were confronted with a series of factual statements, to which they could either agree or disagree. The art in this form of cross examination lay in the attorney's choice of propositions. A good lawyer could frame some questions that were risk free: either the witness agreed, in which case the question was successful, or he disagreed harmlessly. A good example of this was Fitch's inquiry about Behan's "interview" with Billy Allen. At first Behan denied any interview, which was unhelpful but not damaging to the defense. But then he added that the two witnesses had talked about "the difficulty" on the street—a small success for the cross examiner. Sometimes propositional questions could be phrased in a way that made them undeniable; still others could tempt the witness out onto a limb.

The best propositional questions, however, did their work invisibly, inveigling the witness into denying something that could later be proved beyond doubt. These questions did not rely on obtaining an implausible assertion from the witness—such as "cowboy means stockman"—but rather sought to catch him in a lie. These questions might be called "provables," since the witness's uncooperative answer could later be proved false.

Tom Fitch employed many "provables" in his cross examination of Johnny Behan, with the most important one coming at the very end. In fact, it came after the end. Fitch had concluded his questioning of Behan and tendered the witness for redirect when he suddenly asked the court for permission to resume the cross examination. The prosecutors consented to the interruption, allowing Fitch to raise one last point. It was a courtesy that Goodrich and company would later regret.

To a modern cross examiner, Fitch's closing question will seem convoluted, open-ended, and ineffective. But in the context of late-nineteenth-century trial advocacy, it was perfect. After establishing that Behan had paid a visit to the injured Virgil on the evening of the gunfight, Fitch asked,

> (Q) Did you not make use of this language: "I went to see the Clanton crowd and told them to disarm. They would not do it. I went back and met you and spoke to you and you did not stop. I heard you say, 'Boys, throw up your hands, I have come to disarm you.' When one of the McLaury boys said, 'We will,' and drew his gun, and the shooting commenced. I am your friend and you did perfectly right."—or language of such substance and like import?

Behan babbled in response. His long, rambling answer made it seem as though he was thinking out loud, perhaps trying to figure out where the question was leading and how to avoid it. Finally, he got to the point, flatly denying Fitch's proposition:

> (A) I suppose I told him that I heard him say, "Throw up your hands!" I never told him I heard McLaury say anything or that I saw him draw a pistol.

At that moment, Tom Fitch stopped. He had the sheriff right where he wanted him, although the full extent of the "provable," and the success of the cross examination, would not become apparent until the hearing was almost over, more than three weeks later.

On redirect examination, the prosecution was most concerned about the charges of bias. Behan was asked why Wyatt Earp did not get the promised position in the sheriff's office. Again, the witness rambled, telling a complex story about Wyatt's purported interference on an occasion when Behan was trying to serve a subpoena on Ike Clanton.

In an obvious response to one of Fitch's provables, Behan was also asked about the charge that he had misled the Earps into thinking the Cowboys were disarmed. Speaking of his confrontation with Wyatt immediately after the gunfight, the witness said: "There was a conversation on Fremont Street near the Butcher Shop on the sidewalk. Wyatt Earp said, 'Behan, you deceived me,' or 'threw me off. You said you had disarmed them.' I told him he was mistaken, I did not say anything of the kind. Then I related to him what I had said. I said, 'Earp, I told you I was there for the purpose of arresting and disarming them.' He said he thought I had said I had disarmed them."

With that explanation, Johnny Behan left the stand.

Tom Fitch must have been sorely tempted to attack Behan even more stridently on cross examination. The sheriff's well-known antagonism toward the Earps might have provided a fruitful line of questioning. And then there were Behan's Cowboy associations, most notably his employment of robber-cum-deputy Frank Stilwell. But Fitch restrained himself, no doubt a strategic choice based on his assessment of Judge Spicer's tolerance for bombast.

The most interesting question, however, is why Tom Fitch stayed completely away from the subject of Josephine Marcus. Having troubled to establish Johnny Behan's professional rivalry with Wyatt Earp, why not go all the way by exposing his romantic rivalry as well? However much animosity Behan might have felt for Wyatt as a political opponent, that would have paled in comparison to his prejudice against the man who had come to enjoy the attentions of his lover. Behan was a consummate witness, cool and poised, but would he have been able to maintain his composure if confronted with the story of Wyatt and Josie?

Perhaps Fitch was adhering to Victorian decorum, reluctant to bring romance, and sex, into the trial. Or perhaps he was worried that the tactic would backfire, exposing Wyatt—who was still "married" to Mattie Blaylock at the time—as a two-timer. Both reasons are plausible, but neither seems wholly satisfactory. Frontier trials were often filled with tales of passion and betrayal, as would be expected in a society where men were armed and women were scarce. Just a year earlier in Tombstone, Frank Leslie testified about his affair with a married woman, pretty much raising adultery as a defense to the murder of her husband. And later in the Earp trial, Fitch did not hesitate to raise the infidelities of a prosecution witness's wife.[11] After all, Fitch was a worldly man—a native New Yorker and friend of Mark Twain's. There is no reason to suspect him of squeamishness when it came to intimate details.

A more likely possibility is that Wyatt Earp, not Tom Fitch, was responsible for the decision to keep Josie's name out of the proceedings. In later years, both Wyatt and Josephine were extremely protective of her "past," taking pains to keep her name out of Stuart Lake's book *Frontier Marshal*. Lake evidently concluded that Josephine was "the key to the whole yarn of Tombstone," but he decided to "leave that key unturned."[12] There is reason to believe that Lake omitted Josephine from the story only because she threatened litigation, successfully keeping herself out of the picture for decades. In the crucible of Tombstone, there would have been even more reason to safeguard Josie's reputation.

In 1881, Josie Marcus had much to lose by having her name drawn into the trial. She could not exactly be called an adulteress, as none of the parties seem to have been legally married. But there were other names for women who slept with two men, and none of them was complimentary. As an actress and dancer, indeed as an unmarried woman in a boomtown, Josie would have been confronted constantly with the suggestion that she was a prostitute. Such a rumor, in fact, survives to this day, although there is no proof of it. We do know that Josie Marcus flouted the conventions of her time, and it is easy to imagine that Wyatt Earp was not eager to see her exploits further bared in the pages of the *Epitaph,* or worse, the *Nugget.*

But that raises another question. Wyatt was not Tom Fitch's only client. He also represented Virgil and Morgan, whose interests did not necessarily coincide with their brother's. Wyatt, out of chivalry or affection, might have wanted to shield Josie by downplaying her promiscuity, even if it meant letting Johnny Behan off the hook. But were Virgil and Morgan—or Doc, for that matter, who was separately represented and therefore entitled to have his own attorney cross examine every witness— willing to risk their own necks for the sake of Wyatt's love life? This was a serious problem for defense counsel because there could be no compromise solution. For the benefit of three defendants, Behan could be confronted as a jealous liar, thus revealing Josephine's faithlessness. Or for Wyatt's sake, Josie could be kept out of it, thereby passing up an opportunity to undermine the prosecution's star witness.

Counsel had to make a choice. The conflicting interests of Wyatt and his brothers could not be resolved, but they would somehow have to be reconciled. One might expect Fitch to defer primarily to Virgil, the oldest and most important of the brothers. Some writers have since contended that Wyatt was the leader of the brothers, but that is largely an artifact of his fame and longevity. At the time, there is no doubt that Virgil was in charge, at least when it came to law enforcement. On the other hand, it was Wyatt who was present every day in court, sitting at counsel table and observing the proceedings. And it was also Wyatt who was best able to control the unpredictable Doc Holliday, whose cooperation was important to the success of the defense.

Tom Fitch might have solved the problem by deciding that it was just too dangerous to confront Behan with Josie's infidelity, whether or not Wyatt would let him. "It doesn't really matter," he might have thought, "because we don't want to risk offending Judge Spicer." Fitch's wife considered herself the doyenne of Tombstone society, so the lawyer also would have been able to assess the vigor of the local rumor mill. Depending on the measure of ambient gossip, there was a decent chance that the judge already knew all about the "Josie situation" even without testimony. If so, that would give Fitch yet another way out.

It is also conceivable that Tom Fitch was unaware of Wyatt's budding romance with Josie. If one accepts Glenn Boyer's *I Married Wyatt Earp,* purportedly the memoirs of Josephine Marcus, the two lovers kept their relationship discrete and chaste until both were safely out of Tombstone. That account is hardly believable, even on its own terms. For example, it also has Josephine accepting Johnny Behan's invitation to leave San Francisco for Tombstone but never living with him once she arrived. Existing records, however, show that Josephine lived with Behan and cared for his adolescent son. In any event, the authenticity of *I Married Wyatt Earp* has been widely discredited. At the other end of the spectrum, Frank Waters's *The Earp Brothers of Tombstone* depicts Wyatt's courtship of Josie as open and notorious, with the two of them publicly humiliating the abandoned Mattie by prancing into fancy restaurants. Allegedly based on the recollections of Allie Earp, Virgil's widow, Waters's book has also been criticized as unreliable. At the very least, it has a decidedly anti-Wyatt agenda.

Assuming that the truth lies somewhere between Boyer's description of near secrecy and Waters's tale of near exhibitionism, it is unlikely that Wyatt could have kept Tom Fitch totally in the dark about his triangular link to the star prosecution witness. Wyatt certainly did not keep any other secrets from his lawyer, revealing both his aborted deal with Behan and his extended negotiations with Ike Clanton, neither of which were public knowledge. Wyatt appears to have been candid with his counsel, offering much embarrassing information to help the defense. It is unlikely that he would have withheld something as potentially important as his relationship with Josie, especially if others—Virgil and Morgan, for example—already knew about the relationship.

The best we can say is that Tom Fitch made his choice and lived with it. His clients survived the decision. But no lawyer today would pass up the golden opportunity to humiliate Johnny Behan on the stand.

Even without the "personal" element, the cross examination of Behan was proficient and effective. But there was still plenty of life in the prosecution case. Even if Behan was mistaken about the nickel-plated pistol, and even if he was a political rival of Wyatt Earp's, and even if he was reluctant to call a cowboy a Cowboy—well, none of that disproved his main claim that Billy and Tom were shot as they raised their hands in surrender (and the cross examination did not exactly absolve Doc by demonstrating that he killed Tom with a shotgun rather than a six-shooter).

Inevitably, spectators and newspaper correspondents were more impressed by the specifics of Behan's testimony than by the subtleties of Fitch's trial work, and public opinion continued to shift against the Earps. According to one account, "Public feeling, which at first was for the Earps and Holliday, seems to have taken a turn, and now nearly all the people of Tombstone condemn the murderers." The *Arizona Weekly Star* took a more nuanced view, calling the killings dastardly and inexcusable but hoping that "the absence of malice and premeditation upon the part of the slayers may at least be established."[13]

Still, the prosecutors had to make a choice. Recognizing the potential damage done to their star witness, they could temper their case. There was substantial evidence that the Earps fired precipitously, never giving the dead men a chance. Coupled with their brutal treatment of Ike and Tom, that could easily be enough to persuade Judge Spicer that the defendants "acted without due cause or circumspection." In other words, manslaughter. Perhaps Spicer might even find sufficient evidence of second-degree murder, concluding that the Earps acted with "no considerable provocation."[14]

Or the prosecution could move forward aggressively, continuing to press the case for first-degree murder. Behan's testimony was always ambiguous on the question of premeditation—the closest he came was his assertion that Virgil said he would give the Cowboys "a chance to make a fight"—so they could still establish the necessary facts with witnesses yet to be presented.

It is not hard to envision Price and Goodrich debating—or squabbling—over how to proceed, with Price urging moderation and Goodrich out for blood. Behan's position is harder to imagine, though he was probably eager to be rehabilitated even if that meant convicting the Earps on a lesser charge. In the end, however, Price and Goodrich did not have a free hand to resolve their differences. An event outside the courtroom put the case effectively beyond their control.

On the evening of November 3, as Johnny Behan was finishing his second day of testimony, attorney William R. McLaury arrived in Tombstone. The "oldest, most respectable, and certainly the smartest of the McLaury brothers," Will was living and practicing law in Fort Worth, Texas, when he heard of his brothers' deaths.[15] Recently widowed, he made hasty arrangements for the care of his young children and set out for Arizona, where he was determined to obtain "justice."

Wyatt Earp, ca. 1887. Courtesy Arizona Historical Society (No. 1447).

Josephine Marcus Earp, ca. 1921.
Courtesy Craig Fouts Collection.

Doc Holliday, ca. 1887. Courtesy
Craig Fouts Collection.

Virgil Earp. Courtesy Arizona
Historical Society (No. 1444).

Morgan Earp. Courtesy
Arizona Historical Society
(No. 1442).

Ike Clanton. Courtesy Arizona Historical Society (No. 24366).

Frank McLaury. Courtesy
Arizona Historical Society
(No. 24364).

Tom McLaury. Courtesy Arizona
Historical Society (No. 24365).

Frank and Tom McLaury and Billy Clanton in their caskets after the gunfight, 1881. Courtesy Arizona Historical Society (No. 17483).

Johnny Behan.
Courtesy Arizona
Historical Society
(No. 27243).

John Ringo. Courtesy
of the Chafin Brothers.

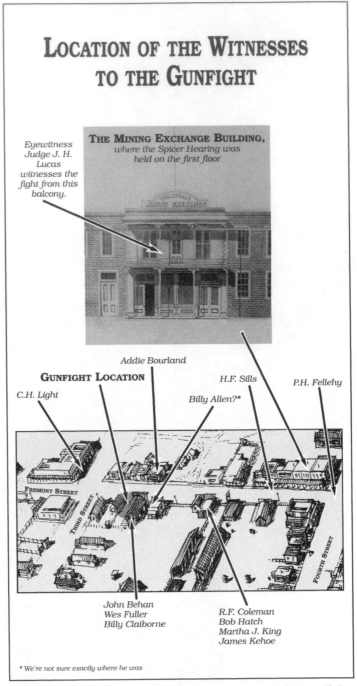

Location of the Witnesses to the Gunfight

The Mining Exchange Building,
where the Spicer Hearing was held on the first floor

Eyewitness Judge J. H. Lucas witnesses the fight from this balcony.

Addie Bourland

Gunfight Location

H.F. Sills

P.H. Fellehy

C.H. Light

Billy Allen?*

Fremont Street

Third Street

Fourth Street

John Behan
Wes Fuller
Billy Claiborne

R.F. Coleman
Bob Hatch
Martha J. King
James Kehoe

* We're not sure exactly where he was

Location of the witnesses to the gunfight. Courtesy Bob Boze Bell Collection.

George Parsons, whose detailed journal is one of the best surviving accounts of life in Tombstone at the time of the shoot-out at the O.K. Corral. Courtesy Arizona Historical Society (No. 1933).

Thomas Fitch, pictured when he was a member of the U.S. Congress, 1869–71.
Library of Congress.

Wells Spicer, 1875, at the time of the
Mountain Meadows trial in Utah. Used
with permission, Utah State Historical
Society, all rights reserved.

Richard Rule, a talented professional
journalist, covered the Earp trial daily
in the *Tombstone Nugget*. Courtesy of
the Chafin Brothers.

Wyatt Earp, about a year before his death in 1929. Courtesy Craig Fouts Collection.

8

"I Think We Can Hang Them"

Will McLaury was raised in Iowa, but he moved to Texas after the Civil War. Although a Republican and a northerner, he managed to establish a successful law practice by entering into partnership with Captain S. P. Greene, a former officer in the Confederate Army. But political parties were the farthest thing from Will McLaury's mind when he arrived in Tombstone. He did not care whether the Earps were Republicans, Democrats, Know-Nothings, or Whigs. He wanted vengeance for his two brothers, who "were very dear to me, and would have walked through fire for me."[1]

McLaury was sworn in as associate counsel for the prosecution on November 4, 1881, in time to watch the conclusion of Johnny Behan's testimony. Surveying the progress of the case thus far, he could not have been pleased by what he saw. The prosecutors had been entirely too accommodating in their conduct of the trial. They failed to vigorously oppose Fitch's bail motion, and they readily consented to the re–cross examination of Sheriff Behan without so much as an objection. In the eyes of an aggrieved brother and Texas lawyer, there had been entirely too much cooperation in the trial and not enough passion. Most infuriating to McLaury was the fact that Wyatt and Doc were free on bond, behaving as though they were still lawmen rather than accused murderers.

McLaury wrote to Captain Greene that Wyatt and Doc were intimidating witnesses by attending court "heavily armed," but it is hard to believe that was true. It would have been illegal for Wyatt or Doc to bring weapons into court, especially since Virgil had been suspended as town marshal and they could no longer claim to be his deputies. And Spicer was hardly the type of man to watch the law flouted in his own courtroom. The hearing was well-covered by many newspapers, including the anti-Earp *Nugget*, none of which reported that the defendants were carrying guns to court.

Perhaps McLaury needed the image of heavily armed defendants to justify his own fantasies of retaliation. His letters—to his law partner in Texas and to his sister and brother-in-law in Iowa—were filled with barely restrained threats of violence. "This thing has a tendency to arouse all the devil there is in me," he wrote, "I could kill them both." He did not hide that sentiment as he spent his evenings in Tombstone's saloons "winning support from the townsmen and defaming the Earps." Gratified by the sympathy he found for his brothers, he speculated more than once about organizing a lynching. "I think I could put an end to this thing in around five hours," he wrote to Captain Greene. To his sister, he was not so oblique: "I find a large number of my Texas friends here who are ready to stand by me and with winchesters if necessary. The only thing now is to keep my friends quiet—their [*sic*] came near being a general killing here last night which had it not been prevented would have closed my business here. I am trying to punish these men through the courts of the country first. If that fails—then we *may* submit."[2]

For a time, however, McLaury focused his fury on the hearing: "It will not bring my brothers back to prosecute these men but I regard it as my duty to my self and family to see that these brutes do not go unwhipped of Justice."[3] He brought renewed zeal to the prosecution team, aligning himself firmly with Ben Goodrich and Ike Clanton, while demolishing the prospect of presenting anything but the most extreme version of the case.

Whether or not Wyatt and Doc were armed, McLaury made it his first order of business to see their bail revoked. He was outraged that Price refused to help him: "The District Attorney was completely 'cowed' and after promising me on the fourth to move the court to commit these men without bail he would not do it and after agreeing in the presence of all our attys. to do so would not do it and none of our attorneys would do so and would not permit me to do so and said they did not want to get me killed and to prevent me from making this motion refused to support me if I made it."[4]

McLaury would shortly get his day in court, despite the reluctance of Price and Goodrich. But first there were more witnesses to examine. Martha King repeated her testimony from the inquest, providing, at least for the time being, a crucial link in the murder case. Standing in Bauer's butcher shop, she watched Doc Holliday and the Earps march down Fremont Street. Doc was trying to conceal a shotgun under his overcoat, carrying it on his left side. As the party passed by the doorway, she heard one of the Earp brothers—she identified him only as "the one on the outside"—say, "Let them have it," to which Holliday replied, "All right."

The witness candidly admitted that she could testify to only a fragment of the conversation, not having heard "any other words" besides the ones she quoted. Over a defense objection, she was then allowed to give her own conclusions about the implications of the phrase "let them have it," and who, precisely, was meant by "them." In her opinion, she knew exactly what the words meant, as well as the intended targets: "When I first went in the shop, the parties who keep the shop seemed to be excited and did not want to wait on me. I inquired what was the matter, and they said there was about to be a fight between the Earp boys and the cowboys."

This was the hearing's first real evidence of premeditation, and it must have seemed significant at the time. Based on diagrams and reconstructions, modern historians generally believe that Morgan Earp was the man "on the outside" who made the remark to Doc Holliday. In the course of the hearing, however, it would have been natural for Judge Spicer to think it was Virgil. As town marshal, he was the acknowledged leader of the band, far more likely than Morgan to be giving instructions to Doc. Previous witnesses testified to the locations of the combatants during the gunfight, but none of them said anything about the order in which the Earps advanced down the street, so there was no reason to assume anything other than the obvious chain of command.

Martha King was a neutral witness if there ever was one. If she could be believed, it appeared that she overheard Marshal Earp (or perhaps Morgan) instructing his posse to shoot down the Cowboys, well before

Frank McLaury ever had a chance to reach for his gun. Of course, there were other possible explanations for King's testimony, but as it stood, she provided the first clear evidence of malice.

The next witness was well-timed to back her up. James Kehoe, a partner in Bauer's butcher shop, testified that he had business dealings with the McLaury brothers. He saw them both on the day of the shootings, noting that Tom did not appear to be armed.

A short time later, watching from the door of his shop, he saw the Earps approach the Cowboys and "heard two shots in quick succession." After the two shots, and possibly as many as three or four, the witness saw Frank McLaury first draw his pistol. In the meantime, Doc Holliday moved into the middle of the street holding a shotgun or rifle. Kehoe's testimony tended to undermine the nickel-plated gun theory, but coming immediately after Martha King he spelled out just what "let them have it" seemed to mean. It was a neat piece of juxtaposition, intentional or otherwise, adding some real starch to the prosecution case as court adjourned for the weekend.

On the morning of Monday, November 7, Wesley Fuller, a local gambler and friend of the Cowboys, continued the prosecution barrage. Fuller was on his way to "warn Billy Clanton to get out of town" when he saw the beginning of the confrontation. Someone from the Earp party shouted, "Throw up your hands," and Billy Clanton quickly complied, crying, "Don't shoot me! I don't want to fight." The Earp party started shooting immediately, firing at least the first five or six shots. The witness saw Billy and Frank draw their pistols, but not until each had already been hit.

At times it seemed that Fuller was confusing Frank and Tom McLaury. He testified at one point, for example, that Frank had "no weapon that I saw on him," although it is certain that Frank was carrying a six-shooter in plain sight, unlike Tom, who was said to be unarmed. And later, Fuller said that Frank "was trying to get the rifle out of the scabbard" on his horse. That would make no sense for Frank, who returned fire with a pistol. Defense witnesses, however, testified that Tom tried to draw a Winchester from a saddle scabbard as the shooting began.

Defense counsel did not raise these discrepancies on cross examination, beginning instead by pointing out that Fuller stopped to speak with a woman named Mattie Webb and did not see the first shot fired. As to what he did see, Fitch pounded away on Fuller about his liquor habit, asking whether he suffered a fit of delirium tremens. The witness would admit only to drinking "considerable" the evening before the fight, which was not at all unusual in Tombstone.

Fuller testified that he saw the Earps and Holliday when they were conferring at the corner of Fourth and Allen Streets, before they headed toward the vacant lot. Fitch got him to admit that they were not carrying their weapons in their hands—Morgan and Doc had six-shooters in their pockets (Virgil had not yet given Doc the shotgun), and Wyatt's was pushed down in his waistband under his coat—suggesting that they were not anticipating an immediate shoot-out.

Then Fitch pulled off an impressive, if underappreciated, legal maneuver. He had a useful bit of hearsay that he wanted to employ in the cross examination, but he could not bring it up unless Fuller "opened the door." Feigning innocence, Fitch asked the witness who fired the initial two shots—a fact the witness had omitted on direct examination. "Morgan Earp and Doc Holliday," Fuller replied, though he could not tell which fired first. That was just what Fitch needed.

"Did you not," the cross examiner asked, "on the fifth day of November, 1881, about 5 o'clock in the afternoon, in front of the Oriental Saloon in Tombstone, say to or in the presence of Wyatt Earp, that you knew nothing in your testimony that would hurt the Earps, but that you intended to cinch Holliday, or words of like import or effect?"

The extreme specificity—date, time, location—was a trial lawyer's feint, intended to suggest that there were multiple witnesses who could nail down his statement. The precise phrasing—"to or in the presence of Wyatt Earp"—also made it seem that others were there at the time.

If Fuller was inclined to lie, he was dissuaded by Fitch's careful technique. "I might have used the words 'I mean to cinch Holliday,'" he admitted, "but I don't think so."

The briefest testimony of the day was Andrew Mehan, a saloonkeeper who testified that Tom McLaury checked his pistol somewhere "between one and two o'clock" on the day of the gunfight—supporting the claim that Tom died unarmed. The defense did not cross examine the witness. There would be other ways to deal with his testimony.

Remanded to Jail

Somewhere in the midst of this, Will McLaury pressed his motion to revoke Doc and Wyatt's bail. If his letters were truthful, the motion was made in unusual circumstances. Not only did Price and Goodrich refuse to support him, but McLaury boasted that he managed to speak to Judge Spicer privately, securing the court's assurance that the motion would be granted. Such "ex parte" contacts were as improper then as they are now, but Judge Spicer was not entirely averse to them. Later, he would conduct a private interview with a defense witness, causing the prosecution to object strenuously. This time, however, the prosecution seemed happy to take advantage of Spicer's loose procedure, if that is what happened.

To the defendants' shock and dismay, Judge Spicer granted McLaury's motion to revoke their bail. It was an unusual step for the court to take, but not an outlandish one. There were two possible bases for Spicer's decision. Since there was no right to bail in capital cases, he might have concluded that he was wrong in his original discretionary ruling. More ominously for the Earps, he also might have been ruling on the quality of the prosecution's case thus far. Bail was prohibited by statute in capital cases "where the proof is evident or the presumption great," meaning that the judge would have been obligated to remand Doc and Wyatt if he believed there was sufficiently compelling evidence of murder.

If Spicer agreed with McLaury that "the proof so far was conclusive of murder," then the defendants were in deep trouble, for at least two reasons. First, the prosecution's case had not been all that strong when it came to proving capital murder (the only crime that precluded bail), so Spicer must have put great stock in Martha King's testimony, followed by the several descriptions of the surrendering Cowboys. Worse, the actual standard of proof in the hearing was only "sufficient evidence," requiring far less than the "conclusive proof" the court seemed already to have found. In other words, the case had gone just about as well as the defendants could have expected, and they were still in a terribly deep hole. They had to hope that Tom Fitch could pull off a miracle, or that the prosecutors would blow their advantage.

Will McLaury had in mind a different turn of events, wondering whether Wyatt and Doc would fight for their freedom rather than submit to jail. "I only hoped they would," he wrote to Captain Greene, "as

I thought I could kill them both before they could get a start." He was even more specific in his letter to his brother-in-law, explaining that he "stood where I could send a knife through their hearts if they made a move. . . . [F]or I was anxious to have an opportunity to send them over the bay."[5]

In fact, Wyatt and Doc accepted the ruling calmly, which McLaury interpreted as fear—"they were quiet as lambs, only looking a little scared"—rather than as composure, or even respect for the law. The defendants had faith in their counsel, who immediately prepared a habeas corpus petition, presenting it that evening to probate judge J. H. Lucas. Defense counsel argued that Spicer's initial grant of bail had to be honored until the conclusion of the hearing, but to no avail. The court agreed with McLaury, giving him another victory after only a few days in town. He was exultant: "Last night after it was known the murderers were in Jail the Hotel was a perfect jam until nearly morning. Everybody wanted to see me and shake my hand."[6]

Suspicions ran high on both sides as Wyatt and Doc were committed to the cold confines of Johnny Behan's county jail. McLaury continued to worry that prosecution witnesses risked being "killed by the friends of these brutes," and Behan, by one report, placed guards around the jail to prevent Earp partisans from staging a rescue attempt. That dramatic apprehension seems unfounded. A jailbreak would have ended any chance that the Earps would be exonerated in court, which was still in the cards despite their recent reverses. And even if Wyatt and Doc planned an escape, that would leave Virgil and Morgan—too badly injured to ride—stuck in Tombstone, almost certain to be convicted. The more real danger was to Wyatt and Doc themselves. Held in the custody of their enemy and accuser, they had good reason to fear "Cowboy justice," and more so because Behan's jail had not exactly proved itself secure over the previous year. As a necessary precaution, "Earp supporters placed more than a dozen armed guards in front of the jail" just in case Clanton and McLaury supporters had ideas of revenge.[7]

Wyatt and Doc spent their first night in jail on Monday, November 7, arriving in court the next morning to see Billy Claiborne, another Cowboy and a Mississippi native, take the stand. Claiborne was the first witness after McLaury's success on the bail motion, and it was obvious that both sides wanted to do their best with him. A strong performance on direct examination would confirm the wisdom of the judge's ruling, but it might give Spicer second thoughts if the witness could be shaken on cross.

Claiborne acknowledged that "I knew Tom and Frank McLaury and Billy Clanton in their lifetime and know Ike Clanton," later adding that he had known them "quite a while." He was standing with them, between Fly's photograph gallery and boardinghouse, when Sheriff Behan came over in his attempt to disarm Frank McLaury. Claiborne watched as Behan frisked Ike for weapons, and he saw Tom McLaury throw open his coat to show that he was unarmed. The Earps approached a minute or two later, and Behan walked up the street to meet them.

According to Claiborne, the Earp party "had their six-shooters in their hands" when they got to the corner of the lot—an important fact that no other witness supplied. Virgil shouted, "You sons-of-bitches, you've been looking for a fight, and you can have it," and then said, "Throw up your hands." That sequence, the reverse of most other testimony, made the Earps look even guiltier.

We do not know which prosecutor interrogated Claiborne, but the examination was notably intense compared to some of the earlier ones. That may have been merely because the hearing had reached a critical stage, or it may have been a sign of Will McLaury's influence. Perhaps McLaury himself put the witness on the stand, although there is no way to verify that. In any event, Claiborne provided one of the most detailed and emphatic descriptions of the gunfight:

> Billy Clanton threw up his hands; Ike Clanton threw up his; and Tom McLaury threw open his coat and said, "I haven't got any-thing boys, I am disarmed." Then the shooting commenced, right then, in an instant, by Doc Holliday and Morgan Earp—the two shots fird by Earp and Holliday were so close together that I could hardly distinguish them. I saw them shoot. Doc Holliday shot at Tom McLaury and Morgan Earp shot at Billy Clanton. When Doc Holliday fired that shot, Tom McLaury staggered backwards and Billy Clanton fell up against the corner of the house and laid himself down on the ground.
>
> There were six or eight fired by the Earp party—they were fired in very quick succession. Billy Clanton was lying on the

ground and drew his six-shooter, rested it across his arm and commenced firing. Frank McLaury at that time was out in the middle of the street with his six-shooter. I did not see Frank draw his pistol; I saw it in his hand. Frank did not have [his] six-shooter in his hand until after six or eight shots were fired by the Earp party.

Billy Clanton fell right against the corner of the window and slid down to the ground; Billy Clanton was standing close to the corner of the house; Morgan Earp shoved his pistol close up to him and fired; Billy then fell as I have described; Billy was standing on one corner and Morgan at the other corner; Morgan shoved his pistol within one foot of Billy Clanton's breast and fired.[8]

Claiborne was the first witness to testify that Morgan Earp shot Billy Clanton at point-blank range, a fact that would assume great significance when Judge Spicer ruled at the end of the case. As it continued, the direct examination became increasingly specific and compelling:

(Q) What was Virgil Earp doing all this time, from the time the first shot was fired?

(A) He was shooting first at one of them, then at the other.

(Q) Did you see him shoot?

(A) Yes sir.

(Q) What was Doc Holliday doing after the first shots were fired?

(A) He was shooting at Frank McLaury out on the street.

(Q) What was Wyatt Earp doing all the time after the first shots were fired?

(A) He was shooting.

(Q) Can you tell who those shots fired by Wyatt Earp were aimed at that you saw?

(A) At Frank McLaury.

(Q) Did you or not, at any time during the shooting, see Tom McLaury with any weapon in his hands, and if so, what kind of arms or weapons?

(A) I did not see any at all.[9]

Over defense objections, Claiborne was allowed to testify that the Clantons and McLaurys had gathered at the corral in order to go home. The last question on direct was whether he had any arms on his person at the time of the shooting—apparently intended to blunt the suggestion that Claiborne was more involved in the fight than he admitted.

"I did not," was his answer.

The cross examination began by focusing on Doc Holliday, challenging Claiborne's testimony that Doc fired the first shot. That emphasis, as well as a few stylistic differences, suggests that it may have been conducted by T. J. Drum rather than Tom Fitch. No matter who the questioner was, the witness proved uncooperative:

> (Q) How was Holliday dressed that day as to his outside coat or garment?
>
> (A) I cannot say. I was not watching his clothing. I was watching the six-shooter in his hand.
>
> (Q) Did you watch him from the first moment of his appearance down the street toward the Clanton party?
>
> (A) No sir, not altogether.
>
> (Q) Did you see him when he first drew any weapon from his person?
>
> (A) I did not see him draw any. He had one in his hand when he came there.
>
> (Q) Did you see him at any time have a shotgun in his hand?
>
> (A) I did not, that I remember.
>
> (Q) What kind of a pistol did he have in his hand?
>
> (A) A nickel-plated pistol.

The claim that Holliday walked down the street with a nickel-plated pistol in his hand was contradicted by nearly every other witness, not to mention the buckshot wounds in Tom McLaury's chest. Even Johnny Behan testified that Doc was trying to conceal a shotgun under his coat, so the cross examination clearly succeeded in luring Claiborne out onto an unsteady limb.

The next step was to attack the witness's credibility. The cross examiner asked Claiborne whether he had been arrested in "a killing scrape" in Charleston, for which he was still under bail. A prosecution objection was overruled, but the witness refused to answer even when pressed.

The subject then turned to bias. Asked whether the witness was "on terms of friendship and intimate" with the Clantons and McLaurys, Claiborne answered that he "liked the boys, [but] not more than I do any of my acquaintances." He denied ever working for the Cowboys but allowed that he had "stopped at their ranches and stayed there all night, once or twice." It was an important admission, given that the Clanton and McLaury ranches were reputed to be transfer stations for stolen cattle. Implying that Claiborne had been more involved in the confrontation than he admitted, defense counsel asked why he had not run when the shooting started. Claiborne gave the implausible answer that he thought "there was more danger in running than in standing there." Always trying to exploit Judge Spicer's aversion to contrived testimony, the cross examiner asked Claiborne whether he had conferred with Johnny Behan before taking the stand, but the witness denied the accusation and counsel had no way of following it up.

The cross examination ended with another example of the "provable" technique. Claiborne was asked whether he saw "any powder marks on Billy Clanton's body after his decease." This one was a win/win proposition for the defense. If the witness testified there were no powder marks, he would undermine his own testimony about Morgan's point-blank shot. On the other hand, Claiborne would be caught in a lie if he tried to invent powder marks, because Coroner Matthews had already testified that there were none. The witness would not give a straight answer—"not that I remember," he said—and the cross examiner's point was made.

The redirect was curious and amusing. Billy Claiborne was asked how he got his nickname, "the Kid." The other "Billy the Kid," of course, was Patrick Henry McCarty (aka William Bonney), a notorious gunslinger and murderer who had been shot down by Sheriff Pat Garrett just a few months earlier in nearby Lincoln County, New Mexico. The prosecution wanted to make it clear that their witness was not the infamous outlaw's namesake.

"Well, I came to Arizona when I was small," Claiborne explained, "when Tombstone was first struck. John Slaughter's men called me 'the Kid' because I was the smallest one in the outfit. That is the way the name originated." As Paula Mitchell Marks observed, he had obviously outgrown the description, causing a skeptical reaction in the courtroom.

The prosecutor quickly moved to solve the problem for the benefit of the presumably incredulous Judge Spicer:

(Q) When did you first come to Tombstone?
(A) About two and a half, or three years ago.
(Q) How much smaller were you then, than you are now?
(A) I have grown nearly two feet since then, in height.

The testimony was not really necessary, but no one was taking any chances at this stage of the proceeding.

The Claiborne examination could easily have been the climax of the prosecution case. His testimony was forceful and effective, providing a clear picture of the gunfight at the most crucial moments. Based on Claiborne's account, Judge Spicer would have had no difficulty envisioning the scene: Doc and Morgan held their guns on the Clantons and McLaurys while Virgil cursed the Cowboys and ordered them to raise their hands. That would explain Billy Clanton's frightened cry, "Don't shoot me, I don't want to fight." He must have seen Doc and Morgan cock their weapons, even as Virgil was calling for surrender. Combined with similar testimony from Billy Allen, Wes Fuller, and Johnny Behan, there was really nothing that could be added to the description of the shoot-out, at least from the prosecutors' perspective.

To be sure, the prosecution case was far from airtight. Tom Fitch and his colleague had done an outstanding job in their cross examinations, pointing out numerous gaps and contradictions in the case against the Earps. In Claiborne's testimony alone they poked substantial holes in the "nickel-plated pistol" theory, showing how the witness, like Behan before him, could not account for the fatal shotgun blast. But that was a problem with the entire premise of the prosecution case, and it could never be resolved by calling more witnesses. As almost always happens, additional witnesses were likely to create still more inconsistencies, rather than clear up existing ones.

The greatest defect in the prosecution case was the proof of premeditation, which rested on three fairly slender assertions: Behan testified to Virgil's angry, pre-gunfight statement that he would give the Cowboys "a chance to make a fight." Martha King added the ambiguous but potentially damning instruction to Doc Holliday—"Let them have it!"

And finally, Billy Claiborne put guns in the hands of the Earps and Holliday as they marched down Fremont Street, suggesting a settled intention to use them even before the Cowboys had a chance to react to Virgil's command. It was far from proof beyond a reasonable doubt, but Judge Spicer's ruling on the bail motion suggested that it could amount to "sufficient reason" for the purpose of the preliminary hearing.

Looking at the preliminary hearing on the afternoon of November 8, the prosecution seemed firmly in command. They had presented plenty of evidence on the lesser charges of manslaughter and second-degree murder, and even the first-degree murder charge was viable. Perhaps they might need a few minor witnesses to add some details, but the real question was whether to risk calling Ike Clanton.

The Surviving Cowboy

Ike Clanton was not a necessary witness. The coroner was required by statute to "summon and examine" every person who "has any knowledge of the facts," but the prosecutors had no similar obligation at the preliminary hearing. They were free to pick and choose their witnesses. While Ike was the only survivor of the Earps' gunfire, he would bring many liabilities with him to the stand. He was the most disreputable of the prosecution witnesses, having spent a full night and morning tramping about Tombstone waving his rifle and threatening the Earps. Allen, Fuller, and Claiborne (and to some extent, Behan) could be tarred as Cowboy confederates, but Ike Clanton was the real thing, likely to draw the ire of Judge Spicer.

A more subtle problem for the prosecutors was Clanton's strong incentive to vindicate himself, which would tend to make him an unreliable witness, or at least to seem that way. Eager to show that he was not wholly at fault for the deaths of his brother and friends, even an honest witness would be tempted to bend the truth. Someone like Ike had every reason to fictionalize his role in the gunfight and the events that led up to it, and he would be suspected of lying no matter what he said. Even if his direct examination could be closely controlled, there was no telling what would happen once he was exposed to one of Tom Fitch's incisive cross examinations.

On the other hand, there were several reasons to call Ike at the preliminary hearing. Will McLaury mentioned one in a letter to Captain Greene: "We are going on with the examination of witnesses before [the] examining court for we fear some of our most important witnesses will be killed by friends of these brutes."[10] If Ike's life was truly in jeopardy, then it was obviously important to get him on the stand before Judge Spicer, if only to produce a transcript that could be used later at trial. McLaury's fear, however, was mostly an invention of his own indignation, believing as he did that the Earps were capable of anything. There is no evidence that prosecution witnesses were being harassed or intimidated, much less assassinated. And even if they had ill intentions, Wyatt and Doc were imprisoned and Virgil and Morgan were bedridden. The other friends of the Earps, including Mayor Clum and most of the local mine owners, were unfriendly toward the likes of Ike Clanton, but they were not the sort who would rub out witnesses.

More realistically, Ike could be used to prop up the first-degree murder charge, especially against Virgil, which remained the weakest link in the prosecution case. The prosecution's strongest case, of course, was against Doc Holliday, who was fingered by nearly every witness as firing the first shot. Morgan, too, was identified as firing in the opening salvo, but the evidence was considerably thinner against Wyatt and Virgil. For the older Earp brothers to be dragged convincingly into the first-degree murder charge, it would be necessary to show that they somehow planned, or at least facilitated, the shooting. That would not be easy because both Virgil and Wyatt had earned considerable respect in Tombstone (and before that, in Kansas) precisely because they enforced the law *without* shooting.

In lawyers' terms, the prosecution needed a "theory of the case" that would explain why Virgil and Wyatt Earp would suddenly turn into killers. What was it about the showdown with the Clantons and McLaurys that would cause upright, straightlaced Virgil Earp to opt for gunplay over an easy arrest? Why would Wyatt Earp—who had buffaloed Curly Bill Brocius, rather than shoot him, after the Cowboy shot Marshal Fred White—participate in an outright assassination? If there was an answer to these questions, it just might have to come from Ike Clanton.

But perhaps that analysis assumes too much strategizing on the part of the prosecution. Ike Clanton was the complaining witness and

Ben Goodrich's personal client. The prosecutors may have felt duty bound to allow him to tell his story. Or they might have thought that they would appear to be hiding something if they refrained from calling him. After all, he testified at the inquest without incident.

For whatever reason, the prosecutors decided to go ahead with Ike, putting all their cards on the table. As it turned out, they could not have played their hand more poorly. Historians have characterized Ike as a blowhard who fell apart on the witness stand. But as we will see, there was much more to it than that.

Ike's testimony began on the morning of Wednesday, November 9. He identified himself as a cattle dealer, which must have raised some eyebrows in the courtroom. Before the irony could sink in, the prosecuting attorney—probably Ben Goodrich—moved quickly to the crucial events.

> (Q) Did you know Frank and Tom McLaury and Billy Clanton?
> (A) Yes sir.
> (Q) Are they living or dead, and if so, when did they die?
> (A) They are dead. They died on the 26th of October, 1881, on Fremont Street, between Third and Fourth Streets, in Tombstone, Cochise County, Arizona Territory.
> (Q) Did they die a natural or a violent death?
> (A) A violent death, they were killed.
> (Q) Were you present at the time they were killed?
> (A) I was.
> (Q) Who else was present at the time, that you saw?
> (A) There was Holliday, Morgan, Virgil and Wyatt Earp, Sheriff Behan, and William Claiborne. No [one] else, that I can remember, at the time they were killed.
> (Q) Who was engaged in the killing of these parties?
> (A) Wyatt, Morgan and Virgil Earp, and Holliday.

Asked to describe the "commencement of the difficulty," Clanton began by detailing Johnny Behan's efforts to disarm Frank McLaury as they were standing near Fly's photo studio and boardinghouse. A defense objection was overruled, and the witness proceeded to testify that Frank refused to give up his pistol "unless the Earps were disarmed," adding Tom's protestation that he had no weapons. The defense objected again, this time to the entire conversation. The McLaury brothers' statements to Behan were indeed hearsay, so the court struck them from the record, but the strategy behind the objection is hard to fathom. Why did the defense want to exclude the evidence? True, Tom's comment supported the claim that he was unarmed, but Behan had already testified to the same facts, making the additional evidence relatively innocuous. Frank McLaury's insistence on keeping his gun, however, was far more helpful to the defendants than to the prosecution since it showed, at a minimum, that Frank was in a combative frame of mind. Sometimes, even good trial lawyers make mistakes, and this appears to have been one of them. Or rather, two of them, given that the prosecutors made a comparable misjudgment, struggling to have the testimony admitted, even though it was ultimately damaging to their case.

For the time being, the attorneys seemed more interested in besting one another than in establishing useful facts. Fitch objected to the next two questions, even though neither was particularly damaging, and the court quickly overruled defense counsel each time. This pattern continued throughout Ike's testimony, with the defense objecting far more frequently than at any other time during the hearing. If the tactic was intended to throw the prosecutors off stride, it clearly failed; the interruptions did not noticeably affect the direct examination.

According to Ike, the Earps and Holliday "pulled their pistols as they got there, and Wyatt Earp and Virgil Earp said, 'You sons-of-bitches, you have been looking for a fight!' and at the same time ordered us to throw up our hands. And they said, 'You have been looking for a fight!' and commenced shooting." Ike testified that Doc and Morgan fired the first two shots, and then he added some details. Virgil, Ike said, immediately fired the third shot, with Wyatt firing next. Thus, he had all four lawmen shooting within seconds of Virgil's command, creating the appearance of a coordinated assault.

In what must have been a painful and awkward moment, Ike was also asked about the exact circumstances of his brother's death. "Morgan Earp shot William Clanton," he began.

> (Q) How do you know that Morgan Earp shot Billy Clanton?
> (A) Because I seen his pistol pointed within two or three feet of his bosom, saw him fire and saw William Clanton stagger and fall up against the house and put his hands on his breast.

(Q) In what position were Billy Clanton's hands at the time Morgan Earp fired at him, and you saw him stagger and fall up against the house?

(A) His hands were thrown up about even with the level of his head—his hands in front of him.

This testimony—about the position of Billy's hands and the distance of Morgan's pistol—would turn out to be extremely important to Judge Spicer's decision, though at the time it was quickly overshadowed by the story of Ike's dramatic confrontation with Wyatt Earp. Unsurprisingly, Ike testified that he bravely wrestled with Wyatt, dodging bullets all the time: "[Wyatt] shoved his pistol up against my belly and told me to throw up my hands. He said, 'You son-of-a-bitch, you can have a fight!' I turned on my heel, taking Wyatt Earp's hand and pistol with my left hand and grabbed him around the shoulder with my right hand and held him for a few seconds. While I was holding him he shot."

Still, there was no avoiding the fact that Ike ran away (and kept running), leaving his friends to face death without him: "I pushed him around the corner of the photograph gallery and then I jumped into the door. I went right on through the hall and out of the back way. I then went on across Allen Street and into the dance hall on that street. As I jumped into the door of the photograph gallery, I heard some bullets pass by my head."

Ike testified for the entire day, telling and retelling the story of the shooting as the prosecution went over the facts in increasing detail. By late afternoon, the examination shifted back to the start of the "difficulty." In Ike's version, the trouble began shortly after midnight when Doc Holliday interrupted his "lunch" and began cursing him for no reason, calling Ike a "son-of-a-bitch of a cowboy" and challenging him to get a gun "if there was any grit in me." Doc accused Ike of threatening the Earps, which Ike denied to no avail. Morgan Earp soon arrived, joining the abuse. Virgil and Wyatt both watched as the curses and threats continued to fly: "Morgan Earp told me if I was not heeled, when I came back on the street to be heeled."

"I walked off," said Ike, "and asked them not to shoot me in the back." And so ended his testimony for the day.

Ordinarily, a court recess is not a particularly significant event. The staccato nature of witness examinations—questions and answers, back and forth—lends itself to interruption, allowing the court to adjourn at any convenient time. In Ike's case, however, the recesses—there would be three of them altogether, including one that lasted for several days—seem to have been more important than usual. The tenor of his testimony would change dramatically after one of the recesses, in ways that suggest a strategy shift for the prosecution.

When court reconvened on Thursday, November 10, Ike resumed his testimony, picking it up at the point of the poker game in the Occidental Saloon. He told of being buffaloed by Virgil Earp, omitting the fact that he was waving a rifle at the time. He also added a new fact, that Morgan Earp "cocked his pistol and stuck it at me" during the arrest. The abuse continued even after Ike was taken to Judge Wallace's courtroom, implicating all three Earp brothers. Wyatt "called me a thief and son-of-a-bitch and told me I could have all the shooting I wanted. . . . Virgil Earp spoke up and told me he would pay my fine if I would fight them," as Morgan threateningly "stood over me and behind me." Ike courageously stood up to them, telling Wyatt "I would fight him anywhere or any way." Miraculously, Ike escaped unscathed, as the Earps allowed him to leave the courthouse once he paid his fine and surrendered his arms.

What brought on the torrent of abuse, which, according to Ike, began when Doc and Morgan "tried to murder me the night before"? Ike had no answer, but it certainly was not his fault. "I never threatened the Earps or Doc Holliday," he said. With that, the direct examination closed.

Ike's testimony rounded out the prosecution case by explaining that the Earps were in a fighting mood well before the gun battle. Their bellicose threats and challenges, if Ike was to be believed, supported the claim that they had a shoot-out in mind, rather than a peaceful surrender, when they confronted the Clantons and McLaurys and demanded that they "throw up their hands." Still lacking, however, was a motive. Apart from Doc's single statement—"You have been threatening the Earps"—Ike as yet offered no reason for their murderous animosity. That gap had to be obvious to everyone in the courtroom, the prosecutors included.

Nonetheless, the direct examiner never asked Ike to explain just why the Earps were so keen to "murder" him, an omission so glaring that it had to be intentional. There was something about Ike's story that the direct examiner chose not to elicit—at least up until that point.

Ike Clanton Runs Wild

After Ike Clanton's direct examination was over, his testimony was "suspended" for two days while he obtained medical treatment for "neuralgia of the head," presumably a headache caused by the pistol whipping he suffered at Virgil's hand more than two weeks previously. When he returned to the stand for cross examination, on Saturday morning, November 12, he would add a series of astonishing elements to his story that must have stunned the court and spectators. At least one of the prosecutors, however, might not have been equally surprised.

The defense theory became apparent right at the beginning of the cross examination. It was the Cowboys who precipitated the fight, not the Earps. Ike's morning of gun-waving bluster was just the first round, perhaps a stalling tactic, until the arrival of Frank and Billy, who had been summoned as reinforcements. Did Ike, at any time on October 25 or 26, send a telegram to Charleston, "directing Frank McLaury and William Clanton to come to Tombstone?" The question had the makings of a great "provable," but Ike denied it flatly, and the incriminating telegram, if it ever existed, was never produced.

The cross examination then turned to more promising territory, challenging Ike's claim that he had never threatened the Earps or Holliday. Didn't Ike tell Ned Boyle, the saloonkeeper at the Oriental, "that as soon as the Earps came on the street, they had to fight"? Ike could not remember speaking with Boyle, or even being in the Oriental that day. His poor memory was no problem for the cross examiner, of course. The question was a "provable," and Ned Boyle was available to testify for the defense.

Moving on to another saloon, Ike was asked whether he was in Kelly's on the morning of the gunfight, Winchester rifle in hand. This time he remembered, and he also remembered Kelly asking him "what was the matter." Didn't he reply that "the Earp crowd had insulted you the night before when you were unarmed,— 'I have fixed,' or 'heeled' myself now, and they have got a fight on sight"? This time, Ike realized his dilemma and admitted that "there was very near that conversation in Kelly's Saloon." Fitch next tried to question Ike about other threats during the previous two months, but the court sustained repeated objections by the prosecution.

There were additional questions aimed at exposing Ike's rustling activities, and some others about his cowardice during the fight. But these were almost second thoughts, with Fitch seldom pursuing Ike's equivocations.

The real heart of the cross examination was devoted to Ike's agreement to rat on Leonard, Head, and Crane, the Cowboy robbers of the Benson stage and the killers of Bud Philpot. The defense theory was that Ike's overnight rampage had nothing to do with unprovoked curses from Doc and Morgan and everything to do with Clanton's fear that he might be discovered as an informer. Until now, Ike had carefully stayed away from any overt reference to his deal with Wyatt. He had mentioned it obliquely at the inquest—calling it a transaction that had "nothing to do with the killing of these three men"—and not at all in his closely cabined direct examination. Fitch was not about to let him get away with that, as he approached the question head-on:

> (Q) Did not Wyatt Earp approach you, Frank McLaury, and Joe Hill for the purpose of getting you three parties to give . . . Leonard, Head and Crane away—in the Arizona parlance—so that he, Wyatt Earp, could capture them?

Ike admitted the approach by Wyatt—to him alone; he disclaimed any knowledge of Frank McLaury or Joe Hill's involvement—but denied that there ever was a deal. Instead, Ike claimed that Wyatt approached for a "private talk" in which he broached a nefarious scheme, offering Ike six thousand dollars to help in a triple murder.

> (A) He told me he wanted me to help put up a job to kill Crane, Leonard and Head. He said there was between four and five thousand reward for them, and he said he would make the balance of the six thousand dollars up out of his own pocket.

Ike also supplied Wyatt's reason for wanting to murder the wanted men, rather than arrest them. The Earps themselves had been in on the robbery, "piping off"—local slang for diverting stolen loot—to Doc Holliday the money from the Wells Fargo box:

> (A) He said that his business was such that he could not afford to capture them. He would have to kill them or else leave the

country. He said he and his brother, Morgan, had piped off to Doc Holliday and William Leonard, the money that was going off on the stage, and he said he could not afford to capture them, and he would have to kill them or leave the country, for they [were] stopping around the country so damned long that he was afraid some of them would be caught and would squeal on him.

And why did Deputy Federal Marshal Wyatt Earp choose to confide his evil deeds to Ike Clanton, rustler and Cowboy?

(A)   He then made me promise on my honor as a gentleman not to repeat the conversation if I did not like the proposition.

Fitch was momentarily caught off guard by Ike's testimony, which charged Wyatt Earp with robbery, embezzlement, murder, conspiracy to commit murder, attempted murder, and murder again. As lawyers do, he briefly changed the subject in order to collect his thoughts. After it was harmlessly established that Ike Clanton was born in Missouri and that Frank and Billy rode into Tombstone from Antelope Springs, the cross examination got back to the point.

Didn't Ike actually have four or five conversations with Wyatt about Leonard, Head, and Crane? Didn't Wyatt explain that he was planning to run for sheriff, and that he was therefore interested in the "glory" rather than the reward money? Hadn't Ike insisted on reassurance that the reward would be paid "dead or alive," because he worried that Leonard, Head, and Crane would "make a fight" when ambushed?

Ike denied everything, even when Fitch confronted him with the telegram from Wells Fargo's San Francisco office, reading aloud, "Yes we will pay rewards for them dead or alive. L. F. Rowell."

On redirect examination, the prosecution shifted gears completely. Having previously stayed far away from Ike's tale of treachery and confession, they now embraced it. Ike's original version implicated only Wyatt Earp, but the prosecutor decided to get more:

(Q)   Please state what Doc Holliday told you upon the subject, and when you have answered as to him, state what Morgan Earp told you, then state what Virgil Earp told you, then state what Wyatt Earp told you.

As it turned out, Ike explained that the three Earp brothers and Doc Holliday had all taken him into their confidence. In addition to Wyatt's admission, Doc Holliday had actually confessed to killing Bud Philpot, shooting him through the heart. Morgan Earp had urged Ike to take the deal, affirming that he had "piped off" fourteen hundred dollars to Doc Holliday. And Virgil admitted that he had helped Leonard, Head, and Crane escape, intentionally leading Behan's posse off their trail.

As the hero of his own story, Ike, of course, would never cooperate in a betrayal. He told Wyatt, "I was not going to have anything to do with helping to capture Bill Leonard, Crane and Harry Head." Then Ike realized that he made a mistake, verifying Wyatt's version of the story rather than his own. He quickly corrected himself, substituting *kill* for *capture*, stating that he refused Wyatt's request to *kill* Leonard, Crane, and Head. Fitch caught the discrepancy, of course, and quickly took advantage of it by asking for a notation on the record. Judge Spicer complied, making and signing the following entry: "At the time of stating the above sentence, the witness first said, 'capture,' and then corrected it to 'kill.' Of which correction and change, Counsel for Defense asked a memorandum to be made, which is here done."

Ike's story was becoming increasingly incredible, even without the capture-kill miscue, and more so because he had not included any of it in his coroner's jury testimony, or even in his direct examination. The prosecutor, however, stayed with him all the way:

> (Q) Why have you not told what Doc Holliday, Wyatt Earp, Virgil Earp, and Morgan Earp said about the attempted stage robbery and the killing of Bud Philpot before you have told it in this examination?
>
> (A) Before they told me, I made a sacred promise not to tell it, and never would have told it, had I not been put on the stand. And another reason is, I found out by Wyatt Earp's conversation that he was offering money to kill men that were in the attempted stage robbery, his confederates . . . and I knew that after Leonard, Crane and Head was killed that some of them would murder me for what they had told me.

That testimony must have set Judge Spicer's teeth on edge, recalling, as it did nearly word for word, the perjured testimony of prosecution witness Jacob Hamblin in the Mountain Meadows case.

Ike did his job, though perhaps too well. He provided the missing element—premeditation—for the capital murder charge, claiming that the shoot-out was a brutal result of the Earps' efforts to silence him. But at what cost to the prosecution's credibility?

And it was not over yet. Fitch saved one of the sharpest lines of questioning for re–cross examination. Even assuming that Ike's testimony was worthless, the defense still had to deal with a half-dozen other eyewitnesses, all of whom testified to criminal acts by the Earps. It was not enough, therefore, simply to discredit Ike Clanton, easy as that might be—the prosecution still had a case without him. Fitch, however, figured out a way to tie Ike's fabulations directly to the prosecutors, placing responsibility for the outpouring squarely where it belonged:

> (Q) Did you relate these conversations . . . to any of the counsel for the prosecution, or any person, before coming upon the stand this afternoon?
>
> (A) I did not communicate this to my counsel until after I was put on the stand. Yes, I did relate it prior to this afternoon.

There it was. At least one of the prosecutors knew full well what Ike intended to say, and he may have been more involved than that.

Fitch ended the recross with some well-placed sarcasm, intended to convey his contempt for Ike's story: "Did not Marshall Williams, the agent of the [Wells Fargo] Express company at Tombstone, state to you . . . that he was personally [involved] in the attempted stage robbery and the murder of Philpot?" "Did not James Earp, a brother of Virgil, Morgan, and Wyatt, also confess to you that he was [a] murderer and stage robber?"

It was not terrific cross examination, or even legally admissible (Judge Spicer sustained objections to both questions), but it drove home the point. The success of the prosecution now rested on the credibility of Ike Clanton.

Requiem for a Witness

Most historians believe that Ike Clanton simply destroyed himself on the witness stand, inventing and elaborating on a far-fetched story of his own devising while dragging down the prosecution case at the same time. Allen Barra suggests that Ike might have visited a saloon or an opium den during one of the recesses. Casey Tefertiller thinks he might even have been on cocaine, explaining that a common treatment for headaches during the 1880s was a solution of cocaine and water. That would account for Ike's display of "overweening confidence" and the fact that he "seemed to glory in his own perceived brilliance" throughout the cross examination.[11] Neither of those possibilities can be ruled out, but another event might also have occurred during one of the first two recesses in Ike's testimony.

Ike's story was hard to swallow, but there was at least one person in Arizona who believed him, and may have urged him on—Will McLaury, the associate prosecutor. On November 9, during the first recess of Ike's direct examination, McLaury wrote a letter to his brother-in-law in Iowa. In that letter, McLaury virtually predicted the very testimony that Ike would give the next morning in court: "The cause of the murders was this—some time ago Holliday one of the murderers attempted to rob express of Wells Fargo & Co., and in so doing shot and killed a stage driver and passenger and the other parties engaged in the murder with him the Earp brothers were interested in the attempt at the Exp. robbery and young Clanton who was killed . . . knew the facts about the attempted robbery and told his brother J. I. [Ike] Clanton and Thos. and Robert [Frank] and they got up facts intending to prosecute him and the Earp Bros. and Holliday had information of it."[12]

Up until that time, it had never been alleged that the gunfight was part of the Earps' efforts to silence potential witnesses against them.[13] Not at the coroner's inquest, and not at any point in the prosecution case, did anyone claim that the Earps were involved in the Benson stage robbery or that they had set out to assassinate the Clantons and McLaurys to prevent them from bringing charges. Just one day earlier, November 8, Will had written a long letter to his law partner with no mention of any connection between the Benson stage and the killing of his brothers. How is it that on November 9, Will suddenly knew the content of Ike's surprising, yet-to-be-given cross examination?

Did Will McLaury and Ike Clanton use one of the court recesses to confer about his testimony? Did McLaury subvert the prosecution case by counseling Ike to broaden his testimony on cross examination, contrary to the plans of Price and Goodrich? The evidence is circumstantial but engaging. There is no direct proof of such a meeting, but in addition to McLaury's letter we also know, from the testimony of Thomas Keefe, that McLaury diligently sought out other witnesses for pretrial conversations.

Ike passed up at least two opportunities to tell his full story under oath—at the coroner's inquest and during his direct examination. We know that he was being counseled by Ben Goodrich on at least the second occasion, and probably the first as well (he testified on cross examination that he "employed counsel to prosecute in this case"). If Ike had shared his story with Goodrich, then it is clear that the lawyer made a conscious determination to keep it out of evidence for fear of undermining the credibility of his client and his case.

The direct examination had proceeded without incident, hewing closely to the events of October 25–26 while avoiding any questions about the background of Clanton's feud with the Earps. Following the first recess in Ike's testimony, Will McLaury wrote a letter that included, in broad outline, the claim that the "cause of the murders" lay in the robbery of the Benson stage. After a second, longer recess, Ike's cross examination began in which he blurted out his charge against Wyatt. Importantly, at that point he did not expand his story to implicate Virgil, Morgan, and Doc. Not yet.

On redirect examination, however, the prosecution abruptly changed course. Rather than shy away from Ike's wild tale, the redirect examiner asked him to repeat it, specifically inviting Ike to add new details about Virgil, Morgan, and Doc. In fact, the redirect brought out the most extravagant version of the story, in which Ike Clanton cautioned Doc "not to take me into his confidence," but Holliday went right ahead and confessed to shooting Bud Philpot "through the heart." We can only wonder whether Ike turned toward Lyttleton Price at that moment, glaring or sneering at the district attorney who had dismissed all charges against Holliday the previous July. Judge Spicer, who had presided over that brief preliminary hearing, must have shaken his head in disbelief at Clanton's audacity, and at the attorney who put him on the stand.

Did Ben Goodrich conduct Ike Clanton's direct examination according to plan, and then yield to Will McLaury for redirect? Or was Goodrich somehow persuaded to adopt McLaury's radical strategy after the cross examination? Either way, it was a critical blunder. McLaury was as zealous as an advocate can be, but his single-minded aggression clouded his judgment, which was already thoroughly impaired by grief and anger. Hating the Earps as he did, McLaury was ready to believe them capable of anything. The more villainous he could make them appear, the more virtuous were his slain brothers. Of course he accepted Ike's story, as most men would in his situation. But because he lacked even a glimmer of dispassion, Will McLaury would have been unable to accept, or even understand, the likelihood that nearly everyone else would regard Ike as an flagrant liar. That was all the more damaging because there might have been some slight truth at the heart of Ike's testimony. Many people believed that Doc Holliday had something to do with the Philpot murder, and Judge Spicer might conceivably have been persuaded as well. But that provable point was obscured by Ike's more outrageous claims about the Earp brothers, and the prosecution did nothing to winnow the wheat from the chaff.

Will McLaury needed Ike Clanton, and not only for reassurance that Frank and Tom had been honest stockmen cruelly murdered by a corrupt town marshal. McLaury needed Ike in order to obtain the fullest possible measure of "justice." The Earps could be executed only if they were charged with and convicted of first-degree murder. And only Ike Clanton could provide the paramount testimony—shaky as it was—of cold-hearted premeditation.

On November 8, Will McLaury wrote to his law partner with the prediction, "I think I can hang them." Writing to his brother-in-law the next day, he expressed the same thought, with a bit more generosity toward to his colleagues: "I think *we* can hang them" (emphasis added).[14] Most researchers consider Will's predictions to be expressions of rage and determination. In fact, they may have been more than that. Will's confidence about the death penalty might also have been a legal judgment, reflecting his conclusion that Ike Clanton could be used to seal the Earps' fate. Once he learned Ike's complete story, and decided to present it to the court, who could blame McLaury if he reveled in the prospect of capital punishment—"Hang them!"

McLaury was right about one thing. Ike's testimony was critical to the case. The more the prosecution departed from its moderate approach, manifest in Johnny Behan's relatively tempered testimony, the more the case became one of first-degree murder or nothing. The chances of convicting the Earps on a lesser charge diminished as soon as Tom Fitch neatly tied Ike's story to the prosecutors themselves. Now the central question, if not the only one, was whether the Earps were brutal assassins, not merely hot-tempered lawmen.

The Prosecution Rests

For all the skill and ingenuity that Tom Fitch brought to the cross examination, the case was far from over. Wyatt and Doc remained in jail, where they had ample time to reflect on the irony of their situation. As much as counsel might assure them that Ike Clanton's testimony damaged the prosecution case, there was no escaping the fact that it also made their situation more dangerous—providing more than enough proof of premeditation, should Judge Spicer choose to accept it. Wyatt had been in enough courtrooms to know that judges could be unpredictable, especially when it came to weighing evidence. Virgil and Morgan were probably even more worried. Still bedridden, they had to rely on second-hand reports of the proceedings, which could never provide enough detail to be completely reassuring.

The prosecutors had four more witnesses to call, all of them concentrating on the treatment of Tom McLaury, in an effort to bring the case back to reality. Tom was the most sympathetic of the Cowboys. Not only had he been subjected to an unprovoked beating by Wyatt Earp—unlike Ike, whose clubbing by Virgil was prompted by his own gun-waving threats—but he also appeared to have been unarmed during the confrontation. Even if Judge Spicer rejected Ike's claims, he might still be swayed by the callous victimization of Tom McLaury.

Apollinar Bauer, a Tombstone butcher, saw Wyatt buffalo Tom outside Judge Wallace's courtroom. As the two men came face to face, Wyatt "raised his left hand or fist-like, and run it into Tom McLaury's face." Tom's hands were in his pockets, and Wyatt asked "are you heeled or not?" As Tom backed away, protesting that he was not armed and had "nothing to do with anybody," Wyatt pursued him, pulling his six-gun and striking Tom three or four times on the head and shoulder. As Tom lay in the street, Bauer heard Wyatt mutter, "I could kill the son-of-a-bitch."

The cross examination focused on Bauer's profession. As a butcher, he was dependent on ranchers for his beef, and on rustlers if he wanted to obtain it as cheaply as possible. The implication of the cross was that butchers were sympathetic to cow thieves, or even in league with them—an idea that presumably made more intuitive sense on the Arizona frontier than it does today. Bauer, however, said that he had known Tom McLaury for only a few weeks, and he denied any dealings with the Clanton family. Of greater ultimate significance was Bauer's description of Wyatt Earp, whom he said was wearing a short coat, not an overcoat, and carrying "an old pistol, pretty large, 14 or 16 inches long."

The next witness, bookkeeper J. H. Batcher, described the same incident, telling a slightly different story. According to Batcher, Tom McLaury was more assertive when Wyatt asked whether he was heeled, saying he was ready "whenever he wanted to fight." Wyatt apparently took him at his word, slapping Tom with his left hand, then striking him once with his pistol. Finally, Thomas Keefe also testified that he saw Wyatt "knock McLaury down with his pistol, twice." Standing about twenty-two or twenty-three feet away from the two men, Keefe did not hear any words pass between them.

There is a saying among trial lawyers that "every fact has two faces." This was certainly true of Wyatt's confrontation with Tom McLaury. Inconsistencies aside, the three witnesses all portrayed Wyatt as a thug who bludgeoned the unresisting Tom to the ground. One inference, therefore, was that Wyatt was out to get Tom; the pistol whipping was preliminary to the gunfight. Another possible interpretation, however, was that Wyatt Earp did not shoot unarmed men. As hostile as he was toward McLaury, he used his pistol only as a club, showing that his first resort was not to firearms. There is no "correct" way to construe ambiguous evidence. Rather, a judge (or a jury, or a lawyer, for that matter) will tend to construe evidence consistently with his own prior experiences. Do pistol whippings generally lead to shootings? The prosecutors apparently thought so, though the influence of Will McLaury's skewed judgment cannot be ruled out. To the Earps' supporters, on the other hand, pistol whippings usually substituted for shootings—knocking the fight out of troublemakers without doing more damage than necessary. Of course, the only interpretation that mattered was Judge Spicer's, and he probably thought that the entire incident was blown out of proportion. Four witnesses testified to the pistol whipping, two of whom were called only for that reason, suggesting that the prosecution might well have been overplaying that particular hand.

Thomas Keefe also testified that he arrived "at the scene of the killing, after the killing was done." He helped Coroner Matthews attend to the dying Tom McLaury after he was removed to Fly's photo gallery. "We searched the body and did not find any arms on him," said the witness. "We examined him close enough to see if there were any arms on him, and there were none on him." As often happened, Keefe also provided some incidental testimony that would later assume greater importance. He described the wound in Billy Clanton's right arm as located "about two inches above the knuckle joint of his wrist," entering at the base of the thumb and passing diagonally to the back.

The defense would contend that Tom McLaury was in fact armed, so it was important to attempt to discredit Keefe, a carpenter who had no known connection to the Cowboys. One possibility was that Keefe failed to notice a pistol that was lying on the floor of Fly's studio. The cross examiner tried mightily to link the pistol to Tom McLaury, but it turned out to belong to Frank (as was confirmed by the final witness, Coroner Matthews, who was recalled for that purpose).

On that note, the prosecution rested. After two weeks of testimony and fifteen witnesses, the outcome was very much in doubt. In simple magnitude, the evidence against the Earps must have seemed overwhelming, but it was not tied together by a unified theme. In modern terms, the prosecution lacked a coherent theory of the case. Were the Earps badge-wearing bullies who let things go too far, or were they rogue lawmen who committed murder to cover up earlier crimes? Were three men killed suddenly in anger, or were they assassinated as part of a settled plan?

In an ordinary preliminary hearing, the prosecution might not have had to answer these questions. The judge's only job was to decide whether there was sufficient evidence to send the case before a grand jury; he did not have to resolve conflicting testimony or determine the defendants' precise intent. Offered a great quantum of evidence, the court might simply conclude that it was perforce "sufficient," allowing a future jury to sort out the theories.

But this was not an ordinary prosecution. The defendants were law officers who claimed to be acting in the line of duty, which added another dimension to the court's decision. In most cases—such as the Benson stage robbery and murder—it is undisputed that a crime has occurred, and the question is whether the defendant committed it. The Earps' trial, however, was very nearly the reverse. There was no doubt that the Earps killed the three Cowboys, but the question was whether it amounted to a crime. Criminality, not commission, was the ultimate issue for the court, and that required a very different weighing of the evidence.

Tom Fitch realized, far better than the prosecutors, that *what* happened was less important than *why* it happened, which became apparent when he called his first witness—Wyatt Earp.

9

"In Defense of My Own Life"

In theory, the defendants were not required to present a case before Judge Spicer. The purpose of the preliminary examination was to test the sufficiency of the prosecution evidence, not to resolve disputed facts. The defense, therefore, might have chosen to remain silent, calling no witnesses and simply arguing that the prosecutors' case was inadequate. That approach, however, almost certainly would have resulted in a finding against the Earps. As much as the prosecution had been damaged by Tom Fitch's cross examinations and Ike Clanton's fantasies, the core of the case remained relatively persuasive, at least for the purpose of committing the matter to a grand jury. On the other hand, the presentation of a defense case involved risks of its own. As a matter of legal strategy, the testimony of witnesses would alert the prosecution to the substance of the defense. Potentially worse, there was also the possibility that defense witnesses, once identified, might be murdered before trial.

Casey Tefertiller believes that Fitch and Drum initially "had no expectation of having the case resolved at the preliminary hearing."[1] After Ike Clanton imploded, however, they made a last-minute decision to "parade" their witnesses before the court in an effort to win the case then and there. While it is certainly true that Ike's self-destruction invigorated the defense, the available evidence indicates that Tom Fitch had always planned to present a full case before Judge Spicer.

In the first place, we have seen that Fitch frequently used "provables" on cross examination, making propositional statements to witnesses and daring them to disagree. This technique works best when a witness can be lured into denying a fact or incident that can later be proved beyond doubt. The necessary corollary, of course, is the subsequent production of defense witnesses who can "prove up" the very propositions that the prosecution witnesses denied.

Most dramatically, Fitch repeatedly confronted both Johnny Behan and Ike Clanton with alternative scenarios that could be established only by one of the defendants. Didn't Behan tell the Earps that he had disarmed the Cowboys? Didn't Ike agree to help Wyatt capture the Benson stage robbers? The clear implication was that someone would later testify that these statements, and many others like them, were true. In the absence of defense witnesses, Judge Spicer would have been left to wonder whether there was any substance to the defense case at all. Or was Tom Fitch just blowing smoke?

Although the physical danger to defense witnesses cannot be overlooked, Wyatt Earp and Doc Holliday were in considerably greater jeopardy as long as they were locked in Johnny Behan's jail. They would be far safer if the case could be ended in Judge Spicer's court, rather than having it drag on for weeks or months following a finding of "sufficient evidence." And if defense witnesses were really likely to be murdered, or perhaps intimidated into silence, it made more sense to get their testimony on paper as soon as possible, given that a preliminary hearing transcript could be submitted into evidence at a later trial.

The most important indicator, however, was the novel legal strategy that Fitch employed in presenting Wyatt Earp's testimony. It was a tactic that could have been used only at a preliminary hearing, and though chancy, it proved devastating to the prosecution case.

Wyatt Earp was called to the stand on the morning of November 16, 1881, as the first witness for the defense. After more than two weeks of unrelenting prosecution testimony, the defendants would begin their explanation of why and how they came to kill three men in broad daylight. It was a moment of high drama that must have created enormous tension in the courtroom, as everyone recognized that the case—and the Earps' lives—might well hang in the balance. In situations like this, a defense lawyer always makes a show of calm assurance, doing everything possible to display confidence in the client. The slightest appearance of distress or anxiety can backfire terribly, casting doubt on the testimony to follow. The judge and prosecutor are free to react more naturally. Wells Spicer must have seemed attentive, perhaps even anxious, as he prepared to hear an account that might allow him to release the town marshal and his deputies. Will McLaury would have been visibly agitated—teeth clenched, muscles taut—straining to maintain his composure as he waited his opportunity to cross examine the man who was responsible for the deaths of his brothers. He was about to be sorely disappointed.

Rather than proceed in standard question-and-answer format, Tom Fitch announced that Wyatt would take advantage of a territorial law allowing a defendant in a preliminary hearing to make a narrative statement without facing cross examination. McLaury, Price, and Goodrich could only watch in frustration as the court made the first few obligatory inquiries—name, age, place of birth, residence, and profession—as required by the statute. Then, in precise statutory language, Judge Spicer invited Wyatt to "give any explanations you may think proper of the circumstances appearing in the testimony against you, and state any facts which you think will tend to your exculpation."[2]

The prosecutors were startled as Wyatt began to read from a lengthy prepared statement. He got only a few words out of his mouth before the objections began. Perhaps the defendant can avoid cross examination, the prosecution fumed, but he has no right to use a "manuscript." The statute itself was silent on the form of the defendant's statement, providing only that the defendant could "make a statement in relation to the charges against him [that is] designed to enable him, if he see fit, to answer the charge and to explain the fact [sic] alleged against him." Perhaps relying on the word "designed," which at least implied advance preparation, Judge Spicer ruled that "the statute was very broad [and therefore] the defendant could make any statement he pleased whether previously prepared or not."

This was a significant legal victory for the defense. Wyatt's story had obviously been carefully fashioned with Tom Fitch's assistance, and it is unlikely that he would have been equally ready to testify extemporaneously. Indeed, many researchers believe, with very good reason, that Tom Fitch himself wrote the statement, leaving Wyatt to read it into the record. However created, the lawyer-assisted story was powerful and compelling.

Tom Fitch's approach to the defense became obvious with Wyatt's very first sentence: "The difficulty which resulted in the death of William Clanton and Frank and Tom McLaury originated last spring." This was going to be a broad story, not a narrow one. The case was not going to be about a single encounter. Rather, Wyatt planned to show that a history of threats and criminality led up to a gunfight that the lawmen had been unable to avoid. As would soon become apparent, the defense intended to characterize the Clantons and McLaurys as dangerous Cowboys who were responsible for—or at least associated with—many of the crimes that had terrorized Cochise County. The prosecutors evidently saw where Wyatt was headed and immediately objected on the ground of relevance. The court overruled the objection and Wyatt continued.

"A little over a year ago," he read, "I followed Tom and Frank McLaury and two other parties who had stolen six government mules from Camp Rucker." The prosecution objected again, arguing that a year-old case of mule rustling was irrelevant to the current murder charge. And again the court overruled the objection. The prosecutors might have been disappointed by that ruling, but they should not have been surprised. Two weeks earlier, Tom Fitch began the hearing by challenging Judge Spicer's authority to exclude evidence, a motion that seemed almost self-defeating at the time. Spicer, of course, had upheld his own authority to rule on objections but promised to "exercise a great liberality in admitting testimony." Now Fitch's strategy was paying off as he cashed in on the court's promise. Wyatt would have the latitude necessary to tell the whole story without interruption.

After detailing the McLaurys' involvement in the theft—including the cunning change of the brand from "US" to "D8"—Wyatt explained how they had double-crossed Lieutenant Hurst, first promising to give him the mules and then threatening an armed "stand-off" rather than return them. Then Wyatt got to the heart of the matter. The McLaurys were so incensed at the Earps' efforts to enforce the law that "Hurst cautioned me and my brothers, Virgil and Morgan, to look out for those men, as they had made some threats against our lives."

From that point on, Wyatt made it seem as though the McLaury brothers had made a vocation of confronting the Earps. "About a month later," he encountered the McLaurys in Charleston, where "they tried to pick a fuss out of me . . . and told me if I ever followed them up again as close as I did before, they would kill me." Then, after the arrest of Behan's deputy Frank Stilwell for robbing the Bisbee stage, Frank McLaury took it upon himself to caution Morgan Earp about the consequences of apprehending Cowboys: "Frank McLaury took Morgan Earp into the street in front of the Alhambra, when John Ringo, Ike Clanton, and the two Hicks boys were also standing by, when Frank McLaury commenced to abuse Morgan Earp for going after Spence and Stilwell."[3] Frank put it bluntly and menacingly, "I have threatened you boys' lives, and a few days later I had taken it back, but since this arrest, it now goes." Indeed, well before the fatal gunfight, it seems that nearly everyone in Cochise County was aware of the Cowboys' threats: "Marshall Williams, Farmer Daly, Ed Barnes, Old Man Urrides, Charley Smith and three or four others had told us at different times of threats to kill us, by Ike Clanton, Frank McLaury, Tom McLaury, Joe Hill and John Ringo."

Despite all the threats, or perhaps because of them, Wyatt decided that Ike Clanton held the key to capturing the men who robbed the Benson stage and murdered Bud Philpot: "It was generally understood among officers and those who have information about criminals, that Ike Clanton was sort of chief among the cowboys; that the Clantons and McLaurys were cattle thieves and generally in the secrets of the stage robbers, and that the Clanton and McLaury ranches were meeting places and places of shelter for the gang."

This sentence, containing Wyatt's first reference to "cowboys," shows just how artful Tom Fitch could be. First, Wyatt tagged Ike Clanton only as "sort of" the Cowboy chief. Fitch planned to convince Judge Spicer that the Cowboys were a dangerous element, but there was no sense in overstating either Ike's importance or the Cowboys' cohesion. The judge might have been part of the Republican establishment, but he was also a former journalist who probably read the *Nugget*, and he might well have been skeptical about whether the Cowboys really had a leader. In fact, it was Ike's father, Old Man Clanton, who was, until his death, the true senior figure among the Cowboys. Wyatt should have known that Ike was never anything more than a loudmouth, but that never came out at the hearing. It was in the defendants' interest to portray Ike as the boss, and the prosecutors, who denied the very existence of Cowboydom, were in no position to suggest an alternative leader. Next, Wyatt gave his reason for suspecting that Ike might know the whereabouts of Leonard, Head, and Crane. They were fellow cattle thieves who were known to stop at the Clantons' ranch. This explained why Wyatt would try to do business with the thoroughly disreputable Ike. Finally, Wyatt referred to the Cowboys as a "gang," raising a theme to which the defense would return again and again.

Turning directly to the Benson stage robbery, Wyatt gave his version of the soured deal with Ike Clanton:

> I had an ambition to be Sheriff of this County at the next election, and I thought it would be a great help to me with the people and businessmen if I could capture the men who killed Philpot. There were rewards offered of about $1200 each for the capture of the robbers. . . . I thought this sum might tempt Ike Clanton and Frank McLaury to give away Leonard, Head, and Crane, so I went to Ike Clanton, Frank McLaury, and Joe Hill when they came to town. I had an interview with them in the back yard of the Oriental Saloon. . . . I told them I wanted the glory of capturing Leonard, Head, and Crane and if I could do it, it would help me make the race for Sheriff at the next election. I told them if they would put me on the track of Leonard, Head, and Crane, and tell me where those men were hid, I would give them all the reward and would never let anyone know where I got the information.

Wyatt told of several additional meetings with Ike, Frank, and Joe Hill, including Ike's insistence on receiving a "dead or alive" telegram from Wells Fargo. According to Wyatt, Joe Hill even went out looking for Leonard, Head, and Crane, only to return with the news that he had found them too late: "Leonard and Harry Head had been killed the day before he got there by horse thieves." Missing no opportunity to score points, Wyatt added that he "learned afterward that the thieves had been killed subsequently by members of the Clanton and McLaury gang."

Wyatt's version of the deal differed sharply from Ike Clanton's. Most important, of course, was the fact that Wyatt adamantly denied that he was involved in the Philpot murder: "The testimony of Isaac Clanton that I ever said to him that I had anything to do with any stage robbery . . . or any improper communication whatever with any criminal enterprise is a tissue of lies from beginning to end." Wyatt also said that he wanted to capture Leonard, Head, and Crane, rather than assassinate them, and he insisted that Ike Clanton willingly agreed to the plan.

What are we to make of Wyatt's statement that Frank McLaury and Joe Hill were also involved in the deal? Was he embroidering his story to drag the Cowboys more deeply into the plot, or was he simply providing facts that Ike Clanton conveniently omitted? As is often the case, the use of details can tell us something about the truthfulness of a witness's testimony. Standing alone, the inclusion of Frank McLaury might have been just one more embellishment, as when Wyatt claimed that the Haslett brothers had been killed by the "Clanton and McLaury gang." If Frank was also a betrayer of the Benson stage robbers, he would have had yet another reason to provoke a confrontation with the Earps, and a dead man could never testify to the contrary.

But Wyatt's version of the plan also included Joe Hill, a Cowboy pal of the Clantons who was very much alive. If Wyatt was lying about the scope of the deal, Hill could have been called as a surprise rebuttal witness by the prosecution. But Tom Fitch was far too smart to chance that sort of scathing impeachment. He would never risk even mentioning Joe Hill unless he believed that Wyatt was telling the truth. Therefore, the reference to Joe Hill (including the very specific detail about his report on the deaths of Leonard and Head) was, in effect, a reverse provable— used to enhance the credibility of Wyatt's story while challenging the prosecution to contradict him if they could. It would not have escaped Judge Spicer's notice that the prosecutors neither produced Hill nor explained his absence, thus turning him into a silent witness for the defense.[4]

Confronting the Cowboys

Turning to the events leading up to the gunfight, Wyatt explained his efforts to reassure Ike Clanton about the secrecy of their bargain. Ike suspected that Wyatt had let Doc Holliday in on the secret, so Wyatt arranged a meeting between the two men at the Alhambra

Saloon: "Unfortunately, Ike and Doc fell to quarreling—each calling the other a liar—and they had to be separated by Virgil and Morgan."

Ike, however, would not calm down. Just a few minutes later he accosted Wyatt on the street, saying that "this fighting talk had been going on for a long time, and he guessed it was about time to fetch it to a close." Wyatt tried to change the subject, telling Ike, "I would not fight no one if I could get away from it, because there was no money in it." Ike refused to relent, warning Wyatt, "I will be ready for you in the morning."

Wyatt dismissed Ike's bluster and eventually went home to sleep. Early the next afternoon, however, he began to get word of Ike's threatening behavior, including a warning from attorney Harry Jones that "Ike Clanton is hunting you boys with a Winchester rifle and six-shooter." Wyatt and Virgil began a search for Ike that ended when Virgil buffaloed Clanton and dragged him off to Judge Wallace's courtroom. Ike's fulminations continued even in court. "I will get even with all of you for this," he said. "If I had a six-shooter now I would make a fight with all of you. . . . I will see you after I get through here. I only want four feet of ground to fight on." By this time Wyatt was taking Ike's threats seriously. "If I had to fight for my life," he figured, "I had better make them face me in an open fight."

It was Tom McLaury's bad luck to show up just as Wyatt was leaving the courtroom. According to Wyatt, Tom was in a belligerent mood and carrying a pistol in plain sight. "I supposed at the time that he had heard what had just transpired between Ike Clanton and myself," he said. "I knew of his having threatened me, and I felt [about him] just as I did about Ike Clanton." When Tom threatened to "make a fight," Wyatt obliged him: "I slapped him in the face with my left hand and drew my pistol with my right . . . and I hit him on the head with my six-shooter and walked away."

The Earps and Doc Holliday gathered at Fourth and Allen Streets to plan how they would handle the Cowboys. As they stood there, citizens continued to report that trouble was brewing. R. F. Coleman anxiously told Virgil, "They have just gone from Dunbar's Corral into the O.K. Corral, all armed, and I think you had better go and disarm them." Realizing that the moment of truth had arrived, "Virgil turned around to Doc Holliday, Morgan Earp and myself and told us to come and assist him in disarming them."

As the Earp party approached within 150 feet of the Clantons and McLaurys, Johnny Behan hurried toward them. "I have disarmed them," Behan said, in an attempt to stop the Earps. Taking Johnny at his word, Wyatt relaxed his guard: "I took my pistol, which I had in my hand, under my coat, and put it in my overcoat pocket. Behan then passed up the street, and we walked on down."

Arriving at the vacant lot, Wyatt observed that "Frank McLaury and Billy Clanton's six-shooters were in plain sight." Virgil called on the Cowboys to surrender—"Throw up your hands, I have come to disarm you"—but Billy and Frank reached for their guns. Virgil shouted, "Hold, I don't mean that," but it was already too late: "I had my pistol in my overcoat pocket, where I had put it when Behan told us he had disarmed the other parties. When I saw Billy Clanton and Frank McLaury draw their pistols, I drew my pistol. Billy Clanton leveled his pistol at me, but I did not aim at him. I knew that Frank McLaury had the reputation of being a good shot and a dangerous man, and I aimed at Frank McLaury. The first two shots were fired by Billy Clanton and myself, he shooting at me, and I shooting at Frank McLaury. I don't know which was fired first. We fired almost together. The fight then became general."

Wyatt carefully testified that he fired only at men whom he believed to be armed. His first shot "struck Frank McLaury in the belly," causing him to stagger, but it did not prevent Frank from firing one shot at Wyatt in return. As to Ike Clanton, on the other hand, "After about four shots were fired, Ike Clanton ran up and grabbed my left arm. I could see no weapon in his hand, and thought at the time he had none, and so I said to him, 'The fight has commenced. Go to fighting or get away,' at the same time pushing him off with my left hand. . . . I never fired at Ike Clanton, even after the shooting commenced, because I thought he was unarmed."

When it came to Tom McLaury, Wyatt was more guarded. Numerous prosecution witnesses testified that Tom was unarmed, and neutral witnesses, including Coroner Matthews, testified that no weapons were found near his body. The killing of Tom McLaury had caused the greatest public outrage, making his death a cornerstone of the prosecution case. Wyatt's testimony cautiously straddled the question: "If Tom McLaury was unarmed, I did not know it, I believe he was armed and fired two shots at our party before Holliday, who had the shotgun, fired and killed him. If he was unarmed, there was nothing in the circumstances or in what had been communicated to me, or in his acts or threats, that would have led me even to suspect his being unarmed."

Given that defense and prosecution witnesses told such sharply divergent stories, Tom Fitch realized that "character" could well be the key to the case. Before Judge Spicer could decide what to believe, he had to decide whom to believe. It was important, therefore, that Wyatt address his failed bargain with Johnny Behan, which he did at some length. Wyatt patiently explained that he kept his own promise to withdraw his application for the Cochise County sheriff's position, but Behan double-crossed him: "I done so, and he never said another word about it afterwards, but claimed in his statement and gave his reason for not complying with his contract, which is false in every particular."

Finally, to bolster his own credibility, Wyatt submitted two sworn statements from the leading citizens of Dodge City and Wichita attesting to his good character and integrity. The Dodge City document was the longer and more effusive of the two, signed by the mayor and four city councilmen, as well as county and federal officeholders. It was also signed by many prominent merchants and businessmen, including two cattle dealers who might have been expected to harbor some resentment over Wyatt's rough treatment of their Texas trailhands. In fact, however, the sixty-two signatories joined in commending Wyatt as a "high-minded, honorable citizen" who "was ever vigilant in the discharge of his duties; and while kind and courteous to all, he was brave, unflinching, and on all occasions proved himself the right man in the right place." As to his current difficulties, the statement continued, "Hearing that he is now under arrest, charged with complicity in the killing of those men termed 'Cow Boys,' from our knowledge of him we do not believe that he would wantonly take the life of his fellow man, and that if he was implicated, he only took life in the discharge of his sacred trust to the people."

The two affidavits provided just the sort of endorsement likely to appeal to Judge Spicer, emphasizing Wyatt's status as an agent of law and order. The prosecution objected to their admission, arguing that "this paper" consisted of irrelevant hearsay. The court ruled, however, that they were properly included in "a statutory statement made by the party charged with [a] crime." Yet again, Tom Fitch's expansive view of the law of evidence prevailed.

In all, Wyatt's prepared statement provided a coherent outline of the defense. The Earps were confronted by a band of outlaws who had been threatening them for nearly a year. Ike Clanton was no harmless blowhard, but rather an armed criminal, in league with other killers and desperadoes. The Earps, therefore, were defending themselves—and Tombstone—against the threat of widespread lawlessness, if only by association: "I knew all these men were desperate and dangerous men, that they were connected with outlaws, cattle thieves, robbers, and murderers. . . . I heard of John Ringo shooting a man down in cold blood near Camp Thomas. I was satisfied that Frank and Tom McLaury killed and robbed Mexicans in Skeleton Canyon."

A prudent lawman could draw only one conclusion: "I naturally kept my eyes open and did not intend that any of the gang should get the drop on me if I could help it." Even so, the Earps first exhausted both peaceful means (separating Ike from Doc Holliday in the Alhambra) and not-so-peaceful means (buffaloing Ike and Tom), leaving them with no alternative but to disarm the Cowboys at gunpoint. In a last-ditch effort, Virgil still called on the Clantons and McLaurys to surrender; the shooting started only when Frank McLaury reached for his six-shooter.

Ever the thorough advocate, Fitch left little to chance or implication. At one point, Wyatt's statement departed from a narrative of the events in order to explain his motives and legal justification:

> I believed then, and believe now, from the acts I have stated and the threats I have related and the other threats communicated to me by other persons, as having been made by Tom McLaury, Frank McLaury and Ike Clanton, that these men last named had formed a conspiracy to murder my brothers, Morgan and Virgil, Doc Holliday and myself. I believe I would have been legally and morally justified in shooting any of them on sight, but I did not do so, nor attempt to do so. I sought no advantage when I went as deputy marshal, to help to disarm them and arrest them, I

went as a part of my duty and under the direction of my brother, the marshal. I did not intend to fight unless it became necessary in self-defense and in the performance of official duty. When Billy Clanton and Frank McLaury drew their pistols, I knew it was a fight for life, and I drew in defense of my own life and the lives of my brothers and Doc Holliday.

It was a neat summary of the law of justifiable homicide, more like a lawyer's closing argument than the testimony of a witness. Just as Tom Fitch planned.

Protecting Wyatt Earp

There has been much confusion concerning Wyatt Earp's statement, much of it due to misunderstandings about the statutory basis for his right to testify without facing cross examination. The law itself was an anachronism. Even though it had been recently amended, and was clearly still in force, it was a legal relic of an earlier time when criminal defendants were prohibited from testifying in their own defense. Odd as it may seem, it was once the law in every U.S. jurisdiction that "interested parties," including criminal defendants, were disqualified as witnesses in their own cases. A defendant, therefore, could not testify to his or her own alibi, or raise any other defense without third-party witnesses. To limit the harsh consequences of this rule, many jurisdictions, including Arizona, allowed defendants to make unsworn statements that could "explain the facts alleged" against them. Because the explanatory statements were not themselves considered evidence, they could not be subjected to cross examination. In 1864, Maine became the first state to abolish the interested party rule, with many other states and territories rapidly following suit. Arizona began allowing defendants to testify in 1871, eliminating the underlying rationale for unsworn statements.[5]

Nonetheless, Judge Spicer was legally obligated to invite each defendant to make such a statement. The statute required him to "distinctly inform the defendant that it is his right to make a statement in relation to the charges against him." It might well have raised eyebrows in the courtroom when Wyatt accepted the offer (although he insisted on taking the oath), invoking a statute that had been substantively superseded for a decade.

As the law required, Judge Spicer himself asked the initial questions, something that many historians have not recognized. Paula Mitchell Marks, for example, says that "the *defense* handed [Wyatt] carte blanche" (emphasis added) by asking him to "give any explanations you may think proper."[6] But far from a slick tactic by Tom Fitch, it was the court's duty to extend the open-ended invitation, using the precise language of the Arizona Criminal Code. The phrase "any explanations you may think proper" was not intended to convey carte blanche, but rather to emphasize the non-evidentiary nature of the statement.

Most historians have accepted Spicer's ruling that Wyatt was entitled to read from a written statement, even though it was obviously prepared with the assistance of counsel, or perhaps simply ghostwritten. In fact, that was far from clear at the time. It is true that one section of the code allowed a witness to make a statement "designed" to enable him to answer the charge, which supports Spicer's decision. Two subsequent code sections, however, make it fairly certain that only oral—that is, extemporaneous—statements were contemplated by the legislature. One section required that the witness's statement be "read to him as it is taken down" and that "he may thereupon correct or add to his answer, and it shall be corrected until it is made conformable to what he declares to be the truth." Another section provided that the "statement must be reduced to writing" and "signed by the defendant, or he may refuse to sign it; but if he refuse to sign it, his reason therefor must be stated as he gives it."[7] None of this would have been necessary if a statement could have been written out in the first place.

This is not to say that Judge Spicer was wrong. Written statements may not have been contemplated by the statutes, but neither were they explicitly forbidden. Faced with a unique situation (an "issue of first impression," in legal terms), Spicer had to make a decision one way or the other. In the end, he exercised his discretion in favor of the defendant, although the ruling could have gone either way.

Tom Fitch had no way of knowing in advance whether Spicer would allow Wyatt Earp to read his testimony, yet he still invested considerable time and energy in creating a statement that he might never get to use.

The extraordinary value of a prepared statement might justify the effort—ensuring that Wyatt's testimony would be comprehensive and persuasive—but there were still risks to this approach. Surely, Judge Spicer would not have believed for a minute that Wyatt had written the statement himself, replete as it was with legal terminology and conclusory language. Wyatt Earp was plenty smart, but he was relatively unschooled and he would never have used phrases such as "these men last named had formed a conspiracy to murder my brothers," or "I believe I would have been morally and legally justified." Perhaps he might have condemned Ike Clanton's testimony as "a tissue of lies from beginning to end," but only a lawyer would have called Johnny Behan's testimony "false in every particular," using a distinctly legalistic locution.

Most judges (and jurors, too) tend to be wary of witnesses who seem to be testifying from a script. Not only does that make it difficult to assess the witness's sincerity, but it also raises the possibility that the details of the narrative have been, shall we say, improved by the intervention of counsel. In the Tombstone case, where prosecution and defense witnesses sharply contradicted each other, and the prosecution's burden was minimal, it was essential that Wyatt's testimony be as believable as possible. It has escaped the notice of historians that Wyatt chose to make his statement under oath, although the statute specifically provided that such statements were to be "without oath." Tom Fitch was looking for every edge he could get.

Given the potential of a prepared statement to diminish, or even undermine, Wyatt's personal credibility, Fitch must have had some reason other than convenience for electing to have his client read from a manuscript. Later in the hearing, Virgil Earp testified in standard question-and-answer form. Why did Wyatt have to rely on a text? Possibilities abound, though none is really satisfactory. Was Wyatt nervous or inarticulate? Was his testimony too broad-ranging to trust to memory (the statute seemed to preclude additional questioning by counsel in the event of forgetfulness)? Were some of the sequences so delicate or precise that they had to be written out for accuracy? Or, as Wyatt's enemies and critics would charge, were crucial parts of the testimony fabricated—requiring a written text so that the witness would not slip up?

Fortunately for the defendants, although they could not have known it at the time, Wells Spicer's own experiences made him unusually sympathetic to lawyer-drafted statements, probably more so than any other judge in Arizona. On January 1, 1875, shortly after he had accepted the representation of John Lee in the Mountain Meadows case, Spicer published a lengthy article in the Salt Lake *Daily Herald* that purported to include an account of the massacre by one of Lee's wives. Written in the first person—under the headline "Rachel's Story as Recorded by Wells Spicer"—Mrs. Lee's narrative absolved her husband by blaming the killings on the Fancher party's own misdeeds, including the patently false claim that the emigrants poisoned a spring and enraged local Indians. Spicer himself defended the practice of attorney ghostwriting: "It is proper here for me to state that in writing this article I do not consider it in the least censurable coming from the attorney of John D. Lee. . . . I think it perfectly proper to write and publish the narration of the occurrence by one who, from her intimate relations with those who are accused of being chief actors, should be supposed to know the facts of the case."[8]

It is implausible, of course, that the article was actually dictated by Rachel. It included information that could have been known only to the defendant himself (much of it untrue, in any event), and it clearly benefited from a lawyer's careful hand. The strategic purpose, however, was apparent. By casting the statement as that of the innocent Rachel, rather than the accused John, Spicer hoped to generate sympathy for his client. He pointed out twice that Rachel was not charged with any crime, which he believed would enhance the credibility of "her" story.

There is no reason to think that anyone in Tombstone was aware of Spicer's 1875 article in the Salt Lake *Daily Herald*. Tom Fitch was living in California at the time, and the story would not have been part of the national coverage of Lee's trial (which did not begin until late July, nearly seven months after the publication of the article). So Fitch probably thought he was taking somewhat of a chance by having Wyatt read his testimony, justified by benefits known only to counsel and client. As it turned out, he was arguing to a judge who was uniquely receptive to the idea, in both law and substance. As attorneys often say, better lucky than good.

Even aside from the question of writing, the decision to protect Wyatt from cross examination carried risks of its own. Especially in light of the fact that Virgil—so badly wounded that court had to convene at his bed-side—was later submitted for cross examination, the unavoidable implication was that Wyatt had something to fear or hide.

Why would Tom Fitch employ such unusual measures to shield Wyatt Earp from questioning? Was he afraid that Wyatt would lose his temper if Will McLaury provoked him? Or was he concerned that he could be forced to make damaging admissions? Perhaps Wyatt knew something that his brothers did not?

It was Wyatt, after all, who was Johnny Behan's great rival, both polit-ically and romantically. What might the prosecution have discovered by digging into Wyatt's version of the failed agreement with Behan over the county sheriff's office? Wyatt painted himself as the injured party in the deal, suffering a double-cross, but perhaps something more lay behind his opaque assertion that Behan's "reason for not complying with his contract . . . is false in every particular." Behan's own story was equally vague, claiming that "something afterward transpired that I did not take him into the office," raising the possibility that all of this had something to do with the sentiments of Josephine Marcus. Defense counsel decided not to cross examine Behan on the subject, despite the potential for impeachment. Perhaps they feared that the prosecutors might raise the matter with Wyatt, to embarrass or anger him, either of which might have damaged his effectiveness as a witness.

Wyatt was also deeply involved in the aborted scheme with Ike Clanton, which eventually led to the gunfight. Was there more to that story than Wyatt was willing to tell? While we can discount Ike's wild claim that the Earps were implicated in the murder of Bud Philpot, some historians and researchers believe that Doc Holliday might have been involved. Doc was present in the courtroom every day, yet the defense never called him to testify (unlike the injured Virgil, who testified as he lay wounded in bed). Was Fitch's maneuver part of a coordinated strata-gem intended to prevent the prosecution from asking any uncomfortable questions about Holliday's role?

Then again, Wyatt might have done more to set off Ike's rampage than he admitted, taunting Clanton rather than trying to reassure him that his secret—the agreement to betray Leonard, Head, and Crane—was still safe. Did Wyatt, as he testified, really ask Doc Holliday to help calm Ike down? Or were the Earps and Holliday having some fun at Ike's expense, tormenting him until matters just got too far out of hand? In Ike's story, Wyatt and Morgan Earp kept challenging him to fight. Cross examination might have revealed that there was more than a little substance to Ike's claim.

As the testimony developed, Wyatt made several other assertions that would have been extremely vulnerable on cross examination. His reference to the "Clanton and McLaury gang," for example, would probably have been exposed as an exaggeration, much as Johnny Behan's credibility had been undermined by his self-serving definition of "cowboy." More substantively, Wyatt would have had to explain the inconsistencies in his story about pistol-whipping Tom McLaury. Wyatt testified that it was Tom who started the trouble, openly wearing a six-shooter and challenging Wyatt to fight. But it was illegal to carry a gun in Tombstone, which meant that Wyatt, an acting city marshal, should have arrested Tom, rather than just beat him up. That is what he and Virgil had done only an hour or so earlier, when they buffaloed the gun-waving Ike Clanton and then dragged him off to Judge Wallace's courtroom. If Tom McLaury did have a gun, then why was there no arrest? If he did not have a gun, then why was he brutalized? We will never know whether Wyatt had a good explanation for the apparent contradiction, because he was never cross examined.

The First Shot

The most serious gap in Wyatt's story was in his account of the fatal gunfight. According to his testimony, Wyatt had put away his gun as he approached the Clantons and McLaurys, misled by Behan's statement that the Cowboys had been disarmed. And he claimed that he kept his gun in his pocket until he saw Frank McLaury and Billy Clanton draw their own weapons:

> I saw that Billy Clanton and Frank and Tom McLaury had their
> hands by their sides. Frank McLaury and Billy Clanton's

> six-shooters were in plain sight. . . . Then Billy Clanton and Frank McLaury laid their hands on their six-shooters. Virgil said, "Hold, I don't mean that! I have come to disarm you." Then Billy Clanton and Frank McLaury commenced to draw their pistols.
>
> I had my pistol in my overcoat pocket, where I had put it when Behan told us he had disarmed the other parties. When I saw Billy Clanton and Frank McLaury draw their pistols, I drew my pistol.

Later, he repeated the claim, "I did not intend to fight unless it became necessary in self-defense and in the performance of official duty. When Billy Clanton and Frank McLaury drew their pistols, I knew it was a fight for life, and I drew in defense of my own life and the lives of my brothers and Doc Holliday."

That sort of careful sequencing carries extra meaning in a lawyer-drafted statement. Wyatt was not simply rambling or accidentally repeating himself. He was intentionally driving home the point that he refrained from drawing his gun until Frank and Billy had already drawn theirs. The point, whether it was Wyatt's or Tom Fitch's, was that the lawmen were not aggressive or trigger happy. They tried to resolve the incident without resort to gunplay, even jeopardizing their own safety by keeping their weapons out of sight and out of reach. Only when Frank and Billy jerked their guns did Wyatt pull his own, beating them to the draw in defense of his life: "The first two shots were fired by Billy Clanton and myself, he shooting at me, and I shooting at Frank McLaury. I don't know which was fired first. We fired almost together."

It is the stuff of legends, but who could believe that it happened that way? The pocket of a leather overcoat is not terribly accessible. It would have taken Wyatt a good few seconds to reach into his pocket and pull out his sizable Colt revolver, which would have weighed more than three pounds fully loaded. Based on the accounts of others, it might have taken him even longer. Apollinar Bauer testified that Wyatt was wearing a short coat, meaning that the pocket would have been higher up on his hip and making his pistol that much less accessible (there is a reason that quick-draw performers keep their holsters strapped to their thighs). Bauer also said that Wyatt used "an old pistol, pretty large, 14 or 16 inches long." Even if Bauer was referring to the gun's overall length, it would have been awkward for Wyatt to pull a firearm that long out of his pocket. Alford Turner suggests that the gun might have been even longer, if Bauer was describing only the part he could see, from the hammer to the muzzle.[9]

Once it was drawn, there was still the matter of aiming and firing the heavy single-action revolver, which had to be manually cocked before every shot, either with one's thumb or the nonshooting hand. At his own preliminary hearing the previous year, Buckskin Frank Leslie explained how difficult that could be, even when the gun did not have to be unpocketed: "I put my hand on a big pistol which I had laid on the porch at my feet when first sitting down, but in trying to cock this pistol it slipped out of my hand."[10]

Various attempts have been made over the years to explain Wyatt's feat of marksmanship. Alford Turner and Paula Mitchell Marks suggest that Wyatt may have really had the gun in his waistband, reaching it "through a slit in the top of the coat pocket." While that might explain how Wyatt quickly got his hand on the pistol, the clumsy position— either drawing the gun back through the slit or firing while his arm was still halfway through his coat—would have made it difficult to aim. Most tellingly, however, Wyatt himself never made such a claim. His testimony was always that the gun was in his pocket, not his waistband, a position that he repeated, with some embellishment, in his 1896 interview with the *San Francisco Examiner:* "I had a gun in my overcoat pocket and I jerked it out at Frank McLaury[,] hitting him in the stomach."[11]

In other words, it would have been all but impossible for Wyatt to get off the first shot if Billy and Frank had already drawn their guns before he even started. Forget the law of the West; the laws of physics were the real problem.

So Wyatt was, at best, playing fast and loose with the truth. Either the gun was not in his pocket, or Frank and Billy did not draw first, or both. Of course, Frank and Billy were too dead to testify, and no other witness claimed to have been able to see all three men at the same time. Nonetheless, a capable cross examiner should have been able to catch this discrepancy and use it to skewer Wyatt.

The question of the first shot was no small matter. The prosecution witnesses were adamant that Doc Holliday fired first, hanging the credibility of their entire case on the rash use of his nickel-plated pistol. By taking responsibility for the first shot (or virtually the first shot), Wyatt did more than just deflect blame from Doc. He turned the case more explicitly into a confrontation between law and outlawry. It would have been one thing for Judge Spicer to believe that Doc Holliday gunned down surrendering men, but far more difficult for him to believe that Wyatt Earp, a deputy federal marshal, began the shooting without provocation. By putting his own reputation on the line, truthfully or otherwise, Wyatt raised the stakes. But how much was he bluffing?

After years of controversy, long after Judge Spicer ruled, the question finally seemed to be resolved by the publication of Glenn Boyer's book *I Married Wyatt Earp,* which was represented to be the edited memoirs of Josephine Marcus Earp. Boyer's Josephine reported that Doc and Morgan fired the first shots, just as Johnny Behan testified, and that Wyatt (and Virgil, too) lied on the witness stand in order to protect them. The false testimony was justified by Behan's "grossly dishonest testimony to the effect that the deceased were shot with their hands in the air." In fact, says Boyer's Josephine, "Frank and Billy were simply beat to the draw," though not by Wyatt Earp. Alas, Boyer's book has been discredited as a "creative exercise" rather than an autobiography, and it cannot be relied upon for Wyatt's veracity, or anything else.[12]

In an exceptionally careful analysis of the sequence of shots at the shoot-out, based on all of the known information, Casey Tefertiller and Jeff Morey concluded that "the frontier's most storied gunfight began just as the Earps testified, with Wyatt Earp firing in response to Frank McLaury's motion for his gun."[13] This seems like the best assessment we will ever have. But it does not fully absolve Wyatt Earp.

Wyatt testified that Billy and Frank actually drew their guns, not that they were merely reaching for them. He also said that his own six-shooter was in his coat pocket, not in his hand. Both of these statements were contrived, perhaps with the help of Tom Fitch, in order to make the story better. Based on the balance of Wyatt's own testimony, the far more plausible scenario is that he approached the Cowboys gun in hand, ready for a fight, and maybe even looking for one. Frank McLaury's "motion" no doubt precipitated the shooting. But who can say whether Frank was really reaching for his six-shooter? That conclusion depends on Wyatt's credibility (Virgil would later corroborate him), and we have seen that he lied, or at least exaggerated, about two other central details.

Of course, Frank McLaury was armed and dangerous, and Wyatt had only a moment to determine his intentions. It would not have constituted murder if Deputy Earp had reacted too quickly, shooting as soon as he saw Frank's ambiguous-but-threatening hand movement. On the other hand, it might well have been manslaughter. According to Arizona law, a killing could not be justified by a "bare fear." Instead, the circumstances had to be "sufficient to excite the fears of a reasonable person" and the "party killing [must have] acted under the influence of those fears, and *not in a spirit of revenge*" (emphasis added).[14]

Here again, a talented cross examiner would have had a grand time exploring the sufficiency of Wyatt's asserted fears and insinuating that any fearfulness was overwhelmed by a "spirit of revenge." In a manslaughter case, it would not have been necessary to show that Frank and Billy were unambiguously trying to surrender but only that Wyatt's judgment, in the moments before he shot, was clouded by anger or vengeance. That would not be an impossible task, in view of the threats and insults he claimed to have suffered. It would be made easier if Wyatt could be goaded into an ill-tempered outburst on cross examination.

But the prosecution did not bother with a manslaughter case, and in any event, the nimble tactics of Tom Fitch saved Wyatt from the perils of cross examination. That combination of prosecutorial misjudgment and defense savvy continued to play itself out as the hearing wound to a close.

10

"I Want Your Guns"

Hoping to capitalize on the momentum created by Wyatt Earp's compelling soliloquy, the defense called two witnesses to corroborate key elements of his testimony. For one of the few times during the hearing, however, Tom Fitch's advocacy fell short.

As a neutral witness, saloonkeeper Robert Hatch could have provided powerful support for Wyatt's testimony, as was certainly expected when he took the stand. Hatch candidly admitted, however, that his view of the events was often blocked and that his account was therefore incomplete. Hatch testified that he saw Billy Clanton shooting his pistol, but only after three or four shots had already been fired. He also saw Doc Holliday shooting Frank McLaury with a pistol (he thought it was bronze, not nickel-plated), but he did not say anything about a shotgun. Most notably, Hatch was unable to identify the sources of the initial shots, or even where "the smoke from the first two or three shots proceeded."

In all, Hatch painted a picture of general turmoil and disorder, in which he could observe only scattered moments of the battle. His inability to describe the entire confrontation caused Will McLaury to gloat about Hatch's perceived failings. Writing to his sister, McLaury said that the witness disappointed the defense, surmising that Hatch got cold feet about "improving" his testimony: "One of their principal witnesses has been on the stand today, and they feel bad his evidence is much stronger for us than it is for them. I think the scoundrel feared to act out his role, and I am of the opinion that his fears are not wholly groundless. I do not think that by perjury these men shall escape."[1]

There is no way to tell whether McLaury was right about Hatch's intentions, but he was wrong about one thing. Far from a weakness, Hatch's testimony of a chaotic scene was intended to help the defense by demonstrating that no person—including prosecution witnesses Johnny Behan and Billy Claiborne—could possibly have seen everything that happened. Fitch tried to stress this point by asking whether Hatch was "satisfied from all you saw that Behan and Claiborne saw nothing of this difficulty." A prosecution objection was sustained, and Fitch tried again: "Would not any man of general intelligence leave the scene of action as soon as the firing commenced?" Judge Spicer was not impressed by the rephrasing, as he sustained another prosecution objection.

Next, bartender Ned Boyle was asked to testify about Ike Clanton's threats against the Earps, "and if any threats were made, whether or not you communicated the same to [the Earps] before the difficulty." If allowed, Boyle's testimony would support Wyatt's claim that the Earps acted in self-defense. But the prosecution objected, claiming that Ike's actions earlier in the day were irrelevant to the gunfight because he made no "demonstration at the time of the killing [that would lead] the defendant then and there to believe that the party making such threats was about to put it [sic] into execution." It was an artful bit of lawyering, arguing that Ike's early morning threats were inadmissible because there was no claim that he acted on them in the afternoon. In fact, Wyatt testified that Ike was unarmed; it was Billy and Frank who reached for their guns. In response, the defense contended that threats against a defendant should always be admissible "on so grave a charge as murder" because they tend to show "the intent of the party committing [the] homicide." The extended legal argument lasted nearly an entire day, with both sides citing court decisions from California to New York. In the end, Judge Spicer disallowed the evidence, ruling that "no threats were yet admissible." The adverb—"yet"—gave some hope to the defense, but it was obvious that Spicer's promise of "great liberality in admitting testimony" was not without limits.

Following this series of tactical defeats, the defense made the bold move of calling Virgil Earp to the stand on Saturday morning, November 19.

Well, not exactly to the stand. Virgil was still incapacitated from his wounds, so Judge Spicer accommodated him by reconvening court at his bedside in the Cosmopolitan Hotel. Unlike Wyatt, Virgil testified in conventional form, declining to exercise his statutory right to make an explanatory statement and avoid cross examination. Perhaps because he was in severe pain, Virgil's answers were frequently disjointed. Without the advantage of a written text, he often seemed to collapse time or skip over important details, requiring counsel to fill in the gaps by prompting him with additional questions.

Virgil's testimony was unlike Wyatt's in another way as well. Rather than begin at the start of the trouble "a little over a year ago," Virgil focused immediately on the events of the gunfight. Thus, Tom Fitch used two of his star witnesses (there would later be a third) to accent two different aspects of his legal theory. Wyatt's job was to lay out the history of Cowboy crimes and threats, emphasizing the peril they represented to the lives of the defendants and the good order of Tombstone. Now it was Virgil's turn to underscore the Earps' role as law officers and protectors of civilization. The first four questions were directed to the authority of his posse:

> (Q) State what official position, if any, you occupied on the 25th and 26th of October last.
>
> (A) Chief of Police of Tombstone and Deputy United States Marshal, and was acting as such on those days.
>
> (Q) State what official or other position, if any, with respect to the police department of Tombstone, was occupied on the 25th and 26th of October last by Morgan Earp.
>
> (A) He was sworn in as Special Policeman and wore a badge with "Special Police" engraved on it, and he had been sworn and acted as a "special" for about a month.
>
> (Q) State what official or other position, if any, with respect to the police department of Tombstone, was occupied on the 25th and 26th of October last by Wyatt Earp.
>
> (A) Wyatt Earp had been sworn in to act in my place while I was in Tucson, and on my return . . . I appointed him a "Special," to keep the peace, with power to make arrest, and also called on

him on the 26th, to assist me in disarming those parties: Ike
Clanton and Billy Clanton, Frank McLaury, and Tom McLaury.
(Q) State what position or deputization, if any, with respect to
assisting you as Chief of Police, was occupied on the 26th of
October last, or anytime during that day by John H. Holliday.
(A) I called on him that day for assistance to help disarm the
Clantons and McLaurys.

When it came to Doc Holliday, both the question and the answer were
carefully phrased. Not without reason, Virgil had been severely criticized
for bringing Doc into the confrontation, and it was important to establish
his bona fides. While Morgan and Wyatt held "official positions," Doc had
been recruited on the spot. Thus, Fitch was careful to ask about Holliday's
"position or deputization . . . with respect to assisting you as Chief of
Police." Some historians have considered Virgil's response evasive, infer-
ring that the request for Doc's "assistance" was something less than deputization and therefore legally questionable. In fact, Virgil was being precise.
A territorial statute allowed him to enlist the aid of "other persons" without the formality of a badge. Such persons were not officially deputies, but
they were nonetheless authorized to assist in law enforcement.[2]

Next, Fitch turned to the events of the gunfight, asking the witness to
"confin[e] your answers for the present entirely to what occurred within
your sight and hearing on the day of the difficulty, on the 26th of
October."

Virgil began by describing a verbal altercation he had with Ike Clanton
in the early morning, at "about six or seven o'clock," as he was headed
home after the all-night poker game. Ike wanted Virgil to carry a challenge to Doc Holliday, "that damned son of a bitch has got to fight."
Virgil refused, cautioning Ike not "to raise any disturbance." As Virgil
turned to leave, Ike called after him, "You may have to fight before you
know it." Ignoring the threat, Virgil went home to bed.

After only a few hours, however, police officer Bronk woke Virgil up
with a warning that there was "liable to be hell! Ike Clanton has threatened to kill Holliday [and] he's counting you fellows in too." Virgil was
apparently unsure about the seriousness of the situation. He took his
time dressing, but he was on the street looking for Ike by about 11 A.M.

A man named Lynch gave Virgil his second warning of the day, informing him that Clanton was threatening to "kill me on sight." Then his
brothers, James and Morgan, found him and added the detail that Ike
was carrying a "Winchester rifle and six-shooter."

Virgil finally found Ike, heavily armed in violation of the law, on
Fourth Street between Fremont and Allen Streets. Wasting no time and
asking no questions, Virgil "walked up and grabbed the rifle in my left
hand. He let loose and started to draw his six-shooter. I hit him over the
head with mine and knocked him to his knees and took his six-shooter
from him. I ask [sic] him if he was hunting for me. He said he was, and
if he had seen me a second sooner he would have killed me. I arrested
Ike for carrying firearms."

Virgil explained that he took Ike to Judge Wallace's courtroom after
confiscating his guns. The clubbing, arrest, and fine, however, did not
cool Ike's temper. For the next few hours, Virgil received a steady stream
of warnings about the behavior of the Clantons and McLaurys. On
behalf of the vigilance committee, a man named W. B. Murray offered
the assistance of "25 armed men at a minutes notice," but Virgil
declined. "As long as they stayed in the corral, the O.K. Corral, I would
not go down to disarm them," he said, but "if they came out on the
street, I would take their arms off and arrest them."

A man named John Fonck made a similar offer. "The cowboys are
making threats against you," he said, and "if you want any help, I can fur-
nish ten men to assist." Again Virgil declined, stating that there would
be no need for a confrontation "as long as they were in the corral" and
did not show up on the street. "Why," said Fonck, "they are all down on
Fremont Street there now."

Realizing that he had to act, Virgil called upon Sheriff Behan for assistance. Behan refused to help, however, but did offer to "go down alone
and see if I can disarm them." Without waiting for Behan to return,
Virgil assembled his brothers and Doc Holliday, and they began their
march down Fremont Street: "When we got about somewhere by
Bauer's butcher shop, I saw the parties before we got there, in a vacant
lot between the photograph gallery and the house west of it. The parties
were Ike and Billy Clanton, Tom and Frank McLaury, Johnny Behan and
the Kid."

It is notable that Virgil included Behan and Claiborne ("the Kid") among the parties, indicating that he associated them with the Clantons and McLaurys. This might simply have been his way of setting the scene, or it might have been an intentional jab at Behan, meant to point out that the sheriff was on the side of the lawbreakers, not the lawmen. As he continued, Virgil's disrespect for Behan became more evident: "Johnny Behan seen myself and party coming down towards them. He left the Clanton and McLaury party and came on a fast walk towards us, and once in a while he would look behind at the party he left, as though expecting danger of some kind. He met us somewhere close to the butcher shop. He threw up both hands . . . and said, 'For God's sake don't go there or they will murder you.'"

Virgil said, "Johnny, I am going down to disarm them." He did not say whether he noticed the apparent contradiction when Behan replied, "I have disarmed them all." Rather, Virgil testified, "When he said that, I had a walking stick in my left hand, and my right hand was on my six-shooter in my waist pants, and when he said he had disarmed them, I shoved it clean around to my left hip and changed my walking stick to my right hand."

As he approached the vacant lot, Virgil caught sight of the four Cowboys, who appeared armed and hostile. Virgil said that Billy Clanton and Frank McLaury had their hands on their six-shooters, while Tom McLaury was reaching for a "Winchester rifle on a horse."[3] Then Virgil gave one of the most dramatic accounts of the hearing, made more so by the fact that he was testifying in his own words:

> As soon as I saw them, I said, "Boys, throw up your hands, I want your guns," or "arms." With that, Frank McLaury and Billy Clanton drew their six-shooters and commenced to cock them and [I] heard them go "click-click." Ike Clanton threw his hand in his breast. . . . At that, I said, throwing both hands up, with the cane in my right hand, "Hold on, I don't want that!" As I said that, Billy Clanton threw his six-shooter down, full cocked. . . . He was not aiming at me, but his pistol was kind of past me. Two shots went off right together. Billy Clanton's was one of them. At that time I changed my cane to my left hand,

and went to shooting; it was general then, and everybody went to fighting.

At the crack of the first two pistols, the horse jumped to one side and Tom McLaury failed to get the Winchester. . . . He followed the movement of the horse around, making him a kind of breastwork, and fired once, if not twice, over the horse's back.

At that point, court adjourned until the following Tuesday, giving Judge Spicer nearly three days to contemplate the image of the Cowboys firing their guns at the brave city marshal and his deputies.

When court reconvened, Fitch moved the examination to other matters, including a threat from Frank McLaury about a month before the shooting. According to Virgil, it began when Frank accosted him on the street, upset about a notice in the paper of the formation of a vigilance committee.

"I understand you are raising a vigilance committee to hang us boys," said Frank.

"You boys?" asked Virgil.

"Us and the Clantons, Hicks, Ringo, and all us Cowboys," Frank replied.

Virgil denied any involvement, reminding Frank of the time that he and Wyatt protected Curly Bill from a lynch mob. "Now do you believe we belong" to the vigilantes, he asked.

"I can't help but believe the man who told me you do."

"Who told you?" Virgil asked.

"Johnny Behan," said Frank, adding, "I'll tell you, it makes no difference what I do, I never will surrender my arms to you. I'd rather die fighting than be strangled."

Virgil's story managed to associate the McLaury brothers with John Ringo, while at the same time implicating Johnny Behan in the feud that led up to the gunfight. It was powerful, but was it true? It was easy to put words in the mouth of a dead man, and Frank's alleged statements— "I never will surrender my arms to you" and "I'd rather die fighting"— seem entirely too convenient, almost a prediction of the gunfight as Virgil described it. The prosecution had another objection; the statement contained no actual threat, and was therefore irrelevant. For once, Judge

Spicer was indecisive. He took the objection "under advisement" and never ruled on it.

Next, Virgil turned to the aborted deal with Ike Clanton, supporting Wyatt's story and adding the detail that Ike had "jumped" Bill Leonard's ranch in Cloverdale, New Mexico, and therefore had a reason for wanting him (and the other two) dead rather than captured.

Finally, as his last question, Fitch asked Virgil to state "any threats communicated to you that you have omitted to state heretofore." In response, Virgil dropped a bombshell, introducing the name of a surprise witness who could blow the case wide open: "There was a man [who] met me on the corner of Fourth and Allen Streets about 2 o'clock in the afternoon of the day of the shooting. He said, 'I just passed the O.K. Corral,' and he said he saw four of [sic] five men all armed and heard one of them say, 'Be sure to get Earp, the marshal.' Another replied and said, 'We will kill them all!' When he met me on the corner he said, 'Is your name Earp?' and I told him it was. He said, 'Are you the Marshal?' and I told him I was. I did not know the man. I have ascertained who he was since. His name is Sills, I believe."

As the judge and spectators wondered about the identity of "Sills," Tom Fitch tendered his client for cross examination.

If the prosecutors had been frustrated by their inability to cross examine Wyatt Earp, they now had their opportunity to question the leader of the posse. Will McLaury, in particular, must have champed at the bit, eager for a confrontation with the man responsible for killing his brothers. As it turned out, however, the cross examination was oddly restrained, no doubt disappointing any spectators who expected fireworks. There were gaps and inconsistencies in Virgil's story, but the prosecutors hardly touched upon them. Perhaps they were unnerved by the introduction of the previously unknown "Sills," as they used their first seven questions to seek information about him.

Next the cross examination turned to Virgil's buffaloing of Ike Clanton, but only to clarify the details. Did Virgil approach Ike from in front or behind? Which hand did he use to grab Ike's rifle? Which way was Ike facing when Virgil struck him? None of the questions amounted to anything, and none of the answers was helpful to the prosecution. Unlike Tom Fitch's calculated, propositional questions to Johnny Behan and Ike Clanton, the cross examination of Virgil Earp seemed aimless. Lacking any apparent theory, the cross examiner raised points and then dropped them without much development or evident purpose.

For example, the cross examiner asked Virgil about his shotgun, a potentially important question in view of the prosecution's "Doc fired first" theory. But the follow-up questions were flaccid: "When and where did you get that shotgun?" and "What did you do with it?" There was no effort to tie it in to the shooting of Tom McLaury, or to show how Holliday might have used both the shotgun and a nickel-plated pistol. In fact, Virgil used the latter question as an opportunity to score points for the defense: "When I called on Morgan Earp, Wyatt Earp, and Doc Holiday to go and help me disarm the McLaurys and Clantons, Holliday had a large overcoat on, and I told him to let me have his cane, and he take the shotgun, that I did not want to create any excitement going down the street with a shotgun in my hand."

The same thing happened when the cross examiner addressed the gunfight itself:

> (Q) You say at the commencement of the affray, two shots went off close together, and that Billy Clanton's was one of them. Who fired the other shot?
> (A) Well, I'm inclined to think it was Wyatt Earp that fired it.
> (Q) How many shots did you fire, and at whom?
> (A) I fired four shots. One at Frank McLaury, and I believe the other three were at Billy Clanton. I am pretty positive one was at Frank McLaury and three at Billy Clanton.

If used by a capable lawyer like Tom Fitch, such questions might have been "provables," setting the stage for another witness who could show that Virgil was exaggerating or lying. But the prosecutors displayed no such strategy, simply accepting the answers even as they bolstered the defense.

The Defense Continues

After Virgil emerged unscathed from cross examination, the defense team pursued a dual strategy with its remaining witnesses. There would be three "substantive witnesses" who testified to the events of the gunfight, each one undermining or refuting an aspect of the prosecution case. In addition, another six witnesses were called to support the general defense theory that the Earps were protecting Tombstone from a "Cowboy menace." These "theory witnesses" provided discrete facts aimed at establishing the dangerousness of the Clantons and McLaurys and their fearsome Cowboy friends.

The first substantive witness was the much anticipated H. F. Sills, whose very existence had been kept secret from the prosecution until the end of Virgil's direct examination. Sills was a furloughed locomotive engineer with the Atchison, Topeka, and Santa Fe Railroad who just happened to be visiting Tombstone on the day of the gunfight. Sills testified that he was passing by the O.K. Corral when he heard four or five men "talking of some trouble they had had with Virgil Earp, and they made threats at the time, that on meeting him they would kill him on sight." One of the men had a bandage around his head; later, at the funeral, that man was pointed out to Sills as Isaac Clanton.

Upon learning that Virgil Earp was the city marshal, Sills sought him out and "told him the threats I had overheard this party make." A few minutes later, Sills saw the confrontation between Virgil and the Cowboys: "I wasn't close enough to hear their conversation, but saw them pull out their revolvers immediately. The marshal had a cane in his right hand at the time. He threw up his hand and spoke. I didn't hear the words, though. By that time, Billy Clanton and Wyatt Earp had fired their guns off and the marshal changed the cane from one hand to the other and pulled his revolver out."

Paying careful attention to detail, Tom Fitch made sure to underscore his witness's credibility:

> (Q) How did you know it was Billy Clanton?
> (A) I saw him after he was dead, and recognized him as the one who fired at Wyatt Earp.

In his very brief testimony, Sills corroborated the Earps almost completely, both as to the Cowboys' threats and the beginning of the gun battle. Unlike nearly everybody else in Cochise County, he was completely neutral, making him an even more valuable witness for the defense.

The prosecutors realized how badly Sills damaged their case and launched into their most extended cross examination of the hearing. Lacking any advance notice of Sills's testimony, however, the cross examination quickly deteriorated into a fishing expedition, more notable for its length than any achievement.

As desperate lawyers often do, the cross examiner began with a series of open-ended questions, playing for time in the hope of deliverance by inspiration. And, as is usually the case, most of the questions led nowhere, simply prompting the witness to repeat—and sometimes reinforce—his direct examination. Asked to describe the armed men he had observed at the O.K. Corral, for example, Sills provided a thorough description of Billy and Frank, accurate in detail down to their ages and facial hair.

At one juncture, it did seem that the wandering cross examination was about to pay off. Asked about the complexion of the man with the bandage about his head, Sills replied, "I could hardly say, because he had his back to me." Encouraged, the prosecutor pursued the point:

(Q) You did not see his face then?
(A) No sir, not at that time.
(Q) When did you first see his face?
(A) On the day of the funeral.

Here, a skilled advocate would have stopped, satisfied that the witness had already conceded that he did not see the man's face, undermining the validity of his later identification. This cross examiner, however, made the classic mistake of reaching for more.

(Q) Can you positively swear that the man you saw at the funeral was the same man that you saw with the bandage around his head in front of the O.K. Corral?
(A) Yes sir I can, by his appearance and by hearing him talk.
(Q) You recognized him by his appearance and by his voice as being the same man?
(A) I recognized him by his appearance and by hearing him talk with this party in front of the O.K. Corral and with other parties at the funeral.

Undeterred by this fiasco, the cross examiner plodded on, exploring Sills's background in excruciating but meaningless detail. At times, it appeared that Sills was facing a memory test, as he was asked about his previous addresses and the names of railroad conductors. Sills was even asked to describe the horses on the wagon that brought him to Tombstone—a test he apparently passed by answering, "there was a white horse and one bob-tailed horse in the team." Although one might generously suppose that this was a provable, no witness was called in rebuttal to contradict him.

After nearly a full session of desultory questioning, the prosecutor was reduced to asking whether Sills ever had a nickname. "Yes sir," he replied, "it was Curley."

Sills was followed by three "theory" witnesses, each of whom testified about threats against the Earps. First, saloon owner Julius Kelley testified that Ike Clanton carried a Winchester rifle into his establishment on the morning of the gunfight: "I asked Clanton what trouble he had been having. He stated that the Earp crowd and Doc Holliday had insulted him the night before when he was not heeled; that he had now heeled himself, and that they had to fight on sight." The prosecution objected briefly to Kelley's testimony and did not cross examine him, evidently saving their ammunition for a renewed confrontation over Ned Boyle, who would be called next.

Boyle had not been allowed to testify earlier in the week when Judge Spicer ruled that threats from Ike Clanton were not "yet" admissible. In the meantime, however, H. F. Sills had established that Ike Clanton—the man with the bandaged head—had been present with the other three Cowboys at the O.K. Corral when they were overheard threatening to kill Marshal Earp "on sight." Hoping that this would provide a sufficient link for Judge Spicer, defense counsel asked Boyle whether, on the morning of October 26, he heard "Ike Clanton make use of any threatening language against Wyatt, Virgil and Morgan Earp and Dr. Holliday, or against any of them."

The prosecutors were not giving up easily. Objecting again, they argued that Ike's alleged threats had no bearing on the conduct of the McLaury brothers or Billy Clanton. Without comment, Spicer overruled the objection and allowed Boyle to answer: "After I went off watch at

8 o'clock in the morning, I met Ike Clanton in front of the telegraph office in this town. His pistol was in sight and I covered it with his coat and advised him to go to bed. He insisted that he wouldn't go to bed: that as soon as the Earps and Doc Holliday showed themselves on the street, the ball would open—that they would have to fight."

Boyle reported the threat to Wyatt, using Ike's own metaphor—the ball would open. The examination then turned to Tom, Frank, and Billy, with Fitch asking whether the witness knew of their reputations for courage and "how expert they were in the use of firearms." This time the prosecution objected to the evidence "on the ground that it is irrelevant, redundant and not responsive to anything proved in the case."[4] Essentially reversing his own earlier ruling, Judge Spicer decided that the evidence was admissible, allowing Boyle to reply that the expertise of the McLaurys and Billy Clanton was "the finest in the country."

The cross examination inquired into the basis for Boyle's knowledge but managed to show only that the Clantons' and McLaurys' reputations were well-known in towns around Cochise County. More successfully, the cross examination established that Boyle never knew Tom, Billy, or Frank to have been involved in any other "difficulty."

The final witness for the day was Rezin J. Campbell, clerk of the board of supervisors, who testified that he was familiar with Ike and Billy Clanton and Frank McLaury, though he knew Tom McLaury only by sight. Continuing the theme begun with Ned Boyle, the direct examiner asked the witness whether he knew the reputations "of the three former during their lives and that of Ike Clanton for coolness and courage and for expertness and dexterity in the use of firearms?" The prosecution objection was duly overruled, and Campbell answered: "The reputation of Frank McLaury was a brave and courageous man and that he was an expert in the use of firearms. Ike Clanton is the same; William Clanton, I can't say for him, only by reputation, that he was an expert in the use of firearms. I did not know Tom McLaury, only by sight."

Campbell was also present in Judge Wallace's courtroom, where he observed the altercation between Wyatt and Ike. "You are a cattle thieving son-of-a bitch," Wyatt cursed, "you've threatened my life enough, and you've got to fight!" "Fight is my racket," Ike snarled back, "and all I want is four feet of ground."

Then Ike apparently turned his attention to Morgan Earp, as Campbell continued to watch: "If you fellows had been a second later, I would have furnished a coroner's inquest for the town." The statement was not really ambiguous, but the direct examiner still tried to "clarify" it, a useful technique for adding a bit of emphasis: "What did [you] gather from the context of the conversation that Ike Clanton meant by, 'a second' later—a second later than what?" This time, an objection was sustained, giving the prosecutors their sole evidentiary victory for the day.

The cross examination of Campbell was easily the best of the day, either because there was a change in personnel—did Lyttleton Price replace Will McLaury?—or because the prosecutors had learned from the experience of questioning the earlier witnesses. Whatever the reason, Campbell was led to concede three significant points. Regarding the fracas in Judge Wallace's court, the witness acknowledged that Ike's weapons had been removed from him, while Morgan Earp hovered over him with a rifle and a six-shooter. Of course, this tended to diminish the seriousness of Ike's threats; he could only have been blustering against the heavily armed Morgan.

Next, the cross examiner took a page from the defense book, getting the witness to affirm that "Virgil Earp, Wyatt Earp, Morgan Earp and Doc Holliday [are] by reputation men of cool courage and experts in the use of firearms." It was a neat turnabout, demonstrating that, in Tombstone at least, a reputation for courage and expertise with firearms was no reason to shoot somebody.

Finally, the prosecutor turned to Wyatt's challenge to Ike, emphasizing the provocative language, "You know you are a cattle thieving son-of-a-bitch, you've got to fight." So it turned out that Wyatt made the first threat in the courtroom.

Notwithstanding that accomplishment, the day ended with the prosecution case in disarray. Sills's testimony had badly damaged their case on the merits, while the court's legal rulings opened the door to expansive defense evidence on the causes of the gunfight. Judge Spicer was no longer looking at the case exclusively as a single incident but was apparently willing to view it, in line with the defense theory, as the culmination of a simmering confrontation between the law-enforcing Earps and the law-defying Cowboys.

There was one more motion yet to be heard. At the close of the day's evidence, defense counsel requested that Wyatt and Doc be released on bail. The court agreed, ordering that both men be "admitted to bail pending the remainder of the examination, in the sum of $20,000 each." The defense obviously anticipated a favorable ruling, because mine owners E. B. Gage and James Vizina immediately posted the required amounts, freeing Wyatt and Doc in time for the four-day Thanksgiving recess.

Endgame

Wyatt Earp and Doc Holliday must have felt encouraged when court resumed on Monday, November 28. For the first time in three weeks they were free of Johnny Behan's jail, able to come and go as they pleased from the courthouse. Still recovering from their wounds, Virgil and Morgan Earp would also have had reason to be optimistic, especially if Tom Fitch had shared with them the final surprise he had in store for the prosecution. Later in the day, Judge Spicer would end up surprising both sides, and probably himself as well, but there was no way to know that when the first witness was called.

Dr. John Gardiner, a surgeon in the U.S. Army, testified that he saw the altercation between Wyatt Earp and Tom McLaury. In appropriately precise and nearly clinical terms, he said that he watched Tom "fall from the effects of a blow from a pistol." A short time later, he saw Tom McLaury enter a butcher shop opposite the Cosmopolitan Hotel. Although every prosecution witness had claimed that Tom was unarmed at the time of the gunfight, Dr. Gardiner thought otherwise: "He entered the butcher shop, and on coming out, I observed to one Albert Billicke that I saw no pistol but supposed at the time, on seeing the right hand pocket of his pants extending outwards, that he had gotten a pistol."

The prosecutors wisely refrained from cross examining Gardiner, probably because his supposition was obviously so flimsy. There were plenty of other explanations for the appearance of McLaury's pocket (even in the days before Mae West made one possibility famous).

Albert Billicke, a hotel owner, would later back up Gardiner, inference for inference. He testified that "when [Tom McLaury] went into the butcher shop his right-hand pocket was flat and appeared as if nothing was in it. When he came out, his pants pocket protruded, as if there was a revolver therein."

That was just too much conclusion-jumping for at least one of the prosecutors to tolerate. Rather than allow Billicke's speculation to sink of its own weight, he launched into an aggressive cross examination, committing the cardinal error of asking a witness for an explanation:

> (Q) How did it happen that you watched [Tom] so closely the different places he went and the exact position of his right-hand pocket when he went into the butcher shop and the exact form of a revolver in the same right-hand pocket when he came out?

The witness was happy to oblige, taking full advantage of the lawyer's mistake:

> (A) Every good citizen in this city was watching all those cowboys very closely on the day the affray occurred, and as he was walking down the street my attention was called to this McLaury by a friend and so it happened that I watched him very closely.

Whether the prosecutor walked into an ambush, or the defense just got lucky, Albert Billicke very neatly summarized Tom Fitch's theory of the case. The Cowboys were a menace to Tombstone, and "every good citizen" knew it. They had to be closely watched and kept under control, which is exactly what Virgil Earp was doing when he called on the Clantons and McLaurys to give up their arms.

The cross examiner tried to repair the damage by resorting to sarcasm, asking Billicke, "Do you know every good citizen of Tombstone, or did you on that day?" Lyttleton Price and Ben Goodrich would have known better than to put such a foolish question to the well-connected operator of the Cosmopolitan Hotel, so it was probably Texan Will McLaury who had to bear the witness's obvious rebuke: "I know not all of them, but a great many." The ill-conceived cross examination managed to turn Albert Billicke's relatively harmless testimony into an embarrassment for the prosecution and another victory for the defense. But as much as Billicke (and Gardiner) contributed to the general theory of the defense, two additional substantive witnesses were far more important to the outcome of the case.

Winfield Scott Williams identified himself only as "a lawyer" when he took the witness stand. In fact, he was an assistant district attorney, having just been appointed the previous week. We do not know whether he alerted his boss, the already-stressed Lyttleton Price, that he was going to testify for the defense, so his appearance may have come as a complete surprise. But even if the prosecutors had advance notice, they may not have anticipated how thoroughly the witness was about to contradict Sheriff Johnny Behan.

More than three weeks earlier, Tom Fitch had cross examined Behan regarding his visit to Virgil Earp on the evening after the gunfight. Behan conceded that he had made the visit but denied telling Virgil that "one of the McLaury boys said, 'We will,' and drew his gun, and the shooting commenced." In fact, insisted Behan, "I never told him I heard McLaury say anything or that I saw him draw a pistol."

It may have seemed at the time that the cross examination was ineffective, as defense counsel did not even try to shake Behan's denial. But when Williams began testifying, it became apparent that Fitch's long-range strategy was about to bear fruit.

Williams testified that he was present at Virgil's residence on the evening of the gunfight and that Johnny Behan was also there. Then Fitch moved in for the kill:

> (Q) Did you hear Behan make use of the following language: "I heard you say, 'boys, throw up your hands, I have come to disarm you,' when one of the McLaury boys said, 'We will,' and drew his gun. The shooting then commenced. 'I am your friend. You did perfectly right,'" or language of like import.
>
> (A) As I remember it, I think either the words or the purport of what was asked, was said by Sheriff Behan to Virgil Earp—excepting the last part, "I am your friend. You did perfectly right," was used in another conversation.

Williams was clearly uncomfortable in his role as defense witness, qualifying his answer as much as possible, but he could not avoid affirming Fitch's provable. Sheriff Behan had indeed said those words. It was a perfect trap, sprung even more tightly because Fitch initially had refrained from asking Behan whether anyone else was present during his visit to Virgil's home.

Either Ben Goodrich or Will McLaury handled the cross examination of Williams; internal references make it clear that the embarrassed Price was on the sidelines.[5] Dumbfounded by the witness's testimony, the cross examiner weakly asked him to repeat it, perhaps hoping that the assistant prosecutor would show some solidarity by hedging a bit. No such luck. Williams was committed to the truth as he knew it, precisely restating Behan's words to Virgil: "I heard you say, 'Boys, throw up your hands! I have come to disarm you.' One of the McLaury boys said, 'We will,' and drew his gun and shooting then commenced. That is as I remember it."

The testimony was devastating to Johnny Behan's credibility. Not only had he been caught in an apparent lie, but the witness was virtually un-impeachable. Even worse for the prosecution, the statement itself—McLaury drew his gun before the shooting commenced—completely substantiated the defense theory of the case.

The most enigmatic episode of the hearing followed when dressmaker Addie Bourland testified about her view of the gunfight from the window of her nearby home. Like all candid witnesses, Bourland could not give a comprehensive account of the events. She explained that she could not tell which party fired first because "I did not know there was going to be a difficulty." She observed a group of men whom she "supposed to be cowboys" standing near Fly's photo gallery as they were approached by four other men—the Earp party—"coming down the street toward them." She said that Doc Holliday, whom she identified by his long coat, "walked up to the man holding the horse and put a pistol to his stomach and then he, the man with the long coat on, stepped back two or three feet, and then the firing seemed to be general."

This was new information. No other witness had seen Doc shove a pis-tol in anyone's belly at the beginning of the fight, so the direct examiner tried to clarify Bourland's testimony:

> (Q) Did you notice the character of weapon Doc Holliday had in his hand?
> (A) It was a very large pistol.
> (Q) Did you notice the color of the pistol?
> (A) It was dark bronze.
> (Q) Was it or was it not, a nickel-plated pistol?
> (A) It was not a nickel-plated pistol.

Satisfied that Bourland had refuted the "nickel-plated pistol" theory, even if she could not distinguish a short-barreled shotgun from "a very large pistol," Fitch moved on to another crucial point:

> (Q) Did you see at the time of the approach of [the Earps] any of the party you thought were cowboys, throw up their hands?
>
> (A) I did not.

By picking up on the witness's own language—"the party you thought were *cowboys*"—the direct examiner used an elegant technique known today as "echoing," no doubt italicizing the word even as he spoke. None of the *Cowboys* threw up their hands, he emphasized.

From a change in the subject matter, it appears that the witness was tendered for cross examination at this point, but the surviving records are not clear and it may have been a few questions earlier or later.[6] In either case, Bourland was echoed one more time, as she was asked, "What did these men that you speak of as cowboys first do when the other party approached them?" It would have been an effective question on direct examination, or a bumbling one on cross, as it served again to accentuate the word *cowboys*. In any event, Bourland simply repeated her earlier testimony: "The man with the long coat on stepped up and put his pistol in the stomach of the man who was holding the horse, and stepped back two or three feet and the firing seemed to be general."

The cross examiner wrapped it up with a series of questions intended to cast doubt on Bourland's observations:

> (Q) About how many shots were fired before you left the window?
>
> (A) I could not tell; all was confusion, and I could not tell.
>
> (Q) Were all of the parties shooting at each other at the time you were looking at them?
>
> (A) It looked to me like it.
>
> (Q) Had any of the parties fallen at the time you left the window?
>
> (A) I saw no parties fall.

Of course, all was confusion with six men firing back and forth at each other, and her view obscured by gun smoke and frightened horses. The difference was that this witness, unlike Behan and company, admitted that she could not keep track of the precise order of the shots. Even so, she was able to say that the parties were shooting at each other *before* any man fell, which refuted the sheriff's claim that the first seven or eight shots all came from the Earps. That was enough for defense counsel, who did not request redirect.

It was not enough for Judge Spicer. During the noon recess he took the extraordinary step of visiting the witness at home for an ex parte interview. Following lunch, the court recalled Bourland to the stand, after making the following statement for the record: "The court voluntarily states that after recess . . . he went to see the witness at her house and talked with her about what she might further know about the case, and that he, of his own motion, says that he believed she knew more than she had testified to on her examination, now introduces her upon the stand for the purpose of further examination without the solicitation of the prosecution or defense."

Defense counsel remained silent while the prosecutors objected mightily; the witness had damaged their case enough and they were not interested in hearing any more from her. The judge predictably overruled the objection to his own conduct, and asked a single question:

> (Q) Please state the position in which the party called the cowboys held their hands at the time the firing commenced; that is, were they holding up their hands, or were they firing back at the other party. State the facts as particularly as may be.
>
> (A) I didn't see anyone holding up their hands; they all seemed to be firing in general, on both sides. They were firing on both sides, at each other; I mean by this at the time the firing commenced.

Granted further cross examination, the prosecution tried to recover by showing that Bourland might have gotten the timing wrong.

> (Q) Did you say this morning, that when the first two or four shots were fired, you were excited and confused, and got up from the window and went into the back room?
>
> (A) I didn't say how many shots were fired, for I didn't know when I went into the other room.

Then the cross examiner blundered in a manner still all too familiar to trial lawyers, by asking one question too many:

> (Q) What conversation did you have with Judge Spicer, if any, with reference to your testimony to be given here since . . . this morning?
>
> (A) He asked me one or two questions in regard to seeing the difficulty, and if I saw any men throw up their hands, whether I would have seen it, and I told him I thought I would have seen it.

Until that moment, it was possible that Addie Bourland had simply missed the cowboys' gesture of surrender in the first few seconds of the confrontation as she heard the shots and looked from man to man. It was the cross examiner's unnecessary question that gave her an opportunity to erase any ambiguity by adding "I would have seen it" if it had happened.

There was one last defense witness, Judge John Henry Lucas of the Cochise County Probate Court. Judge Lucas was sitting in his office, two or three hundred feet from the vacant lot, when his attention was drawn by a "couple of reports of a gun or pistol." Hesitating, he heard several more reports before he went to the door to see what was happening. He observed Billy Clanton, clearly wounded, grasping his pistol as he fell to the ground.

In substance, Lucas's testimony was relatively unimportant. At most, he established only that Billy was still standing and firing well into the gunfight, contrary to claims that he drew his pistol while lying on the ground. But the witness was really called for a tactical reason. Defense counsel wanted to close their case by putting a judge on the stand, simply to show that the Tombstone establishment supported the Earps.

Rebuttal

The defense rested, turning the case back over to the prosecution for rebuttal. Now the prosecutors had one last chance to reinvigorate their case. Now was the time to call Joe Hill to deny Wyatt's version of the deal to ambush Leonard, Head, and Crane. If Hill could not be found, perhaps some other witness could refute Wyatt's claim that Hill came riding into Tombstone with the news that Leonard and Head had been killed by the Haslett brothers. Alternatively, Johnny Behan could have been recalled, giving him an opportunity to rebut the many charges in Wyatt's statement. At a minimum, Behan could have testified about his arrest of Doc Holliday for the Benson stage robbery, detailing the bases for his suspicions and bolstering (a bit) Ike Clanton's testimony.

There was much to refute in Virgil Earp's testimony as well, including his rendition of Frank McLaury's prediction that he would "rather die fighting" than surrender his weapons. That interchange supposedly had been prompted by Behan's mischievous suggestion that Virgil was organizing a vigilance committee—"stranglers"—to hang Frank and the Cowboys. Yet Behan was never brought back to deny the accusation. Rebuttal might also have been the occasion to produce inquest witness P. H. Fellehy, who testified before the coroner's jury that he overheard Virgil saying, "Those men have made their threats. I will not arrest them, but will kill them on sight."

If possible, the prosecution might have called witnesses to contradict the testimony of Ned Boyle and Julius Kelley by showing that Ike Clanton's outbursts were more pathetic than threatening. Or they might even have found someone who could impeach the credibility of Sills and Bourland. But none of that happened.

It would have been one thing if the prosecutors had simply foregone rebuttal, announcing that they were confident about the adequacy of their case. But in fact, they did call one witness, although he had very little to offer.

Ernest Storm was the butcher who operated the Eagle Meat Market opposite the Cosmopolitan Hotel. He was called to refute Gardiner and Billicke, both of whom concluded that Tom McLaury had obtained a pistol while inside Storm's shop. The witness was unequivocal: "I saw Tom coming in about 2 or 3 o'clock. He stayed there about five minutes. He was bleeding on the side of the head when he came in. He stayed there about five or ten minutes and then he went out. He had no arms on his person and did not get any in there that I saw."

Leaving aside the fact that butchers tended to support the Cowboys (as they depended on rustlers for a steady supply of cheap provisions), Storm's testimony was hardly rousing. Gardiner and Billicke were two of the weaker witnesses in the defendants' case, having testified only to their conjectures about the contents of Tom McLaury's pocket. Both of them could be completely discounted without really damaging the defense.

Many lawyers believe that it is essential to call at least one witness on rebuttal, if only to take advantage of the crucial last word. But by calling a witness with nothing to say about the truly important issues, the prosecution only emphasized the fact that so much of the defense case remained untouched.

With that whimper, the evidence closed early on the morning of November 29. The proceeding had lasted one day short of a full month, with testimony from thirty witnesses. Without explanation, the lawyers for both sides waived the right to argument—an unusual step for "Silver Tongued" Tom Fitch—and placed the case in the hands of the Honorable Wells W. Spicer, who announced that he would deliver his decision at two o'clock the next afternoon.

11

Decision

Judge Spicer's job would have been easier if the case before him had been a full trial, where he had to decide the guilt or innocence of the defendants. After Ike Clanton's implosion and Wyatt and Virgil's forceful testimony (not to mention the surprise appearance of H. F. Sills), the evidence surely allowed the court—especially this court—to find reasonable doubt that the Earps committed premeditated murder. But Spicer was not the ultimate fact finder, and the law did not permit him to make that determination, which essentially would have substituted his own judgment for that of a jury.

Quite distinct from a trial, the proceeding was only a preliminary examination in which the prosecutors were not required to prove their case beyond reasonable doubt, or even to present all of their evidence. The only question for Spicer was whether there was "sufficient cause to believe the defendants guilty of a crime," in which case they would be bound over to the grand jury. "Sufficient cause" was a threshold standard, intended to provide defendants with protection against frivolous or baseless accusations, and it was therefore relatively easy for the prosecution to meet.[1] The judge could have his own doubts, even grave doubts, of the defendants' guilt, and yet decide that there was enough evidence to allow a jury to determine their fate.

There was another alternative as well. Judge Spicer could throw out the first-degree murder charge and still find sufficient evidence to support a lesser offense, either second-degree murder or manslaughter. Even in the absence of malice or premeditation, the court could rule that the Earps acted "upon a sudden heat of passion" or "without due caution or circumspection," or perhaps "in a spirit of revenge," any of which was sufficient to bind them over on a lower degree of homicide.[2] Tombstone's Judge James Reilly had done just that in the 1880 prosecution of George Perine for the murder of Mike Killeen. After an eight-day hearing, which was then "the longest criminal investigation ever held in Arizona," Judge Reilly held the defendant to answer only for manslaughter, apparently accepting the defendant's claim that Killeen was the aggressor but rejecting the argument that Perine acted out of more than a "bare fear."[3] Reilly's complex ruling was a clear precedent for Spicer if he chose, or could be persuaded, to follow it.

As confident as they might have been in their attorneys' skillful deconstruction of the prosecution case, the Earps and Holliday still had to worry about the outcome. There were just too many ways for the court to rule against them. In a matter so hard fought and controversial, there was every reason for the defendants to fear—and the prosecutors to hope—that Judge Spicer would simply follow the path of least resistance by submitting the entire case, in some form, to the grand jury.

They did not have to wait long for the answer. Barely twenty-four hours after retiring to consider the matter, Spicer was back on the bench, ready to announce his conclusions. As he began to read from his long, thorough opinion, no one could have realized that it would someday become the most widely debated decision ever delivered in a preliminary hearing by a justice of the peace.

But if Spicer was unaware of his eventual place in history, he was keenly aware of his current status in Tombstone. Although he spent little more than a day writing it, his experience as a newspaper editor and correspondent enabled him quickly to craft a comprehensive review of the case. In keeping with the journalistic conventions of the day, he could not resist filling his opinion with overheated prose, especially when it came to the Clantons and McLaurys, whom he described as "armed and defiant men, accepting their wager of battle and succumbing only in death," whose movements were "as quick as thought and as certain as death," when they found themselves "giving and taking death with unflinching bravery."

Literary excesses aside, Spicer was very interested in the approval of his fellow citizens. After noting the extended length of the hearing and praising the "eminent legal talent employed on both sides," he carefully set out the framework for his opinion:

> The great importance of the case, as well as the great interest taken in it by the entire community, demand that I should be full and explicit in my findings and conclusions and should give ample reasons for what I do.
>
> From the mass of evidence before [me]—much of which is upon collateral matter—I have found it necessary for the purposes of this decision to consider only those facts which are conceded by both sides or are established by a large preponderance of testimony.

Many writers and historians have concluded from the latter statement that Spicer immediately ruled out "the disputed issues of the cowboys having their arms uplifted and of Doc Holliday's purported stage-robbing background."[4] But that is not quite accurate. Without the issue of the Cowboys' attempted surrender, the prosecution had no case at all, neither for murder nor for any other crime, and there would have been no need for the judge to be "full and explicit" in his findings. Far from ruling out crucial issues, Spicer was in fact explaining that he would break down the evidence into three categories.

Naturally, he would accept the facts conceded by both sides, as judges always do. In a mild rebuke to counsel, however, he said that he would disregard a great deal of "collateral" evidence, no matter who had produced it. Spicer's judgment in this regard would prove to be highly controversial, as he later discounted a good deal of hotly disputed evidence—including the entire issue of Tom McLaury's phantom gun—because he considered it beside the point. Finally, the court would analyze the remaining disputed-but-not-collateral evidence to determine which facts were established "by a large preponderance of the testimony." This does not mean that Spicer simply ignored disputed facts, but rather that he would resolve them by considering the weight of the testimony and the credibility of the witnesses.

This was a bold approach, as weighing evidence is usually a job for a jury, not for an examining magistrate. Later in his opinion, Spicer would explain that he was adopting the rule that governed grand juries, allowing an indictment when "all the evidence before them, taken together, is such as in their judgment would, if unexplained or uncontradicted, warrant a conviction by the trial jury." In other words, Spicer preempted the decision of the grand jurors by taking the broadest possible view of his own jurisdiction. That might have led some to brand him a "judicial activist," if the term had been invented in 1881.

A Censurable Act

Moving to the merits of the case, Spicer began with Ike Clanton's overnight rampage, noting that the "prosecuting witness . . . was about the streets and in several saloons of Tombstone, armed with revolver and Winchester rifle, declaring publicly that the Earp brothers and Holliday had insulted him the night before when he was unarmed, and now he was armed and intended to shoot them or fight them on sight. These threats were communicated to defendants, Virgil Earp and Wyatt Earp."

The judge proceeded to recount the series of confrontations, including Virgil's arrest and bludgeoning of Ike, which caused the court only a moment's pause. Making good on his promise to disregard collateral matters, Spicer noted that "whether this blow was necessary is not material here to determine." He paid even less heed to Wyatt's assault on Tom McLaury, remarking only that "the latter was struck by the former with a pistol and knocked down."

By focusing on Ike Clanton's threats and misdeeds—including the claim that fight was his "racket"—Spicer seemed to be endorsing the Earps' version of events. But every fact has two faces, and the tone of the court's opinion quickly shifted. As Spicer went on to explain, Ike Clanton's open hostility, far from justifying the later shooting, should have caused Virgil Earp to take extra measures to avoid a showdown: "In view of the controversies between Wyatt Earp and Isaac Clanton and Thomas McLaury, and in further view of this quarrel the night before between Isaac Clanton and J. H. Holliday, I am of the opinion that the defendant, Virgil Earp, as chief of police, subsequently calling upon

Wyatt Earp, and J. H. Holliday to assist him in arresting and disarming the Clantons and McLaurys, committed an injudicious and censurable act. . . ."

This could have been the key to the prosecutors' case, had they bothered to raise the charge of criminal negligence. Virgil Earp was well aware of the smoldering violence, but his choice of companions added fuel to a fire that might well have burned itself out if he had simply left things alone. Whether or not "Doc fired first," his presence in the posse was a needless provocation, providing significant evidence that Virgil and the others acted improperly in a "spirit of revenge."

But the moment soon passed. Rather than dwell on Virgil's tragic mistake, Spicer went on to excuse it:

> Although in this he acted incautiously and without due circumspection, yet when we consider the conditions of affairs incident to a frontier country; the lawlessness and disregard for human life; the existence of a law-defying element in [our] midst; the fear and feeling of insecurity that has existed; the supposed prevalence of bad, desperate and reckless men who have been a terror to the country and kept away capital and enterprise; and consider the many threats that have been made against the Earps, I can attach no criminality to his unwise act. In fact, as the result plainly proves, he needed the assistance and support of staunch and true friends, upon whose courage, coolness and fidelity he could depend, in case of an emergency.

The prosecutors must have steeled themselves as they saw their chances fade. Judge Spicer had adopted the defense theory that Tombstone was threatened by "bad, desperate and reckless men," implicitly rejecting Johnny Behan's glib answer on cross examination that Cowboys were nothing more than "men who deal in cattle—stockmen." That would lead the court to further conclusions, crippling to the prosecution.

First, Spicer gave great credence to Virgil's testimony that he had acted in response to the Clantons' and McLaurys' threatening movement out of the O.K. Corral and into Fremont Street. Conceding that their purpose "will probably never be known," he accepted the claim that "Virgil Earp, the chief of police, honestly believed . . . that their purpose was [either] to attempt the deaths of himself and brothers [or] at least to resist with force and arms any attempt on his part to perform his duty as a peace officer by arresting and disarming them." The court was also impressed by the series of warnings Virgil received, not only from H. F. Sills, "who had arrived in town only the day before," but also from "several citizens and a committee of citizens" who called on the chief of police to "arrest and disarm the *cowboys,* as they termed the Clantons and McLaurys" (emphasis added).

Perhaps even more important, Spicer took it upon himself to resolve the crucial disputed factual questions, still viewing the issues against the backdrop of "terror in the country." He observed that "witnesses of credibility," presumably including Johnny Behan, had testified that the Cowboys raised their hands when Virgil called for their surrender. Other "witnesses of equal credibility," however, had testified that William Clanton and Frank McLaury responded "by drawing their pistols, and that the discharge of firearms from both sides was almost instantaneous." Therefore, Spicer chose to determine "the important question of whether the deceased offered to surrender before resisting" by accepting the "testimony of persons unacquainted with the deceased or the defendants." This sounds reasonable enough, but in a not-so-subtle reference to Behan, the court went on to reject the competing testimony of "persons who were companions and acquaintances, if not partisans, of the deceased." Cowboy testimony did not get much weight in Spicer's court.

On the specifics, Spicer noted Addie Bourland's testimony "that the firing commenced at once, from both sides." At least one of the prosecutors must have winced, remembering his own botched cross examination when the court continued "that no hands were held up; that she could have seen them if there had been."

The court also pointed out that there were no powder burns on Billy Clanton's clothing (despite prosecution testimony that he had been shot "when the pistol was only a foot from his belly"). In a further display of amateur forensics, Spicer opined that the wound to Billy's wrist was "such as could not have been received with his hands thrown up, and the wound received by Thomas McLaury was such as could not have been received with his hands on his coat lapels." These observations were debatable, to say the least, and they were not directly supported by the medical testimony. But Spicer considered himself a man of science—in his Utah days he had written an article on phrenology, claiming that he could determine criminal character from the shape of a man's skull—and concluded that "these circumstances being indubital [*sic*] facts, throw great doubt upon the correctness of the statement of witnesses to the contrary."

Finally, Spicer stressed that the Clantons and McLaurys had refused Behan's request that they give up their guns. In a sarcastic reproach, the court quoted Behan's testimony "that they 'demurred,' as he said, and did not do it." The judge's emphasis on Behan's word choice— "demurred"—showed disdain for the sheriff's ineffectiveness as a lawman. Even worse was Behan's acquiescence when Frank McLaury stated that he "would not give up his arms unless the Earps were disarmed— that is, that the chief of police and his assistants should be disarmed." That drew the court's outrage, directed nearly as much at Cowboys generally as at McLaury (and Behan): "In view of the past history of the county and the generally believed existence at this time of desperate, reckless and lawless men in our midst, banded together for mutual support and living by felonious and predatory pursuits . . . and at the same time for men to parade the streets armed with repeating rifles and six-shooters and demand that the chief of police and his assistants should be disarmed is a proposition both monstrous and startling!"

This all sounded very much as though the court was exceeding its authority by deciding the ultimate question of guilt or innocence, rather than simply ascertaining "sufficient cause" for further proceedings. Spicer therefore tried to explain that his ruling had a legal, as well as factual, basis:

> Considering all the testimony together, I am of the opinion that the weight of the evidence sustains and corroborates the testimony of Wyatt Earp, that their demand for surrender was met by William Clanton and Frank McLaury drawing or making motions to draw their pistols. Upon this hypothesis my duty is clear. The defendants were officers charged with the duty of arresting and disarming armed and determined men who were expert in the use of firearms, as quick as thought and as certain

as death and who had previously declared their intention not to be arrested nor disarmed. Under the statutes [citation omitted], as well as the common law, they have a right to repel force with force.

Elaborating on the law, Spicer pointed out that the crime of murder required proof "not only [of] the killing, but also the felonious intent. In this case, the *corpus delicti* or fact of killing, is in fact admitted as well as clearly proven." But, he continued, "the felonious intent is as much a fact to be proven as the *corpus delicti*," and that is where the prosecution failed. All of the evidence showed that Virgil and his party were acting under the authority of the law, seeking to accomplish the lawful objective of disarming dangerous men:

> Was it for Virgil Earp as chief of police to abandon his clear duty as an officer because its performance was likely to be fraught with danger? Or was it not his duty that as such officer he owed to the peaceable and law-abiding citizens of the city, who looked to him to preserve peace and order, and their protection and security, to at once call to his aid sufficient assistance and persons to arrest and disarm these men?
>
> There can be but one answer to these questions, and that answer is such as will divest the subsequent approach of the defendants toward the deceased of all presumption of malice or of illegality.
>
> When, therefore, the defendants, regularly or specially appointed officers, marched down Fremont Street to the scene of the subsequent homicide, they were going where it was their right and duty to go; and they were doing what it was their right and duty to do; and they were armed, as it was their right and duty to be armed when approaching men whom they believed to be armed and contemplating resistance.

In other words, Spicer asserted that he was not really *weighing* evidence as much as acting upon the *absence* of evidence. Without specific proof of motive, there could be no "reasonable cause" to believe that the defendants committed murder. That could lead to only one result: "In view of all the facts and circumstances of the case, considering the threats made, the character and positions of the parties, and the tragic results accomplished in manner and form as they were, with all surrounding influences bearing upon the *res gestae* of the affair, I cannot resist the conclusion that the defendants were fully justified in committing these homicides—that it [was] a necessary act, done in the discharge of official duty."

The charge against the Earps and Holliday was dismissed and they were free to go. In the court's language, "There being no sufficient cause to believe the within named Wyatt S. Earp and John H. Holliday guilty of the offense mentioned within, I order them to be released."

What Went Wrong?

When the preliminary hearing before Judge Spicer began on October 31, it certainly seemed that the prosecution had the upper hand. Johnny Behan, Wes Fuller, Billy Allen, and Billy Claiborne were all ready to testify that the Clantons and McLaurys were frantically trying to surrender when they were gunned down, with the first shot fired by Doc Holliday and at least the next four or five also coming from the Earp party. That testimony alone, even if controverted, should have been enough to establish "sufficient cause" to bring the case before a grand jury. And in fact, Judge Spicer made an interim ruling to that effect, on November 7, when he revoked bond for Wyatt and Doc upon a showing that "the proof so far was conclusive of murder." By the end of the hearing, however, the prosecution was reeling, and Judge Spicer's decision upheld the defense on nearly every possible point. From the prosecutors' perspective, things went very badly wrong. But why?

One answer, of course, is that the prosecutors were simply out-lawyered. As we saw at almost every stage of the hearing, Tom Fitch (and T. J. Drum, to the extent he participated) demonstrated a level of proficiency that was almost never equaled by Price, Goodrich, and McLaury. Compare, for example, the cross examinations of Johnny Behan and Virgil Earp.

Tom Fitch, through his deft propositional questions, succeeded in maneuvering Sheriff Behan into a series of implausible statements, most notably when the witness basically denied that the Cowboys of Cochise County were anything more than ranch hands. That assertion later came back to haunt the prosecution, as Fitch surely planned, when Judge Spicer repeatedly based his decision on the existence of "desperate men" who were "a terror to the country" and who "banded together for mutual support [while] living by felonious and predatory pursuits." It was undeniable that Judge Spicer was talking about Cowboys, as he made clear when he referred to the demands of the vigilance committee that the Earps "disarm the *cowboys,* as they [the 'committee of citizens'] termed the Clantons and McLaurys" (emphasis added).

Equally impressive was the way Fitch completely ambushed Behan with Winfield Scott Williams's testimony. Aware of Wells Spicer's bitter experience defending John Lee against perjured prosecution testimony, Fitch must have realized that he could score the most points by catching Behan in a lie. Thus, Fitch cleverly baited the sheriff into denying his post-gunfight acknowledgment that Frank McLaury said " 'We will,' and drew his gun." That gave Fitch an opportunity to prove Behan a liar, by producing Williams's impeaching testimony at the very last moment— a far more effective technique than simply dragging the truth out of Behan in the first place.

In contrast, the prosecution barely touched Virgil Earp on cross examination, although that opportunity provided the best single chance to undermine the defense case. The cross examiner made scant use of "provables" and asked almost no propositional questions. Most significantly, Virgil was never even challenged on his highly suspect assertion that, months before the gunfight, a conveniently prescient Frank McLaury had warned him, "I never will surrender my arms to you" because "I'd rather die fighting." Again, the prosecutors had reason to regret their lapse, as Judge Spicer relied upon that very statement as a reason to exonerate Virgil Earp. In Spicer's mind, the McLaurys and Clantons were "armed and determined men who were expert in the use of firearms, as quick as thought and as certain as death and *who had previously declared their intention not to be arrested nor disarmed*" (emphasis added).

Throughout the hearing, defense counsel adroitly capitalized on their cross examinations, while the prosecutors mostly floundered. Of course, many of the prosecution witnesses had already testified once at the inquest, which gave the defense a great advantage. It is much more difficult to cross examine a witness "cold." But that may not have been the only reason that the defense outperformed the prosecutors.

The Earp hearing, in 1881, occurred during a time of transition in the development of modern cross examination, and it appears that Tom Fitch was on the cutting edge of relatively new techniques. Before the Civil War, every U.S. jurisdiction prohibited "interested parties" from testifying in either civil or criminal cases.[5] Cross examination existed, in the sense that every witness could be questioned by opposing counsel, but lawyers had little reason to develop the sort of sharp, leading questions that are now considered essential. Instead, cross examinations were generally used to fill in gaps in the story, requesting information that was omitted during direct testimony.

In 1864, Maine became the first state to abolish the prohibition against interested party testimony. The three jurisdictions where Tom Fitch practiced all adopted the new rule relatively quickly: California in 1866, Arizona in 1871, and Utah in 1878. Thus, by the time he confronted Johnny Behan in Tombstone, Fitch would have had many years' experience in cross examining hostile or uncooperative witnesses. Texas, however, would not permit interested parties to testify until 1889, meaning that Will McLaury would have had no previous experience in cross examining a criminal defendant, nor could Ben Goodrich have acquired any in the years before he came to Arizona.

Cross examination, of course, is only one part of the story. Contrary to much popular opinion, a trial is not a sporting event or even a drama competition, in which the winner is determined solely on the basis of talent. In fact, a trial (or in this case, an extended hearing) is a contest of ideas in which each side tries to present a comprehensive reconstruction of past events, combining facts and law in a way that leads to a logical result. Modern lawyers call this a "theory of the case," but it is hardly a new concept. Judge Spicer himself recognized the crucial necessity of a case theory when he stated that the "legal character of the homicide" would rest on proof of "felonious intent."

In Tombstone, the prosecutors lost primarily because they failed to present a coherent theory of their case. Although they produced numerous damning facts, the totality of the story never explained *why* Virgil Earp, after years of trustworthy law enforcement, would suddenly turn into a vicious murderer (unless one believed Ike Clanton; more on that later). Nonetheless, the prosecution insisted that all four defendants—Virgil included—were equally guilty of premeditated murder.

The desire to ensnare all four defendants—we can call it an "all for one" approach—led the prosecution to make several serious mistakes, not the least of which was ceaseless reliance on the appearance of Doc Holliday's elusive nickel-plated pistol. While the "Doc fired first" scenario was essential to the murder case against the Earps, it actually deprived the prosecution of an opportunity to build a far stronger case against Holliday alone. Even in pro-defense accounts of the gunfight, Doc Holliday "stalked" Tom McLaury, as Casey Tefertiller put it, and blew him away with both barrels of his shotgun. If Tom was unarmed, which even Wyatt allowed was a possibility, then Holliday's actions could certainly have been characterized as murder, quite apart from the Earps' shoot-out with Billy and Frank.

As it was, however, no prosecution witness could testify about the separate drama that took Tom's life because they were all committed to the tale of the nickel-plated pistol. If there had been a discrete case against Doc, however, Judge Spicer could not so easily have brushed aside the "dispute as to whether Thomas McLaury was armed." As the court noted, that question was "not of controlling importance" in a unified case against all four defendants because his death was incidental to the "felonious resistance" of Billy and Frank. In contrast, a closer—and more honest—focus on Doc Holliday might have been able to establish that Tom McLaury played no greater role in the battle than did Ike Clanton, whose life was spared, as it should have been.

Doc was clearly the least attractive of the four defendants. If Judge Spicer was inclined to be sympathetic toward the Earps, he would have had no such feelings toward the notorious Holliday. Realizing this, the prosecutors evidently thought that they could use Doc's unsavory reputation to tarnish the other three defendants. Ironically, they accomplished just the opposite. By trying to use Doc to drag down the Earps, they ended up sacrificing their best chance for a murder conviction against him.

The decision to rely so heavily on Ike Clanton must also have been driven by the "all for one" strategy. Ike would not have been necessary to support a murder case solely against Holliday, or to establish a lesser charge against the other three defendants. He was essential, however, if the Earps were to be convicted of first-degree murder. Absent Ike, the proof of premeditation was thin indeed. Several witnesses testified to Virgil's statement that he would give the Clantons and McLaurys "a chance to make a fight," and Martha King thought she heard someone (either Morgan or Virgil) tell Doc Holliday to "let them have it." That evidence was hardly conclusive. Virgil's alleged comments were ambiguous, and, in any event, he subsequently agreed that Behan should try to disarm the Cowboys. Martha King's testimony was even less convincing. Standing in a butcher shop as the Earp party passed by, she admitted that she heard only part of the conversation. Moreover, there were at least another half dozen people in or near the butcher shop at the time—many of whom testified that they were paying close attention to the Earps and Holliday—and none of them corroborated King's "let them have it" claim, or anything remotely similar.

The prosecutors may have had no choice about letting Ike Clanton testify—he was, as the court put it, the prosecuting witness—but they did not have to build their case around him. And they surely did not have to use redirect examination to encourage Ike to expand on his sweeping accusations. True, Ike provided the only direct evidence of the Earp brothers' premeditation, but the painfully obvious holes in his story were deadly to the prosecution case. As Judge Spicer observed: "The testimony of Isaac Clanton, that this tragedy was the result of a scheme on the part of the Earps to assassinate him and thereby bury in oblivion the confessions the Earps had made to him about 'piping' away the shipment of coin by Wells Fargo & Co. falls short of being a sound theory, [on] account of the great fact, most prominent in this matter, to wit: that Isaac Clanton was not injured at all, and could have been killed first and easiest, if it was the object of the attack to kill him. He would have been the first to fall; but, as it was, he was known or believed to be unarmed, and was suffered and, as Wyatt Earp testified, told to go away, and was not harmed."

It would never have been less than an uphill struggle to convince Wells Spicer that Virgil Earp was a criminal, but the task was not impossible. Although Spicer's background, instincts, and experiences all disposed him toward the defense, even his critics have credited him with "a fair degree of objectivity."[6] The challenge for the prosecutors, then, was to fashion a case that the judge could accept, even if that had to be less ambitious than the case they preferred.

In sharp contrast to the prosecution, the defense lawyers shaped their case around a single theory that was calculated to appeal precisely to Judge Spicer. Tombstone was imperiled by a band of organized outlaws, and men like the Earps had to take determined action to prevent a disastrous descent into lawlessness. Far from incidental to the defense case, the "Cowboy menace" theory was woven tightly into nearly every direct and cross examination. From the provocative cross examination of Johnny Behan—"Do you regard the Clantons and McLaurys as cowboys?"—to the opening moments of Wyatt Earp's statement—"a little over a year ago, I followed Tom and Frank McLaury and two other parties who had stolen six government mules"—the defense team missed no opportunity to emphasize the difference between lawmen and law breakers.

The long history of confrontations between the Earps and various Cowboys provided an outline for the defense theory, lumping the Clantons and McLaurys along with John Ringo and Curly Bill as "desperate and dangerous men [who were] connected with outlaws, cattle thieves, robbers, and murderers." Wary of possible prosecution objections to too much "irrelevant" background, the defense took care to include most of it in Wyatt Earp's uninterruptable statement, thereby ensuring that Judge Spicer would hear the entire story without distraction.

Fully attuned to the social and political situation in Tombstone, Tom Fitch understood Judge Spicer's concern about the perceived lawlessness in the surrounding countryside. Even if John Clum and the *Epitaph* rather exaggerated the extent of the problem, there can be little doubt that business-oriented (mostly Republican) citizens like Spicer firmly believed that Cochise County's economic health was jeopardized by rustlers and robbers who "kept away capital and enterprise." The Earps, and on that one day, Holliday, stood as defenders of Tombstone's boom-town vitality. It was no accident, then, that Fitch's witness list was a virtual parade of notables, including several businessmen, an army surgeon, an assistant district attorney, the clerk of the board of supervisors, and even a probate judge. The message, as it was fortuitously conveyed by hotel operator Albert Billicke, was that "every good citizen" supported the Earps.

This is not to suggest that Spicer was corrupt or that the outcome of the hearing was predetermined, or even, as some have suggested, that his decisions were driven by his "political and socioeconomic interests." In fact, the judge was scrupulously fair in his rulings, sustaining the prosecution more or less as often as the defense. There can be little doubt that he would not have hesitated to rule against the Earps if he thought there was "reasonable cause" to believe them guilty of murder. But no judge—in fact, no person—is free of biases or preconceptions. In considering the evidence before him, Spicer had no choice but to evaluate the dangerousness of the Clantons and McLaurys. The law required him to view the confrontation from the perspective of the Earps in order to decide whether their actions were reasonable or malicious. There is an inherently subjective element to such a decision. How can one assess "dangerousness," after all, except in light of one's own judgment and experience? Tom Fitch succeeded because he understood that dynamic and pitched his case accordingly.

The prosecutors were not naive or inexperienced. All three men were capable lawyers; Ben Goodrich in particular would go on to enjoy one of the most distinguished legal careers in Arizona. But even if the prosecutors had tried to match Tom Fitch's sophisticated strategy, they were laboring under serious disadvantages. First, of course, they were stuck with the witnesses fate had dealt them. Ike Clanton, Wes Fuller, and Billy Claiborne might all have been Cowboys, who were not exactly endearing to Judge Spicer, but they were in fact witnesses to the gunfight who supported the prosecution case.

An equally serious problem was created by the presence of Will McLaury on the prosecution team, especially if he played a leading role in determining strategy. As an outsider, McLaury would have had no prior knowledge of Tombstone life and politics. He certainly would not have realized the significance of Fitch's "Cowboy threat" theory, much less its capacity to influence Judge Spicer. Believing sincerely that his brothers had been honest ranchers—"universally esteemed as honorable, personable, and brave citizens," as he wrote to his brother-in-law in Iowa—McLaury could not easily have understood how anyone might view the incident as less than "as cold-blooded and foul a murder as has been recorded."[7]

The prosecution's greatest difficulty, however, was caused by the decision to proceed exclusively on the charge of first-degree murder.

Manslaughter

To persuade Judge Spicer to rule against the "regularly or specially appointed" peace officers of Tombstone, the prosecution had to present a sustained counternarrative to the Earps' story of self-defense against a band of desperadoes. As we have seen, the "willful murder" theory proved far too burdensome: It was antagonistic to Judge Spicer's general outlook; it relied much too heavily on Ike Clanton's improbable testimony; and there were far too many ways for the defense to contradict it.

A manslaughter charge, however, would have presented many fewer difficulties for the prosecution. Initially, it would have solved most of the evidentiary problems inherent in the murder charge. The excesses in Ike Clanton's testimony, for example, would have been rendered irrelevant because there would have been no need to establish a prior motive for the shootings. Thus, Ike's outlandish claim of a Wyatt-Doc-Virgil conspiracy to cover up the Benson stage robbery could have been discounted without completely undermining the heart of the prosecution case. In fact, Judge Spicer could have rejected all of Ike's testimony while still deciding that there was sufficient proof of manslaughter.

The same is true of many of the discrepancies in Johnny Behan's testimony, including his inability to explain how Doc Holliday could have fired both a nickel-plated pistol and a shotgun at the opening moment of the gunfight. The "Doc fired first" claim, which was crucial to the murder charge, was severely undermined by Tom McLaury's shotgun wounds—unless one indulges (as Judge Spicer obviously did not) the various theories of firearms acrobatics that subsequent historians have suggested. But that anomaly would have had little bearing, if any, on a lesser charge because the alternative—that Wyatt fired first—was not inconsistent with manslaughter.

In the same way, Martha King's testimony would have been slightly bolstered, while defense witnesses H. F. Sills and Addie Bourland would have been more or less neutralized. King testified that she had heard one of the Earp brothers tell Doc Holliday to "let them have it." That might have been damning, but for her admission that she did not hear the entire exchange, which left open the possibility that the full instruction to Holliday may have been rather more contingent—"If they go for their guns, let them have it." A warning like that was hardly evidence of malice or premeditation; in fact, it was just the opposite. But even a highly conditional statement could have been used as proof of manslaughter because it would show a lack of "due caution or circumspection." The Earps were edgy and ready to shoot at the slightest hint of trouble.

Judge Spicer gave great weight to the testimony from Sills and Bourland that the Cowboys did not have their hands in the air when the shooting began, but that would have mattered much less if the prosecution case had been premised on anything short of deliberate assassination. In fact, a manslaughter charge could actually be supported by the ambiguous nature of Frank and Billy's hand movements: angry and acting in a "spirit of revenge," the Earps literally jumped the gun and began firing at the first sign of an imaginary false move.

Most important, the manslaughter scenario would have been considerably easier for Judge Spicer to accept as a matter of law because it did not require him to believe that the Earps were deliberate killers. As the judge explained in his opinion: "The prosecution claims much upon the point, as they allege, that the Earp party . . . precipitated the triple homicide by a felonious intent then and there to kill and murder the deceased, and that they made use of their official characters as a pretext. I cannot believe this theory, and cannot resist the firm conviction that the Earps acted wisely, discretely and prudentially, to secure their own self-preservation. They saw at once the dire necessity of giving the first shots, to save themselves from certain death! They acted. Their shots were effective, and this alone saved the Earp party from being slain."

First-degree murder, as urged by the prosecution, required proof of "malice aforethought" or "willful, deliberate, and premeditated killing." Forced to decide between Earps-as-willful-pretextual-killers and Earps-as-wise-and-prudent-lawmen, Judge Spicer predictably chose the latter.

But he might well have been open to an alternative story, had it been presented to him, in which the Earps were a little less wise, a little less discrete, and a little less prudent. That would have been enough for manslaughter, which Arizona law generally defined as "the unlawful killing of a human being without malice . . . or without any mixture of deliberation."[8] The further definitions of voluntary and involuntary manslaughter were complex, but they are worth parsing:

> In cases of voluntary manslaughter there must be a serious and highly provoking injury inflicted upon the person killing, sufficient to excite an irresistible passion in a reasonable person, or an attempt by the person killed to commit a serious personal injury on the person killing.[9]

> Involuntary manslaughter [occurs] in the commission of an unlawful act, or a lawful act without due caution or circumspection.[10]

Both offenses (and murder as well) could be negated by a plea of justifiable homicide, defined as "the killing of a human being in necessary self defense," which excluded killings committed out of unreasonable—or "bare"—fear, or in "a spirit of revenge."[11]

It is not hard to see how Judge Spicer might have found reasonable cause to believe that some form of homicide fit the events of the Tombstone shoot-out. Looking first at voluntary manslaughter, the defendants themselves obviously contended that the persons killed (Billy, Frank, and Tom) attempted to commit a serious personal injury on the persons killing (the Earps and Holliday). So the only remaining question was whether the Earp party fired out of justifiable necessity or in an "irresistible passion." And even in the absence of passion, the killings would still have been involuntary manslaughter if the Earps acted lawfully but without due caution or circumspection.

Unlike murder, where there is a huge gulf between guilt and innocence, there is only a thin and subjective line between manslaughter and justifiable homicide, defined almost entirely by the perceived reasonableness or necessity of the defendants' actions. If the prosecutors had not pressed so hard on premeditation, perhaps they could have persuaded Judge Spicer that the Earps' conduct crossed that line.

In fact, Wyatt and Virgil themselves provided plenty of evidence that could have been used in support of a manslaughter finding, beginning with Wyatt's recitation of repeated threats from the Clantons and McLaurys. The defense point, of course, was that the Earps had good reason to be wary of the Cowboys, or as Wyatt put it, they did "not intend that any of the gang should get the drop on [them]." But of course, the Earps' wariness cuts both ways. It might also have meant that they were angry and jumpy, in the mood to shoot first and ask questions later. In that light, Ike's binge of threats and curses might have provoked the Earps to be even more reckless and confrontational, even after they had battered and subdued the hapless Clanton.

The same could be said of the statement Virgil attributed to Frank McLaury, that he would "rather die fighting" than give up his arms. To the defense, Frank's forewarning was proof of the Cowboys' violent intentions. But a capable prosecutor could have given that fact a completely different spin, using it again as proof that the Earps were over-primed for trouble.

And finally, there is the matter of Wyatt Earp's pistol. As we have seen, Wyatt almost certainly lied, or at least exaggerated, when he claimed that he kept his gun in his overcoat pocket until he saw Frank and Billy draw their weapons. It is far more likely that he approached the Cowboys with his gun drawn, shooting when he saw Frank's hand move, either treacherously or innocently. The prosecutors did not bother with that discrepancy because they were busy trying to prove their claim that "Doc fired first." On that theory, Wyatt's actions did not really matter, since Frank and Billy would have been drawing in response to the opening barrage from Doc and Morgan. In a manslaughter case, however, Wyatt's conduct would have mattered quite a bit, especially if it could be shown, or just argued, that he overreacted to an innocent gesture, shooting without even a reasonable moment of hesitation. The prosecution would not have to prove that the Cowboys were surrendering—exposing their witnesses to contradiction and inviting Judge Spicer's disdain—but only that they were never given a decent chance to surrender.

The manslaughter story, then, would go something like this:

In the course of their efforts to become Cochise County's most prominent lawmen, the Earps endured a series of scrapes and confrontations with the Cowboy element, sometimes violent and always troublesome. Although the Clantons and McLaurys were pretty much small-timers compared to John Ringo and Curly Bill Brocius, they were highly visible and, in the case of Ike Clanton, highly obnoxious. As the level of threats and recriminations grew, the Earps became more and more determined to deny the Cowboys free rein in Tombstone.

Wyatt's deal with Ike Clanton was indeed part of a plan to secure the sheriff's office in Cochise County. If it was successful, Wyatt would win acclaim for capturing Leonard, Head, and Crane; if unsuccessful, he would at least be able to squeeze Ike Clanton with threats of exposure. But Ike refused to play his part quietly, showing up in Tombstone on October 25 drunk and in a hostile frame of mind. When Ike seemed about to get out of control, the Earps responded with force, buffaloing Ike and then Tom McLaury, for good measure.

Dazed and confused, the Clantons and McLaurys did not have the good sense to get immediately out of town. For reasons that will never be known, they gathered first at Spangenberg's gun shop, and later at the O.K. Corral. As they crossed through the alleyway and headed to the vacant lot on Fremont Street, at least two of them were armed with six-shooters, and they were leading two horses with rifles in saddle scabbards. Whatever their true purpose, the Cowboys' move appeared defiant or sinister to Virgil Earp, although they had no way of knowing that they were crossing Virgil's unannounced line in the sand.

His patience already wearing thin, Virgil was not willing to tolerate the Cowboys' affront to his lawful, if excessive, authority. Johnny Behan's ineffectual intervention seemed only to make matters worse, but that provided Virgil and Wyatt with an opportunity to show up their rival. When the Earps and Holliday began their march down Fremont Street, they probably intended only to intimidate the Cowboys, or at most to administer new beatings. They did not plan to commit murder.

But then things got tragically out of hand. Already frightened, the Clantons and McLaurys were spooked at the sight of the gunslinger Doc Holliday—maybe more so if they caught sight of the shotgun partially hidden under his long coat. Virgil Earp called out, "Boys, throw up your hands, I want your guns," but Billy and Frank responded slowly. Facing Wyatt Earp, whose gun was already in his hand, they were not foolhardy enough to draw, but their slight hesitation must have seemed suspicious. Still seething over the threats from Ike Clanton, Wyatt let his temper overcome his better judgment. As the Cowboys fidgeted or trembled, he did not wait even a moment to see what would happen next. When Frank McLaury began to move his hand, Wyatt fired the first shot, striking Frank in the belly. At the sound of the gunshot, Morgan Earp also began firing, while Doc Holliday pulled out his shotgun and took aim at Tom McLaury. Then the fight became general and three men were doomed.

The manslaughter story is based entirely on evidence from the hearing, much of it produced by the defense. It requires only a few reasonable inferences—that the Earps were angry enough to shoot without think- ing—and it does not depend at all on proof of malice or intent. It would not have satisfied Will McLaury, of course, who wanted nothing less than a full measure of revenge. But it should have made good sense, at least as an alternative, to a levelheaded prosecutor.

Would Judge Spicer have believed it? Here again we will have to spec- ulate, although it is tempting to say that he could not have believed it any less than he believed the murder case. It is more interesting to ask why the prosecutors waived closing argument, giving up their clearest oppor- tunity to offer manslaughter as a lesser alternative. In the preliminary hearing of George Perine, the attorneys presented summations for five hours, prompting the *Epitaph* to praise their efforts: "For the prosecu- tion, Mr. Anderson wove together the testimony in a net whose meshes seemed so close as to prevent escape to the prisoner, and per contra, Mr. Barke, for the defense, with equal ingenuity unraveled the web and the discharge of the defendant seemed inevitable. The argument, from a forensic point of view, was a brilliant one and was eagerly watched by the prisoner, his features now lighted up with the assurance of hope and anon clouded with the bitterness of despair."[12]

In the end, Judge Reilly was evidently impressed by both attorneys. He rejected the murder case against Perine but bound him over to the grand jury on a charge of manslaughter, as might have happened also to the Earps if Price, Goodrich, and McLaury had posed that alternative to Judge Spicer.

In fact, Spicer came very close to raising the manslaughter issue on his own. Unnoticed for more than 120 years, there is a clear reference to manslaughter at the beginning of his opinion, suggesting that the judge was at least receptive to the idea.

The intriguing comment is found in Spicer's initial criticism of Virgil, where the court comments that Marshal Earp "committed an injudicious and censurable act" in which he acted *"incautiously and without due circumspection"* (emphasis added). Most writers have regarded this statement simply as a rebuke. Allen Barra calls it a "censure," while Casey Tefertiller says it only meant that Spicer "did not condone all of Virgil Earp's decisions."[13] But there was much more to it than that.

In fact, the court was closely paraphrasing the manslaughter statute, which applied to killings that occur "in the commission of . . . a lawful act without *due caution or circumspection*" (emphasis added). In other words, Judge Spicer began his opinion by announcing a prima facie case of involuntary manslaughter against Virgil Earp. The court went on immediately to exculpate the marshal, noting that the "existence of a law-defying element" in Tombstone and the "supposed prevalence of bad, desperate and reckless men" prompted him to "attach no criminality to [Virgil's] unwise act." But of course, that raises a further question: What would have happened if the prosecutors had addressed the manslaughter issue head-on? Could they have done more to negate Spicer's fears, or to show that the Clantons and McLaurys were not really part of the law-defying element? In this context, Spicer's use of the word "supposed" becomes tantalizing. Was the court only "supposing" the prevalence of outlaws based on the Earps' testimony, and even chiding the prosecutors for failing to present sufficient evidence to the contrary?

Later, Judge Spicer seemed to take pains to point out the inadequacy of the prosecution case, perhaps alluding again to the absence of manslaughter evidence: "The evidence taken before me in this case, would not, in my judgment, warrant a conviction of the defendants by trial jury of any offense whatever. I do not believe that any trial jury that could be got together in this territory would, on all the evidence taken before me, with the rule of law applicable thereto given them by the court, find the defendants guilty of any offense."

One reading of this paragraph, of course, is that the judge was implicitly exonerating the defendants of manslaughter as well as murder. On the other hand, the repeated juxtaposition of "the evidence taken before me" and "any offense" could also have been a more pointed comment on the prosecution's failure to present any case for the lesser included offenses. That interpretation is bolstered by the court's final words: "There being no sufficient cause to believe the within named Wyatt S. Earp and John H. Holliday guilty of the *offense mentioned within,* I order them to be released" (emphasis added). In the end, Judge Spicer's only actual ruling was in favor of the defendants on the specific charge of murder.

It was within Spicer's legal authority to reach beyond the official charge and enter a finding of manslaughter, but he had good reasons for passing up the opportunity. In the Mountain Meadows trial, he had seen his client convicted of excessive charges, but only on the basis of contrived testimony. That experience must have left him wary indeed of perjury-enhanced prosecutions. After watching Ike Clanton's stunning dissimulation, he would have been scarcely inclined to help the Tombstone prosecutors rescue some part of their own inflated case. It had been their choice, after all, to offer Ike's testimony, and even to expand on it during redirect examination. As a logical matter, Ike's narrative obliterated the possibility of a manslaughter finding since it denied the very possibility that the Earps had acted out of any motive other than premeditated malice. The prosecutors had a chance to back away from Ike's story, but instead they stuck with it. Judge Spicer then ruled accordingly.

After more than 120 years it is surely impossible to re-create the events of October 26, 1881, in Tombstone, Arizona Territory. At the time, many observers—not only Johnny Behan and the Cowboys—believed that the Earps acted with unnecessary brutality, if not outright malice. Tom Fitch was able to discredit Ike Clanton's murder charge, but only by protecting Wyatt Earp from cross examination and (at least) stretching the truth in the Earp brothers' testimony. Wyatt almost certainly lied on the stand, concealing what might have been the single most significant fact in a manslaughter case—that he was brandishing his six-shooter as he approached the Clantons and McLaurys. Although it is less certain, Virgil, too, seems to have embellished his direct examination, inventing an extremely useful preconfession by the dead Frank McLaury, vowing that he would rather die than give up his arms.

For their part, the prosecutors made one mistake after another. Most seriously, they badly overplayed their case, staking far too much of their credibility on Ike Clanton's tale of a murder conspiracy and paying far too little attention to lesser degrees of homicide. In the end, they even abdicated final argument, leaving Judge Spicer stranded between extremes. Based on the case presented to him, the judge had only the choice of freeing the Earps or committing them to the grand jury on murder charges. Aware of the controversy that was about to erupt, Spicer reflected on the difficulty of his decision, and perhaps his reluctance to reach it: "I have given over four weeks of patient attention to the hearing of evidence in this case, and at least four-fifths of my waking hours have been devoted, at this time, to an earnest study of the evidence before me, and such is the conclusion to which I am forced to arrive."

The case was over. But the war between the Earps and the Cowboys was not.

12

Aftermath

Wells Spicer was keenly aware that his decision in favor of the Earps would outrage a considerable segment of Tombstone and Cochise County society. Making a game effort at advance damage control, his written opinion acknowledged that "it may be that my judgment is erroneous, and my view of the law incorrect." Should that be the case, he continued, "I have the less reluctance in announcing this conclusion because the Grand Jury of this county is now in session, and it is quite within the power of that body, if dissatisfied with my decision, to call witnesses before them or use the depositions taken before me, and which I shall return to the district court, as by law required, and to thereupon disregard my findings, and find an indictment against the defendants, if they think the evidence sufficient to warrant a conviction."

The court was not exactly passing the buck. Following Spicer's extended disquisition on the law and facts, it would have been extremely unlikely for a grand jury to second-guess him, and even less so in this case, given that the grand jury was largely composed of businessmen thought to be sympathetic to the Earps. More likely, Spicer was counting on the grand jury to back him up, using the apology in his opinion as the major premise in what he hoped would be a protective syllogism: If the ruling was correct, the grand jury will not indict the Earps. The anticipated nonindictment would later serve as the minor premise—"the grand jury has not indicted"—leading to the conclusion that Spicer was right all along.

If that was the plan, however, it did not work. It did not even buy Spicer any time. The *Nugget* ran an angry front-page editorial on the same day that it reported the court's decision, all but denouncing Spicer as corrupt, and ridiculing his plea for understanding:

> The examination of Earp and Holliday on the charge of the murder of Frank and Thomas McLaury and William Clanton on the 26th of last month, was concluded yesterday by the discharge of the prisoners by Wells Spicer, the magistrate before whom the examination was conducted. This action was not much of a surprise to any one, inasmuch as Spicer's rulings and action for some days previous to the close of the case had given sufficient indication of what the final result would be. . . .
>
> The remarkable document which appears in another column purports to be the reasons which actuated the Judge in his final action. But the suspicion of reasons of more substantial nature are openly expressed upon the streets, and in the eyes of many the justice does not stand like Caesar's wife, "not only virtuous but above suspicion."
>
> The affair will probably be investigated by the Grand Jury now in session, but from the confessed and known bias of a number of its members, it is not probable that an indictment will be found. While it is well enough for Spicer to say that the Grand Jury are in no manner estopped from consideration of the case, he well knows that his actions will have much influence with those who hedge a magistrate about with a suppositious knowledge of law and rectitude of purpose that he does not always possess.[1]

If they agreed on little else, Spicer and the *Nugget* were both right about the grand jury, which, as expected, quickly declined to indict the Earps and Holliday. Far from calming the waters, however, that decision only exacerbated the situation, with rising tempers on all sides making the threat of continued gunplay a constant possibility. As Clara Brown observed: "There being two strong parties in the camp, of course this verdict is satisfactory to but one of them. The other accepts it with a very bad grace, and a smouldering fire exists, which is liable to burst forth at some unexpected moment. If the Earps were not men of great courage, they would hardly dare remain in Tombstone."[2]

As fighting men, the Earp brothers were not about to be intimidated into leaving town. In fact, Wyatt ostentatiously made a point of registering to vote on the very day of his discharge, signaling an intention to stay in Tombstone (and probably to make good on his undertaking to run against Johnny Behan in the next election). Meanwhile, rumors continued to swirl that the Cowboy faction was plotting armed revenge against everyone even remotely associated with the Earps: Doc Holliday, Judge Spicer, Mayor Clum, Tom Fitch, and others.

On December 14, 1881, John Clum boarded a stagecoach for the first leg of a long-planned trip to Washington, D.C., intending to catch the train in Benson. The stage had traveled only a few miles from Tombstone, however, when it was attacked by bandits, who fired their guns with hardly a warning. Believing the attack to be an assassination attempt rather than a holdup, Clum, who was carrying two six-shooters, jumped out of the coach and hid in the brush, eventually traveling the entire twenty-five miles to Benson largely on foot and partially on a borrowed horse.

Clum had no doubt that he was an intended murder victim. "In the gulch near where the attack was made," he wrote "was ample evidence that horses had been picketed there on several occasions, indicating that these would-be executioners had been anticipating my departure for about a week."[3] In fact, the stage that night was an unlikely robbery target. It had been carrying no "treasure box," as was visibly evident from the absence of a "shotgun messenger," making Clum's deduction even more plausible.

The *Epitaph,* under the command of Charles Reppy during Clum's absence, was furious over the assault on the mayor. Harry Woods's *Nugget,* or course, was wholly unconvinced, basically accusing Clum of self-important paranoia. Stage robberies were endemic in Cochise County, and there was no direct evidence that Clum was the specific target of this holdup. As Allen Barra points out, however, there was definitely an armed attack on the Benson stage that night, wounding one of the drivers and killing one of the horses. Nonetheless, the assailants made no effort to rob the stage, even after it was forced to stop, suggesting strongly that they were more interested in shooting than in stealing.

Even as John Clum was finally making his way back East, Judge Spicer was receiving a series of threatening letters, one of which was reprinted in the *Epitaph:* "Sir, if you take my advice you will take your departure for a more genial clime, as I don't think this one healthy for you much longer. As you are liable to get a hole through your coat any moment. . . . It is only a matter of time you will get it sooner or later."[4] Spicer responded, also in the *Epitaph,* a few days later:

> I am well aware that all this hostility to me is on account of my decision in the Earp case, and for that decision I have been reviled and slandered beyond measure, and that every vile epithet that a foul mouth could utter has been spoken of me, principal among which has been that of corruption and bribery.
>
> Of all such I say, that whenever they are denouncing me they are lying from a low, wicked and villainous heart, and that when they threaten me they do so because they are low-bred, arrant cowards, and know that "fight is not my racket"—if it was they would not dare to do it.
>
> In conclusion, I will say that I will be here just where they can find me should they want me, and that myself and others who have been threatened will be here long after all the foul and cowardly liars and slanderers have ceased to infest our city.[5]

Brave words—including a mild dig at Ike Clanton, who rashly had claimed that fight was his "racket" before he ran away from the Earps. Hardly more than a week later, however, Spicer had good reason to reconsider his bravado.

On December 28, shortly before midnight, Virgil Earp was walking from the Oriental Saloon to the Cosmopolitan Hotel, where he had moved his family for safety. He never made it. As Virgil crossed Fifth Street, he was ambushed by several men who were standing in the shadows next to a burned-out store. Struck by at least two loads of buckshot, Virgil staggered as his assailants ran off into the night.

Wyatt and others carried Virgil to a room in the hotel, where he was attended by two physicians, including Henry Matthews, who had testified at both the inquest and preliminary hearing. The doctors discovered that Virgil's left arm had nearly been ripped off by the shotgun blasts. Removing five inches of bone between the shoulder and elbow, the doctors managed to save the arm from amputation, but it would be nearly immobile for the rest of his life. With Allie at his side, Virgil maintained his composure when he heard the bad news. "Never mind," the lawman told his frantic wife, "I've got one arm left to hug you with."[6]

Others were not so calm. To the *Epitaph,* the attack on Virgil proved "that there is a band of assassins in our midst" threatening "the lives of Judge Spicer, Mayor Clum, Mr. Williams, the Earp brothers and Holliday." George Parsons blamed the "cowardly apathetic guardians of the peace" for failing to pursue the assassins, while surmising that Ike Clanton, Curly Bill, and Will McLaury were responsible for the shooting.[7]

The case against Ike Clanton was strengthened when his hat was discovered at the scene of the crime, and no physical evidence was necessary to make Curly Bill a prime suspect. Parsons's suspicions of Will McLaury, however, seemed to have little if any foundation. Of course, McLaury was sorely aggrieved by the deaths of his brothers, and he made no secret of his hatred of the Earps. His letters home were filled with barely veiled threats of violence, so it is highly probable that he made similar comments during his long evenings in Tombstone's saloons, especially after the grand jury accepted Spicer's judgment and squelched any chance of a successful prosecution. But Will McLaury was a lawyer and a businessman, not a rustler or a saddle tramp. He tried to protect his brothers' reputations as honest ranchers, which would not have inclined him to connive with men like Curly Bill.

In the spring of 1882, McLaury wrote a letter to his father, describing his dismay over the events in Tombstone: "My experience out there has been very unfortunate—as to my health and badly injured me as to money matters—and none of the results have been satisfactory—the only result is the death of Morgan and crippling of Virgil Earp."[8] This has led some to suspect that Will McLaury may have financed the attacks, although the inference is strained at best. McLaury's letter seems more regretful of the legal outcome than boastful of the shootings. In any event, it is known that he left Tombstone several days before the attack on Virgil, never to return.

Wyatt, now the leader of the fighting Earps, believed that the assassination attempt was the work of Ike Clanton and Frank Stilwell, the former deputy of Sheriff Behan, and other Cowboys as well. He immediately sent a telegram to Federal Marshal Crawley Dake in Phoenix: "Virgil was shot by concealed assassins last night. His wounds are fatal. Telegraph me appointment with power to appoint deputies. Local authorities are doing nothing. The lives of other citizens are threatened."[9] Dake responded affirmatively, authorizing Wyatt to organize a posse.

Tombstone held municipal elections on January 3, 1882, just a week after the attempt on Virgil Earp's life. Compromised by the O.K. Corral gunfight, and then crippled, Virgil Earp was not a candidate for a full term as city marshal; nor did John Clum stand for reelection as mayor. Instead, the *Epitaph* supported a ticket of businessman Lewis Blinn for mayor and James Flynn, one of Virgil's former deputies, for marshal. The *Nugget*'s mayoral candidate was blacksmith John Carr, a native of Ireland with considerable political experience. For marshal, the *Nugget* backed Deputy Sheriff David Neagle, who enjoyed a reputation for independence despite his association with Johnny Behan.

The *Nugget* did its best to turn the election into a referendum on the Earps, going so far as to claim that Flynn planned to resign in favor of Virgil if the *Epitaph* ticket won. As it turned out, Virgil's maiming did not result in a sympathy vote. Rather, the assassination attempts against Clum and the Earps seemed only to remind the citizens of the constant violence that afflicted Tombstone, suggesting that the retirement of the Earp faction might settle things down. On election day, nearly every Earp-associated candidate was soundly defeated, with Carr capturing the mayor's seat with more than 70 percent of the vote. "Exeunt Earps!" crowed the *Nugget*'s postelection headline, proclaiming a solid victory over the "ruinous and wanton course" pursued by the *Epitaph* and its allies.

But Wyatt Earp was not ready to exit Tombstone. Not yet. With Virgil's survival still very much in doubt, and municipal government firmly in the control of Johnny Behan's friends, Wyatt relied on his U.S. marshal's badge to assemble a posse in search of Virgil's attackers, whom he believed to be Ike and Phin Clanton, John Ringo, and assorted other Cowboys. At various times, Wyatt's band comprised his brothers Morgan and Warren, Doc Holliday, and several former Cowboys, including Sherman McMasters, Turkey Creek Jack Johnson, and Texas Jack Vermillion. The *Nugget* called the bunch a "Pestiferous Posse" and editorialized against Dake's conferral of federal authority "in the hands of the perpetrators" of the O.K. Corral killings, warning that the Earps carried with them the burden of "the moral guilt, if not the actual."[10]

As Wyatt's crew combed Cochise County, Ike Clanton again proved to be adept at the art of self-preservation. With the assistance of Ben Goodrich, Ike and Phin turned themselves in to another lawman, rather than take their chances in a showdown with the Earps. Brought back to Tombstone, the Clanton brothers were taken before Judge William Stilwell (no relation to Frank), charged with the attempted assassination of Virgil Earp. The case against Phin was quickly dismissed for lack of evidence, but Ike was scheduled for a preliminary hearing on February 2, 1882.

Unlike the Earps' hearing before Judge Spicer, which lasted for nearly a month, the case against Ike Clanton collapsed in about one day. James Bennett testified for the prosecution that he found Ike's hat—it had his name in it—at the scene of the shooting. Sherman McMasters, a sometime Cowboy and later an Earp ally, testified that he overheard Ike talking about Virgil's survival and stating that he "would have to go back and do the job over." That was it. The prosecution had no direct evidence of guilt.

In response, the defense produced a series of alibi witnesses who testified that Ike was in Charleston on the night of December 28. Ike himself testified that he had lost his hat, which was plausible, even if the coincidence of its recovery at the crime scene was damningly suspicious. In the end, Judge Stilwell had little choice but to dismiss the charge, leaving Wyatt and his brothers angry and frustrated.

Ike Clanton was back in court in less than a week, but this time he was on the offensive. On February 9, Ike and Ben Goodrich appeared before Justice of the Peace James B. Smith in Contention and filed new charges against the Earps and Holliday for the murder of the McLaury brothers and Billy Clanton. Because the original charge had been dismissed for lack of "reasonable cause" rather than fully adjudicated by a trial jury, there was no technical bar to a further prosecution—the Constitution's "double jeopardy" clause applies when there has been a final judgment of guilt or innocence, but not when there has been only a preliminary hearing. Apparently hoping for a more sympathetic hearing in Contention than they had received from Judge Spicer, Clanton and Goodrich again presented the maximum possible charge, alleging that the Earps and Holliday did "wilfully, feloniously, premeditatedly and of their malice aforethought, kill and murder . . . William Clanton, Thomas McLaury, and Frank McLaury [by] shooting with guns and pistols then and there loaded with gunpowder and leaden bullets."[11]

Judge Smith seemed more than willing to entertain the new charges, even though the Earps' lawyer, William Herring (Tom Fitch was out of town), argued strenuously that the filing was improper in the absence of any new evidence. Ordered to appear in Contention for a hearing, Wyatt and Doc again found themselves in the custody of Johnny Behan. Refusing to surrender their handguns, they also engaged an escort of a dozen armed friends to protect them on the ride to court. As the legal wrangling intensified, the case bounced back and forth for several days between Contention and Tombstone. Finally, attorney Herring succeeded in bringing a Petition for a Writ of Habeas Corpus before Probate Judge John Henry Lucas. The prosecution had earlier tried to disqualify Lucas, who had been a defense witness at the Spicer hearing, but the judge ruled in favor of his own jurisdiction and determined to hear the writ.

Ben Goodrich presented the affidavit of Ike Clanton, attempting to clean up his original story by rendering his testimony entirely in the baroque legalese typical of the late nineteenth century: "At the time and place aforesaid, J. H. Holliday, Wyatt Earp, Morgan Earp, and Virgil Earp did with guns and pistols, in their hands then and there held, which said guns and pistols were then and there loaded with gunpowder and leaden bullets did shoot at, to and against the bodies of said William Clanton, Thomas McLaury, and Frank McLaury, and did wound, strike, and penetrate the bodies of the said William Clanton, and of the said

Thomas and Frank McLaury with the bullets so shot out of the guns and pistols aforesaid, of which wounds so inflicted as aforesaid, the said William Clanton, Thomas McLaury and Frank McLaury then and there instantly died."[12]

In fewer words, there was nothing new. Judge Lucas allowed that Ike's affidavit would ordinarily be sufficient to require a preliminary examination "if there was nothing else to be considered." In this case, however there had already been an "examination of the parties for the same offense, by a committing Magistrate occupying weeks and then discharged," not to mention the subsequent refusal to indict by a sitting grand jury. The court continued: "Whether [the defendants] are guilty or not, it is apparent to any reasonable being that an examination at this time could serve no good purpose. The evidence of the various witnesses is now in the possession of the District Court, and another examination would simply duplicate them, and when they have been discharged by one Magistrate and a failure to indict by one Grand Jury, it would seem to be unadvisable to enter an examination at this time."[13]

Noting again the absence of any new evidence or changed circumstances, Judge Lucas granted the Writ of Habeas Corpus. Refusing to second-guess Judge Spicer, he discharged the Earps and Holliday once and for all. Tom Fitch's strategy had paid off. By presenting the entire case at the preliminary hearing, Fitch succeeded in winning the Earps' release and preventing any further legal action. The Cowboys, however, were not content to lose in the courtroom; they were determined to continue the battle by other means.

Vendetta

On Saturday night, March 18, Wyatt and Morgan Earp attended a theatrical performance and then repaired to Campbell & Hatch's Saloon for a few rounds of billiards. Wyatt had been warned—by Briggs Goodrich, of all people—that there were strangers in town who might be gunning for the Earps, although the attorney added that John Ringo was not among them. Goodrich's sometime-client Ringo wanted Wyatt to know that he intended to have "nothing to do" with any fight, even if others were planning trouble.

Even forewarned, there was fairly little Wyatt and Morgan could do to protect themselves. Unwilling to cower in their rooms at the Cosmopolitan Hotel, they made a point of carrying guns and staying alert, but they still tried to lead reasonably normal lives.

Just before eleven o'clock, Morgan was finishing his second game of pool with proprietor Bob Hatch. As Morgan stood with his back to the glass door on an outside wall, two rifle shots slammed through an upper window pane. The first bullet struck Morgan, entering "the right side of the abdomen, passing through the spinal column, completely shattering it."[14] The second shot struck the wall above Wyatt's head, doing no additional harm.

The first bullet did harm enough. Morgan would live for only about an hour, despite the efforts of Tombstone's leading physicians to save him. According to Clara Brown, the death scene was heart-wrenching: "The man was surrounded by his brothers and their wives, whose grief was intense. He whispered some words to Wyatt, which have not been given to the public, but spoke aloud only once, when his companions endeavored to raise him to his feet: 'Don't boys, don't,' he said, 'I can't stand it; I have played my last game of pool.' "[15]

Whatever last words were exchanged between the brothers, it was clear that the situation in Tombstone changed dramatically that night, as increasing violence became inevitable. From then on, Wyatt "would have no regard for any law but his own."[16] The ensuing series of killings would become known as Wyatt Earp's "Vendetta Ride."

Almost immediately after Morgan's death, Wyatt began making arrangements to send his brother's remains for burial in Colton, California, where their parents had settled. Too badly injured to fight, Virgil (along with his wife Allie) would accompany the casket by train. But first they had to get safely out of Tombstone. Fearing yet another attack, Wyatt organized an armed escort—consisting of himself, brothers Warren and James, Doc Holliday, Jack Johnson, and Sherman McMasters—to travel with Virgil at least as far as Tucson, where they would change trains for California. Arriving on the evening of March 20, members of the grim party had dinner in a restaurant near the depot before continuing their journey.

As Virgil and Allie settled in on the westbound train, Wyatt caught sight of Frank Stilwell standing near the tracks, perhaps along with Ike Clanton. Stilwell was then, and is to this day, a prime suspect in the murder of Morgan Earp, and Wyatt had good reason to believe that he was lying in wait for Virgil. In fact, Stilwell had a legitimate reason to be in Tucson that day, as he was due in court on the federal charge of mail robbery from the Bisbee stage (for which Virgil had arrested him the previous year). But if Wyatt was aware of that coincidence, it made no impression on him. Acting quickly to protect his brother, Wyatt and his colleagues chased Stilwell down the tracks and virtually shot him to pieces. Passengers and railroad workers reported hearing as many as seven or eight shots, although, oddly, no one seems to have rushed to investigate the shooting. Stilwell's body was not found until the next morning, when it was discovered that he had been hit by as many as three bullets and two loads of buckshot. In later years, Wyatt would freely admit to the killing, claiming to have accomplished it himself in the necessary defense of his crippled brother. The number of Stilwell's wounds, however, make it obvious that he was shot by more than one hand, and without mercy.

That was also the conclusion of the coroner's jury, which issued murder warrants for Wyatt and Warren Earp, Doc Holliday, Sherman McMasters, and Jack Johnson. By that time, however, Wyatt and company were on their way back to Tombstone, where they had unfinished business.

Even as Wyatt was returning to the wars of Cochise County, another coroner's jury was looking into the killing of his brother Morgan. On Tuesday, March 21, Marietta Spence testified against her husband Pete (who had also been arrested for robbing the Bisbee stage), also implicating Frank Stilwell and two other men whom she knew only as "Freeze" and "Indian Charlie." According to Marietta, she had seen her husband and Indian Charlie staking out Morgan on the day before the murder: "Spence nudged the Indian and said, 'that's him; that's him,'" and then Charlie moved down the street "so as to get ahead of him and get a good look at him." On the night of the shooting, Frank Stilwell and Indian Charlie showed up at Spence's home, followed thirty minutes later by

Spence and Freeze, all carrying rifles and speaking in hushed tones. Marietta observed that her husband was trembling and that his teeth were chattering. "Spence didn't tell me so, but I knew he killed Morgan Earp," she said, "I judged they had been doing wrong from the condition, white and trembling, in which they arrived."[17] The next morning, Spence, who had a history of wife beating, threatened to kill Marietta if she said a word to anyone.

The coroner's jury apparently accepted Marietta's testimony, naming Spence, Stilwell, Indian Charlie, and "John Doe" Freeze in the murder of Morgan Earp. The jury didn't know it, but Stilwell was already dead. Spence turned himself in to Johnny Behan, if only to ensure protection from the remaining Earps.

Wyatt arrived in Tombstone only slightly ahead of the warrants for his arrest, which were being transmitted by wire. The manager of Tombstone's telegraph office was apparently an Earp supporter, so he delayed delivering the message to Sheriff Behan until Wyatt had a chance to round up his men and prepare to leave town. Still claiming to be acting under federal authority, Wyatt was determined to track down the men who were responsible for the attacks on Virgil and Morgan. Behan, having just obtained the Tucson warrant, was more or less determined to stop him.

At about eight o'clock on the evening of March 21, there was one final confrontation between the two rival lawmen. "Wyatt, I want to see you," said Behan, as he approached the Earp party on the sidewalk near the Cosmopolitan Hotel. Much had happened in the three days since the murder of Morgan, and Wyatt was in no mood to tolerate Behan's interference, lawful as it was. "You can't see me," he replied, "you have seen me once too often." Then Wyatt added, "I will see Paul," meaning that he would be willing to commit himself to the custody of Sheriff Doug Paul, of Pima County.[18]

The *Nugget* would later charge that Wyatt resisted arrest, drawing his gun on Behan in order to make a getaway. According to the *Epitaph,* however, "no word was spoken by the sheriff that implied a demand for an arrest [and] no weapons were drawn or pointed at the sheriff."[19] The latter version (which is supported by both Clara Brown and George Parsons) makes more sense, as it is unlikely that Wyatt Earp needed firearms to intimidate the ineffectual Johnny Behan. Recall the sheriff's description of his efforts to disarm the Clantons and McLaurys just before the gunfight. He testified to his belief that he had arrested the Cowboys, even though he doubted "whether they considered themselves under arrest or not."

As Wyatt and his men rode off on their vendetta, Behan put together a posse of his own, enlisting John Ringo and Phin Clanton among his deputies. Technically, Behan was invoking Cochise County's authority against a deputy federal marshal, but by that point, many Arizonans must have viewed the situation "as one band of crooks against another." Many believe, however, that Behan's efforts were largely for show. Hardly a fighting man, he would have been less than eager for an armed show-down, perhaps preferring to keep Wyatt disgraced and on the run. George Parsons suspected that Behan was simply building up his expenses, with no intention of catching his man: "Mileage still counting up for our rascally sheriff. He organizes posses, goes to within a mile of his prey and then returns. He's a good one."[20] For whatever reason, Behan never quite succeeded in catching up with Wyatt, or even getting very close.

The Earp posse had considerably more success, beginning on Wednesday, March 22. Searching for Pete Spence (who was actually sitting safely in Behan's jail), Wyatt and his men rode into a wood camp near the Dragoon Mountains. There they located a Mexican worker named Florentino Cruz who was thought to be "Indian Charlie," the alleged lookout for Morgan's murder. Cruz was quickly dispatched—perhaps having first confessed to his involvement—which prompted Parsons to comment, "More killing by Earp party. Hope they'll keep it up."[21] Others were not so sanguine. The *Nugget* and newspapers as far away as San Francisco railed against the killing, and even Earp supporters could not endorse such an obvious murder—without even the pretext of self-defense.

Wyatt's vendetta, however, would claim at least one more life (and perhaps two). On the morning of March 24, the Earp party rode into a clearing known as Iron Springs, where they expected to rendezvous with some allies. Instead, they were surprised when they stumbled across a group of Cowboys—Wyatt would later say there were nine of them—including Curly Bill Brocius. The Cowboys had evidently seen the Earps coming and immediately began firing from the bank of the spring. Texas Jack Vermillion's horse was hit by a bullet, and most of Wyatt's posse retreated to a nearby stand of trees.

But not Wyatt Earp. Grabbing a shotgun, he charged ahead. In Stuart Lake's version of the story, bullets shredded Wyatt's coat as he advanced, heedless of the danger. Catching Curly Bill in his sights, Wyatt let loose with a double load of buckshot, nearly cutting the outlaw in two. Less than a week after Morgan's death, Wyatt had managed to kill three men implicated in the murder.

Curley Bill's body was never recovered—some say that his Cowboy pals buried him secretly, to deprive Wyatt of any glory—so there has always been some question about whether he was really killed in the battle of Iron Springs. Wyatt always claimed credit for the killing, however, and historians generally accept the broad outline of Lake's account, if not the precise details.

Through all of these events, public condemnation of Wyatt, and his methods, continued to build. Even though Wyatt would forever insist that he was acting under federal authority, tracking down wanted bank robbers, there was really no doubt that he was pursuing private vengeance entirely outside the law. While Johnny Behan might never catch him, there was clearly a limit to how long Wyatt could remain at large in Arizona, if only for lack of funds and supplies. Eventually, he would have to ride into Tombstone or some other town where he was liable to be arrested. Or perhaps a serious lawman, either Bob Paul or someone else, would take up the trail and bring him in. At some point, therefore, Wyatt decided that his "work" was done, and he made plans to escape the territory.

By mid-April, Wyatt and his men were in New Mexico. From there, he and Doc headed to Colorado by train, arriving first in Gunnison. The two men split up for awhile, traveling to Trinidad, Pueblo, and Denver, although they remained in touch and on fairly good terms. Eventually, word of their whereabouts reached Arizona, and several attempts were made to extradite them for Stilwell's murder. With the assistance of their friends—including Bat Masterson, who was serving as city marshal in Trinidad—Wyatt and Doc managed to resist extradition, with Colorado Governor Frederick Pitkin finally denying the request, in part, on the ground that Doc Holliday would likely be murdered if returned to Arizona.

There would be no more trials for Wyatt Earp.

There was one last death, however, that might be attributable to the Earp-Cowboy battles. On July 13, 1882, John Ringo was found dead, his body leaning against a large oak tree not far from Tombstone. There was a six-shooter in his hand (with one round expended) and a bullet hole in his forehead. Most strangely, Ringo's boots were missing; his feet seemed to be wrapped in his torn-up undershirt. The coroner ruled the death a suicide, but rumors persisted that John Ringo had been murdered, with Wyatt Earp and Doc Holliday among the logical suspects. Wyatt and Doc are known to have been in Colorado at the time, however, fighting efforts to bring them back to Arizona. Both men were notorious by then, and it is extremely difficult to imagine either one slipping unnoticed across the border and tracking down Ringo, much less killing him and then escaping without once being seen. Stranger things than that happened in Tombstone, however, and it is not out of the question that Wyatt Earp had a hand in Ringo's death, either directly or by proxy. However it came about, the demise of John Ringo marked the end of the Cochise County war.

Denouement

It was not many years before Tombstone lost its "snap" as a boomtown. As early as the spring of 1881, water began to seep into the silver mines that gave the town its economic vitality. While at first the water was treated as a blessing—Arizona was always a fairly parched environment—it soon became clear that the flooded mines could not operate profitably. By 1886, production was in severe decline, made worse by a massive fire that destroyed much of the mining infrastructure. Eventually, Tombstone became a near ghost town, as fortune seekers hunted elsewhere. In more recent years, of course, there has been a tourist-fueled revival, boosted by recurrent interest in Wyatt Earp and the O.K. Corral gunfight.

As to the stalwarts themselves, some lived and prospered while others met tragic fates. Billy Clanton, the McLaury brothers, Morgan Earp, Curly Bill Brocius, John Ringo, Frank Stilwell, and Florentino Cruz all died by gunfire. Ike Clanton, too, was shot to death when he was caught stealing cattle in 1887.

Johnny Behan failed in his bid for reelection as Cochise County sheriff, but he remained a minor figure in Arizona politics, holding a number of offices (some of which he left under a cloud of financial controversy). He eventually served as the warden at Yuma Territorial Prison, an infamous institution where the inmates at various times included Phin Clanton, Pete Spence, and Frank Leslie. Behan died of natural causes in 1912.

John Clum sold the *Epitaph* to saloon owner Milt Joyce, nemesis of Doc Holliday and a prominent Democrat, who quickly changed the newspaper's political orientation. He left Tombstone in the spring of 1882, returning for a few years in 1885–86. Clum moved to California, where he engaged in various business ventures with mixed success. In 1897 he went to Nome, Alaska, with an appointment as a postal supervisor, where he reconnected with Wyatt Earp and George Parsons. After nearly ten years, on and off, in Alaska, he returned to California, where he devoted much of his time to writing. Clum maintained his friendship with Wyatt Earp, serving as an honorary pallbearer at his funeral in 1929. Clum himself died in Los Angeles in 1932.

The lawyers went their separate ways. Will McLaury remained in Tombstone only until December 1881, hoping to obtain a reversal of Judge Spicer's decision. When the grand jury declined to indict the Earps and Holliday, he returned to Texas, where he resumed his law practice and served as a superior court judge. Rumors have persisted that he had some involvement in the attacks on Virgil and Morgan, but they depend on innuendo far more than proof. McLaury died in 1913 in Snyder, Oklahoma. Tom Fitch moved to California in 1886, establishing himself as both a journalist and lawyer. In the 1890s he became an active leader of the "Free Silver" movement, touring the country as a popular (and populist) speaker. He and his wife, Anna, published a successful novel, *Better Days: Or, A Millionaire of Tomorrow,* and they continued to engage in amateur theatricals. Always politically ambitious, Fitch unsuccessfully pursued a senate seat in Utah before traveling to Hawaii in 1901, where he served as legal advisor to Queen Liliukalani. He died in California in 1923. Ben Goodrich remained in Arizona, becoming one of the territory's leading attorneys. He was elected Cochise County treasurer in 1883 and district attorney in 1887. After Tombstone's economic decline, he moved his offices to Phoenix. For a time, he practiced law in California, but he returned to Arizona in 1902 and was elected to the territorial legislature in 1907. He moved to Los Angeles in 1911 (this time for good), where he died in 1923.

Wells Spicer's term as justice of the peace expired in 1882, and he did not seek another. Instead, he devoted time and attention to prospecting, chasing one claim after another. His fortunes rose and fell until, in 1886, he apparently hit rock bottom. Having abandoned his law practice, and without a viable mining claim to work, he evidently drifted into the Sonoran Desert, where he presumably died of thirst or starvation. The *Arizona Daily Star* reported his disappearance as a probable suicide, although rumors circulated that he had really vanished to avoid his debts, trying to start life anew in Mexico.

Despite his injury, Virgil Earp found work as a policeman in Colton, California, where he also served as city marshal. Later, he ran a saloon in San Bernardino before following a gold strike to the Needles area, where he and Allie opened a bar and gambling parlor called Earps' Hall. Returning to Arizona, Virgil held various law enforcement positions in Prescott, and he was also active in Republican politics. He died in bed in 1905.

Doc Holliday remained in Colorado, where he traveled from town to town as an itinerant gambler and sometimes professional faro dealer. In the summer of 1884, in Leadville, he got into a fight with Billy Allen (the former Tombstone Cowboy who testified against Wyatt and Doc in Judge Spicer's court), shooting him in the right arm. Tried and acquitted the following spring (Allen must have been one terrible witness), Doc moved to Denver, though by this time he was sick and broken. He later moved to Glenwood Springs, where he hoped that the waters might restore his health. His tuberculosis, however, was too far advanced for any cure. It is said that he was visited in his last days by Wyatt and Josie. He died of consumption at the age of thirty-six on November 8, 1887.

Another entire book could be written of the further adventures of Wyatt and Josephine. After Wyatt's escape from Arizona, they rendezvoused in San Francisco in late 1882. Mattie Blaylock was by then living in Colton, California, hopefully waiting for Wyatt—a reconciliation that never happened. Instead, Wyatt and Josephine began a life together that would last nearly fifty years, taking them to "every mining camp and racetrack from Texas to Mexico to Alaska."[22] The two are said to have been married in 1888 after Mattie Blaylock's death (from an overdose of laudanum, an opiate, assumed by most to have been a suicide).

Wyatt and Josephine pursued a fast life, moving from one get-rich opportunity to another. Wyatt returned briefly to Dodge City in 1883 at the request of his old friend Luke Short. As a member of the sarcastically named Dodge City Peace Commission, he managed to resolve a political-business-gambling-and-prostitution dispute between Short and the city government. No shots were fired.

Mostly, however, Wyatt and Josephine sought their fortune, from gambling in El Paso to gold hunting in Idaho. For a time they settled in southern California, where Wyatt owned several racehorses and sold real estate. It was not long, however, before they began traveling again. In 1893 they attended Chicago's Columbian Exposition, where Wyatt may have exchanged western reminiscences with Buffalo Bill Cody. In 1885 or 1886 they visited Doc Holliday in Denver, although the legend later developed that they attended Doc at his deathbed two years later.

Wyatt had an additional brush with notoriety in 1896 when he refereed a heavyweight boxing match between "Ruby Robert" Fitzsimmons and "Sailor" Tom Sharkey that was touted as a title bout, due to the temporary retirement of Gentleman Jim Corbett. Although the promoters' championship claim was dubious, that did not prevent the contest from drawing great attention and considerable gambling interest. Brought in as a last-minute stand-in (the two camps could not agree on an acceptable referee), Wyatt was not well-prepared for the event, which was one of the first fights in San Francisco to be conducted under the relatively new Marquess of Queensberry rules. He came straight to the arena from a racetrack, with no time to meet in advance with the fighters or their managers. At the opening bell, he stepped into the ring with a pistol visible in his waistband, and the match was allowed to proceed only after the referee had been disarmed by a police officer.

Notwithstanding that rocky start, the fight seemed to be under control until the eighth round, when Fitzsimmons, who was famed for his "solar plexus punch," appeared to knock out Sharkey with a stiff blow to the body. Writhing on the canvas, the challenger claimed to have been hit below the belt. Stunning the crowd, referee Earp agreed, awarding the match, and the ten thousand–dollar purse, to Sharkey by disqualification.[23] A scandal erupted, as Fitzsimmons's backers, and many San Francisco newspapers, accused Wyatt of participating in a fix. Wyatt defended his decision, but the controversy continued for months. Once again, rival newspapers—in this case, the *Call* and the *Examiner*—alternately attacked and defended Wyatt Earp's integrity, each one invoking his exploits (as either heroics or crimes) in Arizona.

Fitzsimmons's manager brought the matter to court, alleging that Wyatt was part of a conspiracy to fix the fight in favor of Sharkey. During several days of hearings, witness after witness testified to the details of the alleged scheme, often implicating the referee. Wyatt testified in defense of his honor, stating, "I was offered no money . . . to give an unfair decision. I would not have listened to a proposition of that kind to begin with, and everybody who knows me will not doubt my word."[24] In the end, there was no conclusive resolution. Though prizefighting was tolerated in San Francisco, the court determined that boxing was still illegal under California law and therefore refused to enter an order in favor of either party. Wyatt's decision in favor of Sharkey would stand, but it was not exactly upheld. Many boxing historians now believe that Wyatt was duped by Sharkey's theatrics but that he was not part of a plot to defraud Fitzsimmons. Nonetheless, Wyatt's reputation in San Francisco sporting circles took a sharp blow from which he would never recover.

From 1897 through 1901, Wyatt was frequently in Alaska, running saloons and gambling halls while intermittently prospecting for gold (he often wintered in San Francisco). In Nome, he was reunited with George Parsons and John Clum and thereafter stayed in touch with his old friends for the rest of his life.

By 1905, Wyatt and Josephine were living in southern California, staking mining claims in the Mojave Desert. Fortune continued to elude them, however, as Wyatt's various business efforts never quite fulfilled their promises. Settling in Los Angeles, Wyatt found that the stories of his Arizona exploits followed him, this time to some advantage. He became a fixture on the Hollywood sets of the early cowboy films; some say he was an "advisor," others say he was just hanging out. Toward the end of his life, Wyatt made several efforts at publishing his biography—for the sake of the historical record as well as his own finances—eventually producing a clumsy manuscript with the assistance of a friend named John Flood. Finally, Stuart Lake managed to arrange several interviews with Wyatt, resulting in the publication of *Wyatt Earp: Frontier Marshal* in 1931.

Wyatt did not live to see his story told. He died just short of his eighty-first birthday in January 1929, one day after he received a final visit from his old friend John Clum. Josephine arranged for Wyatt to be buried in the Jewish section of the Hills of Eternity Cemetery in Colma, California, though she was too distraught to attend the funeral. Wyatt's pallbearers included John Clum and George Parsons, as well as cowboy stars Tom Mix and William S. Hart.

Josephine lived another fifteen years, until 1944, spending much of her time defending Wyatt's reputation and threatening legal action against his would-be biographers, including Stuart Lake. Determined to safeguard her privacy and sense of propriety, she managed to keep herself almost entirely out of the public record, including Lake's book, during her lifetime. Her grave is next to Wyatt's.

Retrospect

By any measure, Virgil Earp's leadership of the Tombstone police force was a disaster. Not only did he fail to bring the Cowboys under control, but his tactics actually created a good measure of sympathy for the rustlers and enhanced legitimacy for their supporters. By the time Wyatt Earp left Arizona, Ike Clanton and John Ringo were riding in a sheriff's posse, with much support from the citizenry—an event that would have been unimaginable even a few months earlier.

As to the famous gunfight, Judge Spicer was absolutely correct that Virgil handled it, at best, "incautiously and without due circumspection." Rather than ratchet down the potential for violence, he exacerbated the situation by recruiting Doc Holliday, even though he had other deputies—including Officers Bronk, Campbell, and Flynn—who could have been enlisted to help. Instead of relying on the official police force, Virgil made the confrontation seem personal, and therefore more threatening to the Cowboys, by arming his brothers and Holliday. He interrupted Sheriff Behan's efforts to disarm the Clantons and McLaurys, although there did not appear to be any urgent necessity (even if the four men had been staking out Holliday's rooming house, Virgil obviously knew that Doc was not home). Perhaps worst of all, Virgil decided to enforce an ultimatum—planning to disarm the Cowboys if they stepped out of the O.K. Corral—that was never communicated to Billy, Frank, Ike, or Tom. Or even to Johnny Behan, for that matter.

On previous occasions, both Virgil and Wyatt had been able to maintain order in difficult circumstances without resort to lethal force, yet their encounter with the Clantons and McLaurys resulted in almost immediate gunplay. The McLaury brothers were dealers in stolen cattle, but they were not professional gunslingers like Curly Bill and John Ringo, or stagecoach robbers like Frank Stilwell and Pete Spence. Nothing known about the McLaurys' background suggests that they were planning a shoot-out with the Earps, although, along with Billy Clanton, they certainly ended up provoking one. Still, it is hard to escape the conclusion that Virgil could have avoided the killings if only he had been more willing to wait out the Cowboys, rather than face them down.

None of this amounts to murder, of course. But Virgil's actions (and those of his deputies) still raise a crucial question: Why did they choose to force the issue, rather than allow the tension to dissipate? One answer is that the Earps were angry or fed up with the Cowboys in general and Ike Clanton in particular—and they were therefore determined to prove just who ran the streets of Tombstone. Could the Earps have been angling for a physical confrontation? Hoping to send a message to Curly Bill and John Ringo (not to mention Johnny Behan and Harry Woods), did they decide to make a nondeadly example out of the hapless, and relatively less dangerous, Clantons and McLaurys? If so, their conduct was uncomfortably close to manslaughter. More to the point, a capable prosecutor could have used the history of animosity between the Earps and the Cowboys to establish that the posse acted in a "spirit of revenge," if not malice.

But the prosecutors pursued a murder charge, impelled not only by the angry public reaction to the shootings, but also by motives of political opportunism and personal revenge. Murder, however, requires proof of malicious intent that the prosecution was not able to produce. The defendants were all duly released. They may not have been completely blameless, but they turned out to be just innocent enough.

Notes

The longhand transcript of the proceedings in *Territory of Arizona v. Morgan Earp, et al.* survived until the 1930s, when it came into the possession of a Works Projects Administration writer named Hal L. Hayhurst. As part of a never-finished book or article, Hayhurst typed out an edited version of the transcript that included much of the verbatim record along with his own summaries and editorial comments. Unfortunately, Hayhurst never returned the original document to the court file, and it was evidently destroyed along with his personal effects when the writer died. The Hayhurst typescript was edited and published in 1981 by Alford Turner under the title *The O.K. Corral Inquest.* Turner himself critiques the Hayhurst document as incomplete and anti-Earp, but it is nonetheless the most widely available version of the hearing record.

Daily accounts of the proceeding, often verbatim, were also published in Tombstone's competing newspapers, the *Nugget* and the *Epitaph.* Of these, the *Nugget*'s reports are generally considered the most complete, as they were written by Richard Rule, an exceptionally talented professional journalist. While there are frequent discrepancies between the *Nugget* and the Hayhurst/Turner transcripts, the differences are by and large irrelevant to the larger questions of trial strategy. Because it is more accessible, all quotations to the hearing record are therefore taken from Hayhurst/Turner, unless otherwise indicated. I have cited the *Nugget* only where its report is significantly more extensive or where other indications establish it as more reliable.

One of the more noticeable, though less important, differences between the *Nugget* and the Hayhurst/Turner typescript is in the spelling of surnames, which had not been standardized in the 1880s. This is true of many other sources as well, leading to variations such as McLaury/McLowery, Ringo/Ringold, and Earp/Erp. For the sake of readability, I have adopted the most common modern usages throughout,

and have emended quotations for consistency, rather than pepper the text with vari-
ant spellings followed by parenthetical Latinisms (*sic*).

For historical context, other than the legal proceedings, I have relied primarily on
Allen Barra's *Inventing Wyatt Earp: His Life and Many Legends,* Paula Mitchell
Marks's *And Die in the West: The Story of the O.K. Corral Gunfight,* and Casey
Tefertiller's *Wyatt Earp: The Life Behind the Legend.* The writers have different per-
spectives and interpretations, but there is a general consensus among them regarding
most of the major events.

Chapter 1. Slap Leather

1. Garry Wills, *A Necessary Evil,* 247.

Chapter 2. From Dodge City to Tombstone

1. *Dodge City Times,* July 7, 1877, cited in Bob Boze Bell, *The Illustrated Life and
Times of Wyatt Earp,* 25; *Ford County Globe,* June 18, 1878, cited in Bell *(Wyatt
Earp),* 27.
2. Cited in Casey Tefertiller, *Wyatt Earp: The Life Behind the Legend,* 28.
3. Allen Barra, *Inventing Wyatt Earp: His Life and Many Legends,* 85.
4. Tefertiller, 29.
5. Cited in Bell *(Wyatt Earp),* 29; Barra, 86; cited in Tefertiller, 30.
6. "How Wyatt Earp Routed a Gang of Arizona Outlaws," *San Francisco
Examiner,* August 2, 1896, reproduced in Alford Turner, *The Earps Talk,* 5.
7. Bell *(Wyatt Earp),* 31.
8. Clara Brown, *Tombstone from a Woman's Point of View,* 17.
9. Barra, 95.
10. George Parsons, *The Private Journal of George W. Parsons,* 120; Clara Brown, 20.
11. Stuart Lake, *Wyatt Earp, Frontier Marshal,* 253–54.
12. Cited in Tefertiller, 45.
13. Barra, 95.
14. Tefertiller, 92, 99.
15. Clara Brown, 40.
16. Parsons, 178, 179.
17. January 27, 1881; cited in Steve Gatto, *The Real Wyatt Earp: A Documentary
Biography,* 76–77; March 17, 1881; cited in Tefertiller, 79; October 8, 1881, cited in
Tefertiller, 110.
18. Quoted in Tefertiller, 112.
19. Parsons, 118.
20. Paula Mitchell Marks, *And Die in the West: The Story of the O.K. Corral
Gunfight,* 94; Tefertiller, 43, 107.
21. October 3, 1881, cited in Tefertiller, 111.
22. Richard Maxwell Brown, *No Duty to Retreat: Violence and Values in American
History and Society,* 71.

23. Parsons, 108.

24. Tefertiller, 36.

25. John Clum, *Apache Days and Tombstone Nights: John Clum's Autobiography, 1877–1887*, 23.

26. August 13, 1881, quoted in Douglas Martin, *Tombstone's Epitaph*, 150.

27. April 16, 1881, quoted in Martin, 151.

28. Richard Maxwell Brown, 71.

Chapter 3. Prelude to a Gunfight

1. Quoted in Richard Erwin, *The Truth about Wyatt Earp*, 204.

2. August 5, 1880, quoted in Tefertiller, 44; quoted in Marks, 91.

3. Tefertiller, 44.

4. *San Francisco Examiner*, August 2, 1896, quoted in Turner (*Earps Talk*), 5; Barra, 288.

5. Bob Boze Bell, *The Illustrated Life and Times of Doc Holliday*, 17, 31–32.

6. *Tombstone Nugget*, October 12, 1880, quoted in Marks, 102.

7. Martin, 177.

8. Quoted in Tefertiller, 51.

9. November 8, 1880, quoted in Tefertiller, 54.

10. Sippy also won a regular election in January 1881, in which Virgil Earp did not run.

11. Boyer, *I Married Wyatt Earp*, 11, 12.

12. Quoted in Barra, 113.

13. Parsons, 134.

14. Parsons, 137.

15. March 18, 1881, quoted in Erwin, 259.

16. Arizona Compiled Laws, 1864–77, sections 19 and 40; quoted in Tefertiller, 80.

17. Karen Holliday Tanner, *Doc Holliday: A Family Portrait*, 151. Allen Barra writes that Behan acted from partisan motives and that "Behan's County Sheriff's Office had been at cross-purposes with the town marshal and federal marshal from the beginning." Barra, 144. Bob Boze Bell calls "the rivalry between Johnny Behan and Wyatt Earp . . . a rough and tumble political brawl." Bell *(Doc Holliday)*, 43.

18. July 10, 1881, quoted in Erwin, 246.

19. September 13, 1881, quoted in Erwin, 255.

20. Stilwell did not live to stand trial. He was killed in the aftermath of the O.K. Corral gunfight, one of the many victims of the feud between the Earps and the Cowboys.

21. September 20, 1881, quoted in Tefertiller, 111–12.

Chapter 4. Thirty Shots in Thirty Seconds

1. John Clum, *It All Happened in Tombstone*, 1.

2. October 27, 1881, quoted in Casey Tefertiller and Jeff Morey, "O.K. Corral: A Gunfight Shrouded in Mystery."

3. Parsons, 188.

4. Martin, 188.

5. Martin, 189–90.

6. October 27, 1881, quoted in Barra, 184.

Chapter 5. Invitation to an Inquest

1. Quoted in Tefertiller and Morey.

2. October 28, 1881, cited in Martin, 190.

3. Clara Brown, 43.

4. Tefertiller, 126.

5. Arizona Statutes, Chapter IV, section 4 (1877).

6. Interestingly, one member of the coroner's jury is identified in some surviving documents as B. S. Goodrich. Two Goodrich brothers lived in Tombstone at the time, Ben and Briggs. Both men were Texas lawyers and Confederate veterans, almost certain to be unsympathetic to the Earps. Ben Goodrich would join the prosecution team as associate counsel, and he was probably already advising Ike Clanton by the time of the inquest. Briggs was active in Democratic Party politics and would later serve as the territory's attorney general. The *Nugget*, however, identified the juror as "W. S. Goodrich," who is not known to have been related to Ben and Briggs. If the juror's first name was William, then the error could be attributed to his likely nickname, Bill. *Tombstone Nugget*, October 29, 1881.

7. Arizona Statutes, Chapter IV, section 7 (1877).

8. Arizona Statutes, Chapter X, section 21 (1877).

9. October 30, 1881.

10. Arizona Statutes, Chapter IV, sections 9–12 (1877). A finding of "criminal means" further obligated the coroner to issue an immediate warrant for the arrest of the accused. Section 12.

11. Arizona Statutes, Chapter X, section 22 (1877).

12. Tefertiller, 130; Barra, 191.

13. No copy of the complaint appears to have survived, but all evidence indicates that it did not distinguish among the defendants. The prosecution in the criminal case made no effort to establish separate levels of culpability, treating each defendant as fully responsible for the acts of the others. The following February, after the initial case against the Earps was dismissed, Ike Clanton filed yet another murder charge, this time in Contention rather than Tombstone. That complaint, clearly drafted by a lawyer, again probably Ben Goodrich, did not distinguish among the four defendants.

14. Clara Brown, 43; Parsons, 189.

Chapter 6. Judge Spicer's Court

1. Arizona Statutes, Chapter XI, sections 142, 143 (1877); Chapter XI, section 128 (1877).

2. October 31, 1881, quoted in Martin, 191.

3. Bat Masterson, "Famous Gun Fighters of the Western Frontier," *Human Life,* Vol. IV (April 1907), 10, quoted in Joseph Rosa, *The Gunfighter: Man or Myth?* 141; Parsons, 129.

4. Quoted in Martin, 83.

5. Quoted in Tefertiller, 44.

6. Arizona Statutes, Chapter XI, section 11 (1877).

7. Richard Maxwell Brown, 76.

8. Tefertiller, 156.

9. Lynn Bailey, *A Tale of the "Unkilled": The Life, Times, and Writings of Wells W. Spicer,* 63.

10. Sally Denton, *American Massacre: The Tragedy at Mountain Meadows, September 1857,* 222.

11. Will Bagley, *Blood of the Prophets: Brigham Young and the Massacre at Mountain Meadows,* 300.

12. Quoted in Bagley, 302.

13. Quoted in Bagley, 305. Until his death, Lee would refer to Hamblin as "Dirty Fingered Jake." Denton, 229.

14. Eric Moody, *Western Carpetbagger: The Extraordinary Memoirs of "Senator" Thomas Fitch,* vii.

15. Moody, 81.

16. Parsons, 159.

17. "Statement of Thomas Fitch" (1838–1923), Bancroft Library, 4–5.

18. Moody, 110.

19. He is not, for instance, included in Lynn Bailey and Don Chaput, *Cochise County Stalwarts: A Who's Who of the Territorial Years.*

20. Quoted in Tefertiller, 68.

21. Jay Wagoner, *Arizona Territory, 1863–1912: A Political History,* 452.

Chapter 7. "I Don't Want to Fight"

1. Arizona Statutes, Chapter XI, section 478 (1877); Chapter XI, section 479 (1877).

2. *Tombstone Epitaph,* quoted in Erwin, 268; Gary Roberts, "The Gunfight at the O.K. Corral: The Wells Spicer Decision," *Montana: The Magazine of Western History,* 66; Arizona Statutes, Chapter XI, section 140 (1877).

3. Tefertiller, 132.

4. The cross examinations of Wes Fuller and Thomas Keefe both covered the location of the wound on Billy Clanton's wrist. In each case, the record notes that the witness was asked to point out the corresponding spot on Fitch's wrist, indicating that he was the cross examiner. Billy Allen described "the character of the wound on Billy Clanton's wrist by pointing to Mr. Fitch's wrist"; Thomas Keefe illustrated "upon the arm of Mr. Fitch, the direction in which the ball passed through the arm of Billy Clanton."

5. *Tombstone Nugget,* November 3, 1881.

6. Roberts, 66.

7. *Tombstone Epitaph,* November 3, 1881, quoted in Roberts, 66.

8. Turner, quoted in Barra, 195–96; Marks, 227; Barra, 196–97.

9. Lake, 250: "Wyatt threw his shotgun before him, left hand on the fire-end, right on grip and triggers."

10. The majority of nickel-plated Colts were short-barreled, some as short as three inches, making them much less accurate than the standard seven-inch model. Ron Graham, John Kopec, Kenneth Moore, *A Study of the Colt Single Action Army Revolver,* 71–73. The self-cocking, or double-action, models were not only hard to aim, but weak mechanisms also made them unreliable. According to writer and publisher Bob Boze Bell, Samuel Colt himself disfavored double-action revolvers because they could not be fired accurately. Bell *(Doc Holliday),* 34.

11. The witness was Thomas Keefe. Fitch cross examined him about an arrest in Bodie, occasioned when Keefe suspected another man of "being intimate with my woman." A fight ensued, for which the witness was jailed and then "honorably acquitted."

12. Quoted in Barra, 385.

13. *San Francisco Examiner,* November 7, 1881, quoted in Tefertiller, 134; *Arizona Weekly Star,* November 10, 1881, quoted in Tefertiller, 134.

14. Arizona Statutes, Chapter X, section 21 (1877).

15. Barra, 200.

Chapter 8. "I Think We Can Hang Them"

1. Quoted in Marks, 265.

2. Tefertiller, 135; quoted in Erwin, 273; quoted in Tefertiller, 146; quoted in Marks, 265–69.

3. Quoted in Erwin, 273.

4. Quoted in Marks, 266.

5. Quoted in Marks, 268.

6. Quoted in Marks, 268–69.

7. Barra, 200.

8. *Tombstone Nugget,* November 9, 1881.

9. *Tombstone Nugget,* November 9, 1881.

10. Quoted in Erwin, 273.

11. Barra, 202; Tefertiller, 138.

12. Quoted in Marks, 265.

13. Ike later admitted that he told the story to County Recorder Jones on Sunday, November 13, which was after his direct examination had ended. Ike might have told it to others as well in the weeks between the gunfight and the hearing, although there is no record of that. Paula Mitchell Marks says that rumors were flying around Tombstone of the Earps' involvement in the Benson stage robbery, though she gives no examples. But even if Ike's story, or versions of it, had been discussed in saloons and dance halls, it was most definitely omitted from his direct examination and

introduced only after he had an opportunity to confer with counsel—Will McLaury?—during court recesses.

14. Quoted in Erwin, 273; quoted in Tefertiller, 135.

Chapter 9. "In Defense of My Own Life"

1. Tefertiller, 155.

2. Arizona Statutes, Chapter XI, section 133 (1877); Chapter XI, section 135 (1877).

3. *Tombstone Nugget,* November 17, 1881.

4. According to Stuart Lake, Joe Hill later rode into Tombstone and "substantiated in detail Wyatt's account of the conspiracy in which Hill, Ike Clanton, and Frank McLaury had agreed to betray Leonard, Head, and Crane and had exonerated Doc Holliday from all connection with the attempt to rob the Benson stage." Lake, 319.

5. See *Ferguson v. Georgia,* 360 U.S. 570, 577 n.6 (1960); Arizona Statutes, Chapter XLVIII, section 393 (1877). In other regards, Arizona witness law was not so progressive. Neither Indians nor "Negroes," or persons having "one-half or more" of such blood, could testify in "an action or proceeding to which a white person is a party." Arizona Statutes, Chapter XLVIII, section 396 (1877).

6. Marks, 280.

7. Arizona Statutes, Chapter XI, section 136 (1877); Chapter XI, Section 137 (1877).

8. Salt Lake *Daily Herald,* January 1, 1875, quoted in Bailey, 58.

9. Turner *The O.K. Corral Inquest,* 125.

10. Martin, 88.

11. Turner *(Inquest),* 125; Marks, 221; *San Francisco Examiner,* reproduced in Turner *(Earps Talk),* 7.

12. Boyer, 92; Tefertiller and Morey, 38.

13. Tefertiller and Morey, 38.

14. Arizona Statutes, Chapter X, section 266 (1877).

Chapter 10. "I Want Your Guns"

1. Quoted in Tefertiller, 146.

2. Arizona Statutes, Chapter XI, section 19 (1877): "Whenever the officers of justice are authorized to act in the prevention of public offenses, other persons who, by their command, act in their aid are justified in so doing."

3. This is one of the passages in which there is a substantive difference between the *Nugget* report and the Turner/Hayhurst document. According to Turner/Hayhurst, Virgil's next comment was "I don't hardly know how Ike Clanton was standing, but I think he had his hands in an attitude where I supposed he had a gun." Turner *(Inquest),* 193. In the *Nugget,* however, Virgil's testimony is, "I *don't* think he had his hands in an attitude where I supposed he had a gun." *Tombstone Nugget,* November 20, 1881 (emphasis added). Although the difference is not crucial for our purposes, the likelihood is that the Turner/Hayhurst version is correct, as

Virgil comments in the next paragraph that "Ike Clanton threw his hand in his breast," as though he was reaching for a gun. Turner *(Inquest)*, 193.

4. *Tombstone Nugget,* November 24, 1881.

5. In answering questions, the witness twice referred to Price in the third person.

6. Both the Hayhurst transcript and the account in the *Nugget* are clear that Bourland was cross examined and dismissed from the stand before the noon recess. Additional questioning, by Spicer and then by the prosecution, was initiated when court reconvened.

Chapter 11. Decision

1. There appears to be no definitive Arizona case defining "sufficient evidence" as of 1881. Other contemporary authorities, however, make it clear that the standard was a low one, roughly the equivalent of the modern concept of "probable cause." *Blackstone's Commentaries,* perhaps the leading source of law during a time when books were scarce, suggested that sufficient evidence could be found unless "it manifestly appears that no such crime has been committed, or that the suspicion entertained of the prisoner was wholly groundless." Cited in *In re Van Campen,* 28 F.Cas. 954 (S.D.NY 1868). The courts in other jurisdictions articulated various tests in analogous situations. One Missouri court looked for "circumstances sufficiently strong to induce such belief [in guilt] in the mind of a reasonable and cautious man." *Vansickle v. Brown,* 68 Mo. 627 (1878). A California court defined the standard as "positive evidence of facts tending to show guilt." *Ex Parte Dimmig,* 74 Cal. 164 (1887).

2. Arizona Statutes, Chapter X, sections 22 and 30 (1877).

3. *Tombstone Epitaph,* August 27, 1880, cited in Martin, 91. See also Arizona Statutes, Chapter X, section 30 (1877).

4. Tefertiller, 152. Barra put it this way: "Testimony regarding the Cowboys having their hands in the air, which was disputed by the Earps and unsupported by neutral testimony, would not be considered." Barra, 210.

5. Johnny Behan, although rather obviously biased, was technically a neutral witness rather than an "interested party." He would have been permitted to testify, and subjected to cross examination, even in jurisdictions that had not abolished the interested party disqualification.

6. Marks, 295.

7. Quoted in Barra, 200.

8. Arizona Statutes, Chapter X, section 21 (1877); Chapter X, section 22 (1877).

9. Arizona Statutes, Chapter X, section 23 (1877).

10. Arizona Statutes, Chapter X, section 22 (1877).

11. Arizona Statutes, Chapter X, sections 29 and 30 (1877).

12. Quoted in Martin, 90.

13. Barra, 211; Tefertiller, 152.

Chapter 12. Aftermath

1. *Tombstone Nugget,* December 1, 1881.
2. Clara Brown, 47.
3. Clum *(It All Happened in Tombstone),* 26.
4. Quoted in Erwin, 371.
5. Quoted in Tefertiller, 170.
6. Parsons, 199.
7. Quoted in Martin, 215; Parsons, 199.
8. Quoted in Tefertiller, 175.
9. Quoted in Tefertiller, 175.
10. Quoted in Tefertiller, 185.
11. Reproduced in Turner *(Inquest),* 230.
12. Reproduced in Turner *(Inquest),* 244.
13. Reproduced in Turner *(Inquest),* 242.
14. Quoted in Martin, 217–18.
15. Clara Brown, 57.
16. Marks, 341. Allen Barra agrees that "he saw the powerlessness of the law in this time and place. Now he would settle matters himself." Barra, 233. If possible, Casey Tefertiller puts it even more bluntly: "By his way of thinking, Wyatt Earp would have to become a justice unto himself to avenge Morgan's death." Tefertiller, 201.
17. Quoted in Marks, 342–43; quoted in Barra, 250.
18. Martin, 224.
19. Quoted in Martin, 224.
20. Tefertiller, 233; Parsons, 213. Behan was evidently paid by the mile for his posse work.
21. Parsons, 213.
22. Barra, 101.
23. To this day, there has been only one other time that a putative heavyweight title has changed hands on a foul. In 1930, Max Schmeling won the vacant title from Jack Sharkey (no relation) by disqualification in an elimination match following Gene Tunney's retirement. Mike Tyson's more recent ear-biting disqualification came when he was trying to regain the championship from Evander Holyfield.
24. Quoted in Tefertiller, 298.

Bibliography

Sources Cited

Books and Articles

Bagley, Will. *Blood of the Prophets: Brigham Young and the Massacre at Mountain Meadows*. Norman: University of Oklahoma Press, 2002.

Bailey, Lynn R. *A Tale of the "Unkilled": The Life, Times, and Writings of Wells W. Spicer, the Man Who Defended John D. Lee and Exonerated the Earps and Doc Holliday*. Tucson, Ariz.: Westernlore Press, 1999.

Bailey, Lynn R., and Don Chaput. *Cochise County Stalwarts: A Who's Who of the Territorial Years, Volumes I and II*. Tucson, Ariz.: Westernlore Press, 2000.

Barra, Allen. *Inventing Wyatt Earp: His Life and Many Legends*. New York: Carroll & Graf Publishers, Inc., 1998.

Bell, Bob Boze. *The Illustrated Life and Times of Doc Holliday*. Phoenix, Ariz.: Tri-Star Boze Publications, 1995.

———. *The Illustrated Life and Times of Wyatt Earp*. Phoenix, Ariz.: Tri-Star Boze Publications, 1995.

Boyer, Glenn G. *I Married Wyatt Earp: The Recollections of Josephine Sarah Marcus Earp*. Tucson: The University of Arizona Press, 1976.

Brown, Clara Spalding. *Tombstone from a Woman's Point of View: The Correspondence of Clara Spalding Brown, July 7, 1880, to November 14, 1882*. Edited by Lynn R. Bailey. Tucson, Ariz.: Westernlore Press, 1998.

Brown, Richard Maxwell. *No Duty to Retreat: Violence and Values in American History and Society*. New York: Oxford University Press, 1992.

Clum, John. *It All Happened in Tombstone*. Flagstaff, Ariz.: Northland Press, 1965.

———. *Apache Days and Tombstone Nights: John Clum's Autobiography, 1877–1887*. Edited by Neil B. Carmony. Silver City, N.M.: High Lonesome Books, 1997.

Denton, Sally. *American Massacre: The Tragedy at Mountain Meadows, September 1857.* New York: Knopf Publishing, 2003.

Erwin, Richard. *The Truth about Wyatt Earp.* Carpentera, Calif.: The O.K. Press, 1992.

Gatto, Steve. *The Real Wyatt Earp: A Documentary Biography.* Edited by Neil B. Carmony. Silver City, N.M.: High Lonesome Books, 2000.

Graham, Ron, John Kopec, and Kenneth Moore. *A Study of the Colt Single Action Army Revolver.* N.p., 1976.

Lake, Stuart N. *Wyatt Earp, Frontier Marshal.* Boston: Houghton Mifflin Co., 1931.

Marks, Paula Mitchell. *And Die in the West: The Story of the O.K. Corral Gunfight.* Norman: University of Oklahoma Press, 1989.

Martin, Douglas D. *Tombstone's Epitaph.* Albuquerque: University of New Mexico Press, 1959.

Moody, Eric N. *Western Carpetbagger: The Extraordinary Memoirs of "Senator" Thomas Fitch.* Reno, Nev.: Great Basin Press, 1978.

Parsons, George W. *The Private Journal of George W. Parsons.* Tombstone, Ariz.: Tombstone Epitaph, 1972.

Roberts, Gary L. "The Gunfight at the O.K. Corral: The Wells Spicer Decision," *Montana: The Magazine of Western History,* vol. 20 (Winter 1970): 63–74.

Rosa, Joseph G. *The Gunfighter: Man or Myth?* Norman: University of Oklahoma Press, 1969.

Tanner, Karen Holliday. *Doc Holliday: A Family Portrait.* Norman: University of Oklahoma Press, 1998.

Tefertiller, Casey. *Wyatt Earp: The Life Behind the Legend.* New York: John Wiley & Sons, Inc., 1997.

Tefertiller, Casey, and Jeff Morey. "O.K. Corral: A Gunfight Shrouded in Mystery," *Wild West* (October 2001): 38.

Turner, Alford. *The Earps Talk.* College Station, Tex.: Creative West Publishing, 1980.

———. *The O.K. Corral Inquest.* College Station, Tex.: Creative West Publishing, 1981.

Wagoner, Jay. *Arizona Territory, 1863–1912: A Political History.* Tucson: University of Arizona Press, 1970.

Waters, Frank. *The Earp Brothers of Tombstone.* New York: Clarkson N. Potter, 1960.

Wills, Garry. *A Necessary Evil: A History of American Distrust of Government.* New York: Simon & Schuster, 1999.

Other Materials

Arizona Compiled Laws, 1864–77, sections 19, 40.

Arizona Statutes, Chapter IV, sections 4, 7, 9–12 (1877).

Arizona Statutes, Chapter X, sections 21–23, 29, 30, 266 (1877).

Arizona Statutes, Chapter XI, sections 11, 19, 128, 133, 135–137, 140, 142, 143, 292, 478, 479 (1877).

Arizona Statutes, Chapter XLVIII, sections 393, 396 (1877).

Blackstone's Commentaries.

Ex Parte Dimmig, 74 Cal. 164 (1887).

Ferguson v. Georgia, 360 U.S. 570, 577 n.6 (1960).

Fitch, Thomas. "Statement of Thomas Fitch" (1823–1923) Bancroft Library, Berkeley, Calif., undated.

McLaury, Will. Letters, New York Historical Society, New York City.

Tombstone Epitaph, November 1881.

Tombstone Nugget, November 1881.

In re Van Campen, 28 F.Cas. 954 (S.D.NY 1868).

Vansickle v. Brown, 68 Mo. 627 (1878).

Further Reading

The following is a fairly extensive, but still incomplete, list of the many published books devoted to "Earpiana" and related subjects. Inclusion in this compilation should not be taken as an endorsement or a guarantee of reliability.

Adams, Andy. *The Log of a Cowboy: A Narrative of the Old Trail Days.* Boston: Houghton Mifflin Co., 1903.

Adams, Ramon F. *Burs under the Saddle: A Second Look at Books and Histories of the West.* Norman: University of Oklahoma Press, 1964.

Aggeler, Geoff. *Confessions of John Ringo: A Fictional Memoir of Johnny Ringo, Guerrilla and Outlaw.* New York: E. P. Dutton, 1987.

Alagna, Magdalena. *Wyatt Earp: Lawman of the American West.* New York: Rosen Publishing Group, 2004.

Alexander, Bob. *John H. Behan: Sacrificed Sheriff.* Introduction by Paula Mitchell Marks. Silver City, N.M.: High Lonesome Books, 2002.

Altshuler, Constance Wynn. *Starting with Defiance: Nineteenth Century Arizona Military Posts.* Tucson, Ariz.: Arizona Historical Society, 1983.

Backus, Anna Jean. *Mountain Meadows Witness: The Life of Bishop Philip Klingensmith.* Spokane, Wash.: Arthur H. Clark, 1995.

Bailey, Lynn R. *Henry Clay Hooker and the Sierra Bonita.* Tucson, Ariz.: Westernlore Press, 1998.

———. *The Valiants: The Tombstone Rangers and Apache War Frivolities.* Tucson, Ariz.: Westernlore Press, 1999.

Ball, Larry D. *The United States Marshals of New Mexico and Arizona Territories, 1846–1912.* Albuquerque: University of New Mexico Press, 1978.

———. *The High Sheriffs of New Mexico and Arizona Territories, 1846–1912.* Albuquerque: University of New Mexico Press, 1992.

Bartholomew, Ed. *Wyatt Earp, 1848–1880: The Untold Story.* Toyahvale, Tex.: Frontier Book Company, 1963.

———. *Wyatt Earp, 1879–1882: The Man and the Myth.* Toyahvale, Tex.: Frontier Book Company, 1964.

Bechdolt, Frederick R. *When the West Was Young.* New York: The Century Co., 1922.

Benjamin, Stan. *Tombstone Lawmen, 1880–1999*. Privately published by the author, 1999.

Bourke, John Gregory. *An Apache Campaign in the Sierra Madres*. New York: Scribner's Sons, 1886; Lincoln: University of Nebraska Press, 1987.

Bowman, John S., ed. *The World Almanac of the American West*. New York: Pharos Books, 1986.

Boyer, Glenn G. *Suppressed Murder of Wyatt Earp*. San Antonio, Tex.: The Naylor Company, 1967.

———. *Wyatt Earp's Tombstone Vendetta*. Honolulu, Hawaii: Talei Publishers, 1993.

———. *Wyatt Earp: Facts—Early American Ancestors (1680 to Wyatt's Birth in 1848)*. Rodeo, N.M.: Historical Research Associates, 1996.

———. *Wyatt Earp: Facts—By Wagon Train from Iowa to California, 1864*. Rodeo, N.M.: Historical Research Associates, 1997.

———. *Wyatt Earp: Facts—Wyatt Wears His First Badge Lamar, Mo*. Rodeo, N.M.: Historical Research Associates, 1997.

———. *Wyatt Earp, Family, Friends & Foes, Vol. I: Who Was Big Nose Kate?* Rodeo, N.M.: Historical Research Associates, 1997.

———. *Wyatt Earp, Family, Friends & Foes, Vol. II: Who Was Sheriff Johnny Behan?* Rodeo, N.M.: Historical Research Associates, 1997.

———, ed. *Wyatt Earp by Wyatt S. Earp*. Sierra Vista, Ariz.: Yoma V. Bissette, 1981. (The text of this book was written by John H. Flood around 1926.)

Breakenridge, William M. (ghostwritten by William MacLeod Raine). *Helldorado: Bringing Law to the Mesquite*. Boston: Houghton Mifflin Co., 1928.

Brent, Lynton Wright. *The Bird Cage: A Theatrical Novel of Early Tombstone*. New York: Dorrance & Co., 1945.

Brooks, Juanita. *The Mountain Meadows Massacre*. 1950; Norman: University of Oklahoma Press, 2003.

Brown, Mrs. Hugh. *Lady in Boomtown*. New York: Ballantine Books, 1972.

Brown, Robert L. *Saloons of the American West*. Silverton, Colo.: Sundance Publications, 1978.

Burns, Walter Noble. *Tombstone: An Iliad of the Southwest*. New York: Doubleday, 1927.

Burrows, Jack. *John Ringo, the Gunfighter Who Never Was*. Tucson: University of Arizona Press, 1987.

Butler, Anne M. *Daughters of Joy, Sisters of Misery: Prostitutes in the American West, 1865–90*. Urbana: University of Illinois Press, 1987.

Canton, Frank M. *Frontier Trails*. Norman: University of Oklahoma Press, 1966.

Carmony, Neil B. *Next Stop: Tombstone—George Hand's Contention City Diary, 1882*. Tucson, Ariz.: Trail to Yesterday Books, 1995.

———. *Tombstone's Violent Years, 1880–1882, as Remembered by John Pleasant Gray*. Tucson, Ariz.: Trail to Yesterday Books, 1999.

Chafin, Earl, ed. *Wyatt's Woman. The Unvarnished Memoirs and Recollections of Josephine Sarah Marcus Earp*. Riverside, Calif.: Earl Chafin Press, 1998.

————, ed. *The O.K. Corral Testimony*. Riverside Calif.: Earl Chafin Press, 2001.

Chaput, Donald. *Virgil Earp: Western Peace Officer*. Encampment, Wyo.: Affiliated Writers of America, Inc., 1994.

————. *Dr. Goodfellow: Physician to the Gunfighters, Scholar, and Bon Vivant*. Tucson, Ariz.: Westernlore Press, 1996.

————. *"Buckskin Frank" Leslie*. Tucson, Ariz.: Westernlore Press, 1999.

————, ed. *The Earp Papers: In a Brother's Image*. Encampment, Wyo.: Affiliated Writers of America, Inc., 1994.

Chase, C. M. *New Mexico and Colorado in 1881*. Fort Davis, Tex.: Frontier Book Co., 1968.

Churchill, E. Richard. *Doc Holliday, Bat Masterson, & Wyatt Earp: Their Colorado Careers*. Denver: Timberline Books, 1974.

Cilch, Kenneth R. *Wyatt Earp, The Missing Years: San Diego in the 1880's*. San Diego, Calif.: Gaslamp Books, 1998.

Clum, Woodworth. *Apache Agent: The Story of John P. Clum*. Boston: Houghton Mifflin Co., 1936.

Collins, Charles. *The Great Escape: The Apache Outbreak of 1881*. Tucson, Ariz.: Westernlore Press, 1994.

Cox, William R. *Luke Short and His Era*. Garden City, N.Y.: Doubleday & Co., 1961.

Cresswell, Stephen. *Mormons, Moonshiners, Cowboys & Klansmen*. Tuscaloosa: University of Alabama Press, 1991.

Cunningham, Eugene. *Triggernometry: A Gallery of Gunfighters*. New York: The Press of the Pioneers, 1934.

DeArment, Robert K. *Bat Masterson: The Man and the Legend*. Norman: University of Oklahoma Press, 1979.

DeLafosse, Peter, ed. *Trailing the Pioneers*. Logan: Utah State University Press, 1994.

DeMattos, Jack. *The Earp Decision*. College Station, Tex.: Creative Publishing, 1989.

Dempsey, David, with Raymond P. Baldwin. *The Triumphs and Trials of Lotta Crabtree*. New York: Morrow, 1968.

Dillard, Margaret, and Gary Dillard. *Tales of Old Tombstone*. Tucson, Ariz.: Frontera House Press, 1995.

Dodge, Fred. *Under Cover for Wells Fargo*. Boston: Houghton Mifflin Co., 1969.

Dolph, Jerry, and Arthur Randall. *Wyatt Earp and Coeur d'Alene Gold! Stampede to Idaho Territory*. Eagle City, Idaho: Eagle City Publications, 2000.

Drago, Harry Sinclair. *Wild, Wooley & Wicked: The History of the Kansas Cow Towns and the Texas Cattle Trade*. New York: Clarkson N. Potter, 1960.

Dunn, J. P., Jr. *Massacres of the Mountains: A History of the Indian Wars of the Far West, 1815–1875*. New York: Harper Brothers, 1886; Mechanicsburg, Pa.: Stackpole Books, 2002.

Dykstra, Robert R. *The Cattle Towns*. New York: Knopf, 1968.

Earp, Wyatt. *How I Routed a Gang of Arizona Outlaws and Other Stories*. Edited by Neil B. Carmony. Tucson, Ariz.: Trail to Yesterday Books, 1995.

Everitt, David. *Legends: The Story of Wyatt Earp*. Knightsbridge, Mass.: Knightsbridge Publishing Co., 1990.

Fattig, Timothy W. *Wyatt Earp: The Biography.* Honolulu, Hawaii: Talei Publishers, 2003.

Faulk, Odie B. *Tombstone: Myth and Reality.* New York: Oxford University Press, 1972.

———. *Arizona: A Short History.* Norman: University of Oklahoma Press, 1974.

———. *Dodge City: The Most Western Town of All.* New York: Oxford University Press, 1977.

Fielding, Robert Kent. *Unsolicited Chronicler: An Account of the Gunnison Massacre, Its Causes and Consequences.* Brookline, Mass.: Paradigm Publications, 1993.

Fielding, Robert Kent, and Dorothy S. Fielding. *The Tribune Reports of the Trials of John D. Lee for the Massacre at Mountain Meadow.* Higganum, Conn.: Kent's Books, 2000.

Fischer, Ron W. *Nellie Cashman: Frontier Angel.* Honolulu, Hawaii: Talei Publishers, 2000.

———. *The Jewish Pioneers of Tombstone and Arizona Territory.* Ron W. Fischer Enterprises, 2002.

———, ed. *The Tombstone Business Directory, 1880–1884.* Ron W. Fischer Enterprises, 2002.

Flood, John Henry, Jr. *Wyatt Earp.* Riverside, Calif.: Earl Chafin DBA New Media Communications, 1997.

Ganzhorn, Jack. *I've Killed Men: An Epic of Early Arizona.* New York: Devin-Adair Co., 1959.

Gard, Wayne. *Frontier Justice.* Norman: University of Oklahoma Press, 1981.

Garrett, Patrick Floyd. *The Authentic Life of Billy the Kid.* Santa Fe: New Mexican Printing Co., 1882.

Gatto, Steve. *John Ringo: The Reputation of a Deadly Gunman.* Tucson, Ariz.: San Simon Publishing Company, 1995.

———. *Wyatt Earp: A Biography of a Western Lawman.* Tucson, Ariz.: San Simon Publishing Company, 1997.

———. *Johnny Ringo.* Protar House, 2002.

Gibbs, Josiah. *The Mountain Meadows Massacre.* Salt Lake City, Utah: Salt Lake Tribune Publishing Co., 1910.

Goff, John S. *Arizona Territorial Officials I: The Supreme Court Justices, 1863–1912.* Cave Creek, Ariz.: Black Mountain Press, 1975.

———. *Arizona Territorial Officials II: The Governors, 1863–1912.* Cave Creek, Ariz.: Black Mountain Press, 1978.

———. *Arizona Biographical Dictionary.* Cave Creek, Ariz.: Black Mountain Press, 1983.

———. *Arizona Territorial Officials IV: The Secretaries, United States Attorneys, Marshals, Surveyors General, and Superintendents of Indian Affairs, 1863–1912.* Cave Creek, Ariz.: Black Mountain Press, 1988.

———. *Arizona Territorial Officials VI: Members of the Legislature, A–L.* Cave Creek, Ariz.: Black Mountain Press, 1996.

———. *Arizona Territorial Officials VII: Members of the Legislature, M–Z*. Cave Creek, Ariz.: Black Mountain Press, 1998.

Granger, Byrd Howell. *Arizona's Names: X Marks the Place*. Tucson, Ariz.: Falconer Publishing, 1983.

Green, Carl, and William Sanford. *Wyatt Earp: Outlaws and Lawmen of the Wild West*. New York: Enslow Publishers, 1992.

Griswold, Don L. *The Carbonate Camp Called Leadville*. Denver: University of Denver Press, 1951.

Haley, James L. *Apaches: A History and Cultural Portrait*. Garden City, N.Y.: Doubleday & Co., 1981.

Hand, George. *Whisky, Six-guns & Red-light Ladies: George Hand's Saloon Diary, Tucson, 1875–1878*. Edited by Neil B. Carmony. Silver City, N.M.: High Lonesome Books, 1994.

Hatley, Allen G. *Texas Constables: A Frontier Heritage*. Lubbock: Texas Tech University Press, 1999.

Heller, Herbert. *Sourdough Sagas*. New York: Ballantine Books, 1972.

Hickey, Michael M. *"Los Dos Pistoleros Earp": The Way It Happened*. Privately published by the author, n.d.

———. *Street Fight in Tombstone near the O.K. Corral*. Honolulu, Hawaii: Talei Publishers, 1991.

———. *The Cowboy Conspiracy to Convict the Earps*. Honolulu, Hawaii: Talei Publishers, 1994.

———. *The Death of Warren Baxter Earp: A Closer Look*. Introduction and political overview by Richard Lapidus. Honolulu, Hawaii: Talei Publishers, 2000.

———. *John Ringo: The Final Hours—A Tale of the Old West*. Honolulu, Hawaii: Talei Publishers, 2001.

Hoggatt, Norman Lee. *On the Trail of Wyatt Earp*. Mound House, Nev.: Mound House, 1999.

Hooker, Forrestine Cooper. *An Arizona Vendetta: The Truth about Wyatt Earp*. Riverside, Calif., 1998.

Hunter, J. Marvin. *The Story of Lottie Deno: Her Life and Times*. Bandera, Tex.: Four Hunters, 1959.

Jahns, Pat. *The Frontier World of Doc Holliday: Faro Dealer from Dallas to Deadwood*. Lincoln: University of Nebraska Press, 1979.

Johnson, David. *John Ringo*. Stillwater, Okla.: Barbed Wire Press, 1996.

Jones, A. T. *Great Register of the County of Cochise Territory of Arizona, for the Year 1882*. Tombstone, Ariz.: Cochise County Recorder's Office, 1882.

Kasdan, Lawrence, and Jake Kasdan. *Wyatt Earp: The Film and the Filmmakers*. New York: Newmarket Press, 1994.

Kelly, George H. *Legislative History of Arizona, 1864–1912*. Phoenix, Ariz.: Office of the State Historian, 1926.

Kintop, Jeffrey M., and Guy Louis Rocha. *The Earps' Last Frontier*. Reno: Great Basin Press, 1989.

Lair, Jim. *The Mountain Meadows Massacre: An Outlander's View*. Harrison, Ark.: Carroll County Historical and Genealogical Society, 1986.

Lake, Carloyn. *Undercover for Wells Fargo: The Unvarnished Recollections of Fred Dodge*. Boston: Houghton Mifflin Co., 1969.

Lamar, Howard R., ed. *The Reader's Encyclopedia of the American West*. New York: Harper & Row, 1977.

Lockley, Fred. *History of the First Free Delivery Service of Mail in Alaska at Nome, Alaska, in 1900*. Privately published by the author, 1928.

Lockwood, Frank C. *Pioneer Days in Arizona*. New York: The Macmillan Company, 1932.

Lutrell, Estelle. *Newspapers and Periodicals of Arizona, 1857–1911*. Tucson: University of Arizona Press, 1949.

Lynch, Slyvia D. *Aristocracy's Outlaw: The Doc Holliday Story*. New Tazewell, Tenn.: Iris Press, 1994.

Lyon, William H. *Those Old Yellow Dog Days: Frontier Journalism in Arizona, 1859–1912*. Tucson: Arizona Historical Society Press, 1994.

Marcot, Roy M. *Spencer Repeating Firearms*. Livonia, N.Y.: R & R Books, 1990.

Masterson, Bat, and Jack DeMattos. *Famous Gunfighters of the Western Frontier*. Monroe, Wash.: R. M. Weatherford, 1982.

McGrath, Roger D. *Gunfighters, Highwaymen and Vigilantes: Violence on the Frontier*. Berkeley: University of California Press, 1987.

Miller, Joseph Henry. *Arizona: The Last Frontier*. New York: Hastings House, 1956.

Miller, Nyle H., and Joseph W. Snell. *Why the West Was Wild*. Topeka: Kansas State Historical Society, 1963.

———. *Great Gunfighters of the Kansas Cowtowns, 1867–1886*. Lincoln: University of Nebraska Press, 1967.

Miner, H. Craig. *Wichita: The Early Years, 1865–80*. Lincoln: University of Nebraska Press, 1982.

Monaghan, Jay. *The Great Rascal: The Life and Adventures of Ned Buntline*. Boston: Brown and Company, 1951.

Myers, John M. *Tombstone: The Last Chance*. New York: E. P. Dutton, 1950.

———. *Doc Holliday*. Boston: Little, Brown & Co., 1955.

Myrick, David F. *Railroads of Arizona, Vol. I: The Southern Roads*. Berkeley, Calif.: Howell-North Books, 1975.

Noel, Thomas J. *The City and the Saloon: Denver, 1858–1916*. Lincoln: University of Nebraska Press, 1982.

O'Connor, Richard. *Bat Masterson*. New York: Doubleday & Co., 1957.

Olsson, Jan Olaf. *Welcome to Tombstone*. Translated by Maurice Michael. London: Elek Books, 1956.

O'Neal, Bill. *Encyclopedia of Western Gunfighters*. Norman: University of Oklahoma Press, 1979.

Otero, Miguel Antonio. *My Life on the Frontier: 1864–1882*. New York: Press of the Pioneers, 1935.

Parker, Basil G. *Recollections of the Mountain Meadows Massacre.* Plano, Calif.: Fred W. Reed, American Printer, 1901.

Parry, Richard. *The Winter Wolf: Wyatt Earp in Alaska.* Forge Publishers, 1998.

Parsons, George W. *A Tenderfoot in Tombstone: The Private Journal of George Whitwell Parsons: The Turbulent Years: 1880–1882.* Edited by Lynn R. Bailey. Tucson, Ariz.: Westernlore Press, 1996.

———. *The Devil Has Foreclosed: The Private Journal of George Whitwell Parsons: The Concluding Arizona Years, 1882–1887.* Edited by Lynn R. Bailey. Tucson, Ariz.: Westernlore Press, 1997.

Patterson, Richard. *Historical Atlas of the Outlaw West.* Boulder, Colo.: Johnson Books, 1985.

Pendleton, Albert S., Jr., and Susan McKey Thomas. *In Search of the Hollidays.* Valdosta, Ga.: Little River Press, 1973.

Penrose, Charles W. *The Mountain Meadows Massacre: Who Were Guilty of the Crime?* Salt Lake City, Utah: Juvenile Instructor Office, 1884.

Rea, Ralph R. *The Mountain Meadows Massacre and Its Completion as a Historic Episode.* Harrison, Ark.: n.p., 1957.

Rogers, W. Lane, ed. *When All Roads Led to Tombstone: A Memoir by John Plesant Gray.* Boise, Idaho: Tamarack Books, 1998.

Ruffner, Melissa. *Prescott: A Pictorial History.* Prescott, Ariz.: Primrose Press, 1981.

Samuels, Charles. *The Magnificent Rube: The Life and Times of Tex Rickard.* New York: McGraw-Hill, 1957.

Schellie, Don. *The Tucson Citizen: A Century of Arizona Journalism.* Tucson, Ariz.: Tucson Citizen, 1970.

Sellers, Frank. *Sharps Firearms.* North Hollywood, Calif.: Beinfeld Publishing, 1978.

Sheffer, H. Henry III, and Sharyn R. Alger. *"The Mountain Meadows Massacre": The Oppression of the Saints.* Apache Junction, Ariz.: Norseman Publications, 1995.

Shillingberg, William B. *Wyatt Earp and the "Buntline Special" Myth.* Tucson, Ariz.: Blaine Publishing Company, 1976.

Shirley, Glenn. *Guardian of the Law: The Life and Times of William Matthew Tilghman.* Austin, Tex.: Eakin Press, 1988.

Slotkin, Richard. *The Myth of the Frontier in Twentieth Century America.* New York: Atheneum, 1992.

Sonnichsen, C. L. *Billy King's Tombstone: The Private Life of an Arizona Boom Town.* Tucson: University of Arizona Press, 1972.

———. *I'll Die Before I Run: The Story of the Great Feuds of Texas.* Lincoln: University of Nebraska Press, 1988.

Stanley, F. (Father Stanley Francis Louis Crocchiala). *Desperadoes of New Mexico.* Denver: World Press, 1953.

———. *Dave Rudabaugh: Border Ruffian.* Denver: World Press, 1961.

Stokes, George W., and Howard R. Driggs. *Deadwood Gold: A Story of the Black Hills.* Chicago: World Book Co., 1926.

Streeter, Floyd Benjamin. *Prairie Trails & Cow Towns: The Opening of the Old West.* New York: Bonanza Books, 1971.

Theobald, John. *Arizona Territory: Post Offices & Postmasters.* Phoenix: Arizona Historical Foundation, 1961.

Trachtman, Paul. *The Gunfighters.* New York: Time-Life Books, 1974.

Traywick, Ben T. *The Clantons of Tombstone.* Tombstone, Ariz.: Red Marie's Bookstore, 1996.

———. *John Henry (The "Doc" Holliday Story).* Tombstone, Ariz.: Red Marie's Bookstore, 1996.

———. *Wyatt Earp's Thirteen Dead Men.* Tombstone, Ariz.: Red Marie's Bookstore, 1998.

———, ed. *Historical Documents and Photographs of Tombstone.* Tombstone, Ariz.: Red Marie's Bookstore, 1994.

———, ed. *Death's Doings in Tombstone.* Tombstone, Ariz.: Red Marie's Bookstore, 2002.

Trimble, Marshall. *A Panoramic History of a Frontier State.* New York: Doubleday & Co., 1977.

Underhill, Lonnie, ed. *Tombstone, Arizona, 1880 Business and Professional Directory.* Tucson, Ariz.: Roan Horse Press, 1982.

Urban, William L. *Wyatt Earp: The O.K. Corral and the Law of the American West* (The Library of American Lives and Times). New York: Rosen Publishing Group, 2003.

Urquhurt, Lena M. *Glenwood Springs: Spa in the Mountains.* Glenwood Springs, Colo.: Taylor Publishing Co., 1970.

Waldman, Scott. *Gunfight at the O.K. Corral: Wyatt Earp Upholds the Law* (Great Moments in American History). New York: Rosen Publishing Group, 2004.

Walker, Henry P., and Don Bufkin. *Historical Atlas of Arizona.* Norman: University of Oklahoma Press, 1979.

Wallace, Robert. *The Miners.* New York: Time-Life Books, 1976.

Walling, Emma, compiler. *John "Doc" Holliday: Colorado Trials and Triumphs.* Privately published by the author.

Walters, Lorenzo. *Tombstone's Yesterday: True Chronicles of Early Arizona.* Glorieta, N.M.: Rio Grande Press, 1968.

Wharton, David. *The Alaska Gold Rush.* Bloomington: Indiana University Press, 1972.

White, Brooks. *Galeyville, Arizona Territory, 1880: Its History and Historic Archaeology.* Raleigh, N.C.: Pentland Press, 2000.

Willison, George F. *Here They Dug the Gold.* New York: Reynal and Hitchcock, 1946.

Wise, William. *Massacre at Mountain Meadows: An American Legend and a Monumental Crime.* New York: Crowell, 1976.

Wright, Robert M. *Dodge City, the Cowboy Capital and the Great Southwest.* Wichita, Kans.: Wichita Eagle Press, 1913.

Wukovits, John F. *Wyatt Earp* (Legends of the West). New York: Chelsea House
   Publications, 1997.
Young, Frederick R. *Dodge City: Up Through a Century in Story and Pictures.* Dodge
   City, Kans.: Boot Hill Museum, 1972.
Young, Roy B. *Cochise County Cowboy War: A Cast of Characters.* Apache, Okla.:
   Young & Sons, Enterprises, 1999.

Acknowledgments

This book is dedicated to my late father, Fred Lubet. He helped me with this project from inception almost to the very end. I am certain it would be a better book if I had been able to show him the manuscript just one more time.

I am indebted to many others for their advice and encouragement. Special thanks go to Allen Barra, who generously shared his knowledge and insight regarding Wyatt Earp and Tombstone. My agent, Lydia Wills, helped me turn an idea into a reality. My editors at Yale University Press—Larisa Heimert, Keith Condon, and Jessie Dolch—provided invaluable professional input. Bob Boze Bell, Craig Fouts, and the Chafin brothers graciously allowed me to use photographs from their private collections.

I am also grateful for the support of the Northwestern University School of Law Faculty Research Program, particularly the Spray Trust Fund and the Stanford Clinton, Sr., Fund. Among many others at Northwestern, I relied greatly on the exceptional assistance of Marcia Lehr, Alisa Johnson, and Brett Perala.

Linda Lipton, Natan Lipton-Lubet, and Sarah Lipton-Lubet indulged me at every turn. I would get nothing done without them.

Index